To our Nurse Management Team:

We appreciate your commitment to
our patients and staff, and your
contribution to our excellence.

THE NURSE EXECUTIVE TEAM

UCLA Healthcare

ORDINARY PEOPLE, EXTRAORDINARY LIVES

ORDINARY PEOPLE, EXTRAORDINARY LIVES: THE STORIES OF NURSES

Edited by Carolyn Hope Smeltzer and Frances R. Vlasses

Sigma Theta Tau International
Honor Society of Nursing

Sigma Theta Tau International

Publishing Director: Jeff Burnham
Book Acquisitions Editor: Fay L. Bower, DNSc, FAAN
Graphic Designer: Jonathan Sarmiento
Proofreader: Linda Canter

Printed in the United States of America
Composition and cover design by Graphic World
Printing and Binding by Walsworth Publishing Company

Sigma Theta Tau International
550 West North Street
Indianapolis, IN 46202

Visit our Web site at www.nursingsociety.org for more information on our books and other publications.

ISBN: 1-930538-10-3

Library of Congress Cataloging-in-Publication Data

Ordinary people, extraordinary lives : the stories of nurses / edited by Carolyn Hope Smeltzer and Frances R. Vlasses.
      p. ; cm.
  ISBN 1-930538-10-3
  1. Nurses—United States—Biography. 2. Nursing—United States.
  [DNLM: 1. Nurses—United States—Biography. 2. Nurses—United States—Personal Narratives. 3. Nursing—United States—Biography. 4. Nursing—United States—Personal Narratives. WZ 112.5.N8 O65 2003] I. Smeltzer, Carolyn Hope. II. Vlasses, Frances.
  RT34 .O73 2003   610'.92'2—dc22
                                                                          2003

03 04 05 / 9 8 7 6 5 4 3 2 1

ORDINARY PEOPLE, EXTRAORDINARY LIVES: THE STORIES OF NURSES

by

Carolyn Hope Smeltzer

Frances R. Vlasses

DEDICATIONS

CAROLYN HOPE SMELTZER'S DEDICATION

This book is dedicated to my many nurse friends who were willing to share their stories. Two of my best friends need special mention, because they were extraordinary individuals and nurses who died when they were young. One is Linda DuBien, a pediatric nurse practitioner, who left behind a husband and three children. She was a wonderful nurse who always made her patients, family, and friends feel peaceful. The other is Paula Dumas Vrba, a nurse educator and administrator. She was the mother of two boys, a daughter, a sister, an aunt, and a friend to many. She was a logical, perceptive nurse with a knack for getting things done and, although opinionated, never judgmental.

FRANCES R. VLASSES' DEDICATION

To the nurses whose stories remain untold. May this book initiate a dialogue to share what is in your hearts with others.

ACKNOWLEDGEMENTS

CAROLYN'S ACKNOWLEDGEMENTS

Many have supported and influenced my life, career, and story as a nurse. First, as a student at Evanston Hospital School of Nursing (1962 to 1972), I met Marjorie Beyers and Sheila Haas. I still brainstorm with and receive support from both. As a student at Purdue University's BSN Completion Program (1972 to 1974) I met my lifelong friend, Anne Solak. My first faculty position at Ravenswood Hospital (1974 to 1978) is when I became friends with Paula Vrba's family, Charles, Chas, Geoffrey, and Ruth. And it was during this same time that I met Kathleen Archibald Simon, now my godmother. Kathleen not only became my friend, but brought me into her circle of friends, Nancy, Rosemary, Barbara, Patty, and Maureen. During my doctorate program (1978 to 1983), I gained a "pseudo" nurse-friend—Joan Meyer—"pseudo," because she has "hung around" with me and my nurse friends for over 25 years. Now she talks, walks, and acts like a nurse.

During my Loyola years (1978 to 1984) in the Medical Center, School of Nursing, and School of Education, I met professionals who supported my creativity and leadership—Father Baumhart, Julia Lane, Mary Ann McDermott, Anne Juhasz, Otto Simon, Trudy Harnell, Bernie Rimgale, Cathy Corso, Terry Koepke, Barbara Feltman, Carol Debiase, and Carol Wrabl. At the University of Arizona Medical Center (1984 to 1987), I met Becky Hull, who still helps me seek great care for my retired friends and family in Tucson, Tim Vicarrio, and Sue Roberts. Linda Harty and Cheryl Vajkid, as well as Mable Purham and Sharon Massey, became my friends at the University of Chicago Hospitals (1987 to 1990). My consulting life enabled me to meet both consultants and clients who influence my life—Ruth Williams Brinkley, Nancy Formella, Heather Beebe, Beth Joosten, Jennifer Jackman, and Pamela Reid. At PriceWaterhouseCoopers, I have become close to yet another set of clients and professionals-turned-friends—Mary Ann Stabile, Rita Klint, Rita Turley, Caroline Martin, and Beth Kaminski as well as with colleagues Donald Shaw, Cayce Truong, Gloria J. Mangialardo, and Polly A. Smith.

I would be remiss to not acknowledge others who have contributed to my life and to my story, long-term friend and support, Robert Kelly, and my family, Mary, Harry, Mary, Charles, and Jim.

FRAN'S ACKNOWLEDGEMENTS

My heartfelt thanks go to Dean Sheila Haas, Dr. Ida Androwich, and other members of the leadership team at Loyola University Chicago Niehoff School of Nursing for encouraging me to pursue this project. Mickey Hade deserves a special mention for providing needed technology assistance on her own time. My children, Christopher and Jessica, are to be commended for their contributions in ways that were uniquely theirs in support of another of their mother's writing adventures. They learned this from their father, Peter, who I credit with providing superb editorial and technological assistance and, most importantly, patience and support throughout the book birthing process.

THANK YOU

FROM CAROLYN AND FRAN

To the many nurses who had stories that needed and were waiting to be told. Through these stories, both authors have found new friendships. You truly have taught us to listen in a new and different way. You have taught us the art and power of storytelling. You have taught us the importance of "your story" and how "your story" truly has impacted others in a lasting and meaningful way. You affirmed what we already believed, that nurses have stories that need to be heard and that, through your stories, we appreciate the power of caring in a very tangible way.

To the many others who made this book possible and gave it "their all." Included are the authors, many first-time writers, who captured the "nurse's story"; the photographers who illustrated the nurses' stories through photography.

To the creative art director, Jonathan Sarmiento, who dedicated himself to making the photography an extension of each nurse's story. Jonathan was relentless in making the book's "look and feel" be as beautiful and powerful as the stories themselves. He never stopped thinking and designing to perfection while completing a double major, graphic design and art history at the University of Illinois. Despite a very busy schedule, he volunteered his time and talents to be part of the team, in part because he grew up listening to and valuing the stories of his mother, a nurse, and his father, a physician. Jonathan always understood the mission of the book. He brought the stories to life with his layout and art.

To the unrelenting, unflappable, and artfully diplomatic internal editor, Janet Gill, of the Marcella Niehoff School of Nursing, Loyola University Chicago. We were continually encouraged in this endeavor by her generous and gracious donation of personal time and considerable talents.

To the nurses who helped to gather stories and provide enthusiasm: Beth Brooks, Marjorie Beyers, Marilyn Schaffer, Suzanne P. Smith, and Cindy Saver. To Jeff Burnham, who offered consistently good advice and insisted on quality throughout the project, and to Fay Bower for believing in our vision that nurses had valuable stories to tell. To Sigma Theta Tau International for making our vision come alive in this book.

ABOUT THE AUTHORS

CAROLYN HOPE SMELTZER

Carolyn Hope Smeltzer has been a nurse for over 30 years. Her story is a simple one. Her young uncle was dying of leukemia at the age of 23, and Carolyn spent much of her time with her Uncle Danny in the Veterans' Hospital in downtown Chicago. She watched her uncle and other patients being cared for by nurses.

Nurses alleviated her uncle's pain, comforted him, and provided cold packs when he had a fever. A nurse even held his hand when he died. During his illness, the Richard Speck killing of student nurses occurred. Carolyn and her uncle watched television coverage of the event in the hospital lounge almost every day. One of the student nurses killed was a friend of her Uncle Danny. Carolyn soon learned the respect and needs that patients, including her uncle, had for nurses. The anguish and disbelief patients expressed with regard to anyone harming or taking a nurse's life will never leave Carolyn's mind.

Before her uncle died, Carolyn turned 14, and it was at that time she knew she wanted to be a nurse. At the age of 15, Carolyn was a "candy striper" and at the age of 16, a nurse aide. At 21, she graduated from a hospital diploma school of nursing. Throughout her career, she performed a variety of nursing roles, such as staff nurse, nurse educator, administrator, consultant, and author. In addition, she is a friend, sister, and daughter. Carolyn is currently a partner at PriceWaterhouseCoopers in Chicago.

Carolyn loves to watch movies, lives healthy, and enjoys life. She focuses on having fun. She continually uses her nursing skills and knowledge to guide and counsel friends with health dilemmas. Carolyn currently volunteers as a member of the Board of Ancilla Health Care System's Elderly Housing Project (Linden House); the Sisters of Charity of Leavenworth Health System, Kansas; Advocate Healthcare System Board, Oak Brook, Illinois; the President's Advisory Board of Loyola University Chicago; and the Illinois Liver Association. When she is not working, writing, or coaching, she is reading with Barbara, golfing with Emma, laughing with Abigail, horseback riding with Erin, or swimming.

FRANCES R. VLASSES

Fran Vlasses has enjoyed a rich career in administration, service, and education. Currently Fran is a nurse educator; she is also an inveterate student of nursing. She has been and continues to be taught by the profession's finest, who she continually meets in her own everyday life. Early in her career, she was fortunate to work within a community of caring that opened her eyes to the delicacy and intricacy of good nursing care. With her vision cleared, she was able to accept instruction from nurses who mentored her career, shared their excitement about their work in her research, presented their patient-care challenges in consultation, worked side-by-side with her on a variety of community volunteer projects—some not so obviously related to health—and provided care to her own family. It is her hope that meeting the nurses in this book clears your sight lines to a future of giving and receiving care.

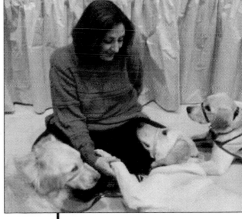

FOREWORD

A s a young girl growing up in a farming community in southern Ohio, I never thought about being a nurse—I wanted to be a teacher. As I grew up, I realized what an important role nurses played in the community. They were respected for their talents and knowledge of the individual patients they saw and of the families to which the patients belonged.

As a trustee of the W.K. Kellogg Foundation, I have traveled to see health projects funded by the Foundation in the United States, in Latin America and the Caribbean, and in southern Africa. For example, in southern Africa nurses (dressed in their British uniforms) in the small rural communities are the only link to health care as we know it. They treat all the citizens of that community and are loved and revered by all. Sometimes they are the final authority on matters facing that community that are not health related. They are amazing people.

When I was appointed to the Board of Trustees of The Ohio State University in 1982, nursing education was organized in a school of nursing. Soon after, the school of nursing petitioned to become a college of nursing, which was another step on the road to professionalism. Now in addition to their nursing education, faculty members are doing research (the scientific side of nursing) to improve nursing practice and additional teaching. This book is so important because it illustrates and highlights the caring, nurturing side of the nursing profession, a side that is easily lost in the high technology world in which we live.

I have known and admired so many great nurses . . . Marguerite Wilson, who cared for me when our first child was born; Dr. Grayce Sills, who has been a mentor and friend from my days at Ohio State; Dr. Helen Grace; Dr. Gloria Smith; and Barbara Sabol, whom I have traveled with to visit health projects both in this country and in South America and Africa. To them and to the authors of this book . . . I thank you for all the services you so lovingly give to your patients, families and friends.

—*Shirley Dunlap Bowser*
Trustee of the W.K. Kellogg Foundation

INTRODUCTION

Everyone knows a nurse. It could be a family member, a neighbor, or someone who cared for them or their loved one. But do you really know a nurse? Do you know what motivates nurses or why this profession, with all its challenges and stresses, was chosen over others? Can we really understand the rewards, joys, and pain individuals experience in nursing?

In many ways nurses are stereotyped. The stereotype is positive but simplistic; for instance, nurses are good, caring, hardworking, and compassionate people. While this description can be confirmed, there is much more to be said about nurses. At the very least, a nurse could be described as kind, nurturing, intelligent, and caring, as well as overworked and performing functions that many would avoid.

In reality, and because of the service they provide, nurses should be treated with reverence. After all, these are people who are at our sides during the first moments of life, throughout life, during human suffering—sometimes to the point of wishing for death—and at life's final moments. Yet nurses remain grounded in the sameness of their practice, helping others with activities of daily living despite the circumstances of age or health status, sometimes taming the horrific with a cloak of ordinary caring activities. And, like the rest of us, nurses continue to be about the business of composing their own personal lives. Surely, nurses must be transformed by the sacredness of their calling.

The nurses in this book tell us the stories of how they reconcile these extraordinary experiences. Through their stories they teach us how they have learned to walk with equanimity, always in close proximity to the human experience of joy and suffering, and how this walk informs their own personal activities of daily living. They tell us the story of living life as a nurse.

These are the stories we have asked nurses to share with you. For, in the course of any day, a nurse can care for individuals, families, and communities in paid jobs, volunteer jobs, and personal relationships. We have asked nurses to allow us to see what it is like to live life as a nurse.

It is our hope that this book will serve as both a tribute and an honor to those chosen by their colleagues as examples of ordinary people with extraordinary lives. But, more importantly, these stories provide text for us, teaching us what it is like to be with both human suffering and joy and what it is like to experience life to its fullest.

It is often in their personal lives that nurses reveal their most profound acts of caring. Carolyn was recently at a spa where she heard the stories of four nurses. One was a pilot, one a photographer, another was a nurse dealing effectively with an undiagnosed disease and feeling guilty about not being able to function as a nurse. The fourth was searching for a way to use her skills as a nurse since she had been laid off as a pediatric nurse practitioner.

Nurses have extraordinary lives that are unseen, thus the reason and importance of this book. This book contains stories of nurses written by friends, patients, and families who have an awareness and interest in those who have cared for them. These stories are diverse; they are written about men and women, nurses of different ethnic groups, and nurses of one or more generations. All of the stories have one thing in common they portray the qualities of selflessness, service, hope, courage, authentic presence, and the drive to make a difference. These are the stories we feel compelled to share, for these are the stories that represent the extraordinary lives of nurses that have gone largely unseen and unnoticed. These stories will enhance our understanding of nurses as people and how their contributions reach far beyond their jobs. The true goal of this book is to clear our eyes and ears of stereotypical nurse representations and provide an open mind to view nurses as individuals.

TABLE OF CONTENTS

PART I: NURSES RESPECTING EACH OTHERS' STORIES

PART IV: NURSES DEFINING THEMSELVES THROUGH PATIENTS' STORIES

PART V: NURSES REFLECTING ON THEIR STORIES

PART VI: TRIBUTE TO A SPECIAL NURSE

respecting

PART I

NURSES RESPECTING EACH OTHERS' STORIES

A BLEND OF PROFESSION AND FAITH: SISTER HELEN KYLLINGSTAD

by Pam Berreth and Linda Knodel

"Nursing and my devotion to God have the same elements, whether it's the passion, caring, or desire," says 85-year-old Sister Helen Kyllingstad as she recounts in vivid detail her 55-year career in nursing. When she professed her vows in 1947, she joined a rich tradition of healthcare providers, the Sisters of St. Benedict, determined women who, in 1885, established the first hospital in Dakota Territory, now St. Alexius Medical Center in Bismarck, North Dakota.

The profession of nursing came first, the profession of faith second. In 1938, Helen graduated from nursing school in St. Paul, Minnesota, and spent a year as a psychiatric nurse before being persuaded to return to her home state of North Dakota as a public health nurse. In those post-Depression years, children made the biggest impression on her. She visited the schools and saw children with red creases from the corners of their eyes, mouths, and noses (rhagades), and with gums that were red and bleeding from a lack of vitamin C. "Within a month of providing grapefruit and canned orange juice for the school lunch programs, I couldn't believe the difference," she said. Some families had never seen grapefruit and didn't know what to do with it. "One mother put them in a kettle and was going to boil them," she says. "We had to teach them to squeeze the grapefruits and drink the juice."

She also saw to it that families were provided with cod liver oil, a source of vitamin D. "Sometimes you would note they had it, but the parents wouldn't make sure the children got it. I remember a man at the Farmers Union Meeting telling how his cattle had improved so much because he gave them cod liver oil. I was just furious and said, 'Sure, you can get some money for your cattle, but you can't for your children!'"

She also remembers the births in families who had very little. There was a home with two kids lying on a mat with scarlet fever. Their only nourishment was cherries and gravy made of flour and water.

And there was a mother of six who had only one diaper in the house for the twins she was expecting. "There were days during that time I thought I couldn't do it," she recalls. But those days were also an affirmation of her vocation.

In 1947, she joined the sisters of Annunciation Monastery. That year, the sisters approached her about serving as administrator of a hospital they had decided to manage in the mining town of Beulah, North Dakota. They thought her public health training provided the necessary background. She started to laugh and said, "I don't know anything about running a hospital." She later proved herself to be wrong.

The operating room was on the upper floor of a three-story converted hotel. With no elevator and stairs so steep a patient couldn't be carried on a stretcher, the staff had to seat the patients on chairs and carry them in chairs up and down the steps. A fully anesthetized, 110-pound patient was carried down the stairs by Sister Helen because there wasn't an available bed on the upper floor.

Despite the challenges, Sister Helen has stated she had more fun at Beulah than anywhere else because everything was improvised. They sterilized in a 20-quart pressure cooker on the kitchen stove. The physicians scrubbed in a small bathroom sink and held their arms over the bathtub as someone poured alcohol over them. X-rays were developed in a closet.

While she was a public health nurse, a physician showed her how to use ether and chloroform. When the physicians at the hospital learned of this, she was asked to provide anesthesia. She decided she needed formal training, so she attended anesthesia school. After that, for 20 years she traveled to rural hospitals as a nurse anesthetist while also serving as administrator at Richardton Community Hospital. In 1964, she started the school of anesthesia at St. Alexius Hospital. After her retirement, she directed the sisters' health center from 1986-1990.

Even after her retirement, nursing is still the core of her being. After she diagnosed a case of pemphigus, which was missed by local physicians, a physician came to the switchboard, where she now worked, and shook her hand. After that encounter, every time he talked with new physicians, he would tell them, "If you have tough cases, listen to these old nurses. They know what they're talking about."

Sister Helen's life of devotion to nursing and her faith has made an impact on the health and well-being of many people. She has clearly done what was impossible. Her persistence, devotion, and ingenuity have given hope and help to many. She is a remarkable woman who has been able to blend faith with nursing and to use both to provide a better life for many.

Newborns were placed in laundry baskets that were painted white. Some had blue trim, some pink. When premature twins arrived, Sister Helen converted a cardboard box into an incubator by putting hot water bottles on the bottom, hanging a light inside for warmth, and covering the top with a windowpane.

To start the hospital, Sister Helen was given $500. "I never used the money," she recalls. Imagine having $500 to start a hospital and never having to use it! She kept a ledger on her roll-top desk, recording what a patient used each day. In 1947, while insurance hadn't been implemented, she doesn't recall any problem with payment; the day the patient was discharged, she received payment. That first year, they performed 45 appendectomies and 20 tonsillectomies. They also cared for victims of accidents from the coal mines and had "lots" of newborn deliveries.

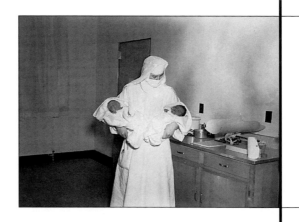

ALEX

by Carole L. Hamm

lex was born in 1948 to immigrant parents (Sicilian mother and German father) and raised in Cincinnati, Ohio. One of four children, with an older brother and two younger sisters, Alex was never short on familial responsibilities. Although monetary means were not in abundance, family loyalty, personal values, and love for one another permeated their home. Each and every influence in Alex's life was strong and strict. His father, a popular local baker, instilled in the family a fierce work ethic and unwavering moral fortitude. His stubborn German ways did not allow for a flexible upbringing. Alex's animated side can be solely attributed to his mother's Sicilian heritage. Although extremely varied in style, both parents provided a united team in maintaining charge of their children. Escaping this structure at school was not optional, as Alex and siblings spent their educational years under the tutelage of stern nuns in the Catholic school system.

One of Alex's earliest loves was cooking. If he wasn't on the playing field, he could always be found in the kitchen with his mother or at his dad's bakeshop, acting as the "assistant" cook or baker. This information may not stimulate much interest until you factor in Alex's imposing 6' 5", 250-pound stature, with exaggerated Sicilian features, a German constitution, and a proclivity for mischief or the fact that he lettered in football, basketball, swimming, and track. Now, revisit that scene in the kitchen, and see if you can visualize Alex over the stovetop, stirring the comfit. Not exactly the same image you may have seen on the Cooking Channel with Pasquale or Emeril. However, given his family history, Alex was destined for great culinary creations until one year post-high school.

Chef school went on hold when Alex was called by his country to report for duty in Vietnam. He refers to this time in his life as an 18-month camping trip and the saddest day of his father's life. At the age of 19, mentally prepared by his parents and the nuns and physically prepared by his brother and high school teammates, Alex traveled thousands of miles from Cincinnati to engage in an unpopular and often confusing war.

As with many veterans, Alex possessed a quiet dignity about his time in the war. Instead of focusing on his own experiences or merits, he focused his comments about Vietnam on his comrades and their contributions and, for many, their losses. As the crew chief on a helicopter gunship, Alex experienced many tragedies. It was being exposed to numerous catastrophic medical emergencies and crises that prompted him to reconsider his life's direction. Feeling helpless and frustrated at his limited abilities to help or save his comrades, Alex was drawn to the nursing profession. This 18-month "camping trip" changed his course from the bakeshop to the bedside.

After considerable struggle and inner conflict, Alex applied and was accepted to nursing school. As the first male to enter through those portals, he created much controversy and unease. Back then, his presence could be compared to a female fighter pilot in today's military.

Alex was chastised and ostracized by all of the females in his class. They consistently gave him bedpan duties and other undesirable responsibilities. He accepted these but went on to gain their affection and respect by graduating at the top of the class. He also scored the highest on the state board exam! Alex's first job was in the city mental hospital. He loved his role there and felt proud that his efforts were having positive effects on the patients.

One morning, Alex went with his father to visit his closest friend, Johnny, a fellow baker. At 8:30 a.m., they found themselves around the corner at the local bar. It was then that Alex crossed paths with Jack, a sergeant at the jail across the street. This meeting changed the course of his career and life. Jack asked what Alex did for a living. He proudly replied, "I'm a nurse!" (Although with his shaved head, goatee, and WWF appearance, he'd more readily pass for a biker from Hell's Angels.) Jack then eyeballed his brawny frame appreciatively and said, "You want a job?" "At *that* place?!" Alex asked. "Sure, why not? Where do you work now?" responded Jack. When Alex informed him that he was working at the mental hospital, Jack yelled, "Perfect! You'll fit right in. Everybody's crazy in my place, including the jailers!" Needless to say, Alex initially resisted the magnetic pull of the offer but ultimately caved in to his inevitable destiny

At the jail, Alex encountered many different kinds of inmates. James had been a homeless man for the past 10 years. He lost his family in a fatal car accident and steadily digressed to a debilitating existence. He engaged in petty crimes for the sole purpose of securing warm shelter, food, and medical attention during harsh winter months. Sidney was sentenced to 15 years in jail for armed robbery. Walter was back again for drug trafficking. He had 12 previous arrests and incarcerations for the same crime. LaShawn, who was small for his age and looked 13 as opposed to his actual 16 years, was in for crack cocaine possession. He was buying it for his addicted parents when

the Cincinnati police picked him up and brought him in. These are the people who broke Alex's heart time and again.

His first day on the job was an interesting one. The medical staff consisted of Alex and a physician. Alex was given a key ring weighing over 10 pounds and a clipboard. He picked out his uniform off a rack of light blue shirts and dark blue pants, none of which fit him exactly, but at least distinguished him from the inmates. After "suiting up," he was taken over to Judge Black's chambers and sworn in as a deputy. Sick call began at 10:00 a.m., where Alex had the unique, but not infrequent, opportunity to witness an all-out brawl among the inmates, the physician, and the jail deputies. Once these initial unpleasantries were over, Alex and the physician got down to the business of seeing the inmates for their healthcare problems. The physician wrote all the orders on 3 × 5 index cards and handed them to Alex as he left. Alex asked the physician what he should do with the cards. The doctor replied, "I don't know. That's your problem!"

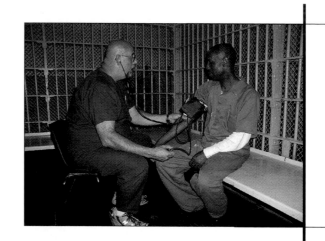

When sick call was completed, Alex had to let the inmates out through the iron bar door so they could go back to their cells. While attempting to open the heavy door, he dropped his set of keys. Out of nowhere, the warden appeared like a tornado and threatened him, using numerous expletives, with a three-day suspension should he have the misfortune to drop the keys again or create any other security breach. On his way home, Alex seriously wondered about his sanity if he continued to work in such an environment. Yet, he continued to return each day and repeated much the same process over and over.

The worst day of Alex's career occurred on 7/7/77. Jail staff placed an inmate in a straight jacket when he became unmanageable. The 90-degree heat and high humidity on the top floor, with no air conditioning, eventually overcame him. Alex found him dead in his cell. Later that morning, he was delivering medications to another cellblock. He opened a cell door and stepped in, noticing that his shoes were sticking to the floor. As he flipped on the lights of the cell, he found a bloodied body at his feet. The two remaining inmates in the cell were simultaneously pointing at the other and stated, "He did it!" Alex took the rest of the day off. On 8/8/88 and again on 9/9/99, he didn't go to work. He says that this phenomenon won't occur for some time again, at least until 10/10/10.

When Alex started at the jail, there was very little to work with; there were no equipment, systems, or policies in place. The medical department existed in name only and was basically an empty shell. Over the course of his 29-year career, Alex pioneered many services for the jail. He achieved first-time accreditation, hired additional staff, implemented a medical records program, and wrote all of the healthcare policies, procedures, and protocols. He is very proud of these accomplishments and the progress gained within the jail's healthcare system. But Alex's greatest satisfaction comes when the inmates tell him, "Thank you. What you did for me here means a lot." He now gets calls saying, "Alex, my son/grandson is in there. Could you look out for him?" And he does.

Alex balances the crazy demands of his job with much more low-key hobbies. He's an avid bird watcher and loves to plant a variety of flowers in his yard. He's devoted to wife, Evie, and their four sons and their families. When asked how he relieves some of the stress, Alex admits to a weakness for the Play Station II "Grand Theft Auto 3" game. "I get to kill everything in that game. It's a lot of fun!" And, with a twinkle in his eye, he says, "Hey, just don't tell Sheriff Leis I do that!"

Over the course of his 29-year career, Alex pioneered many new services for the jail. He achieved first-time accreditation, hired additional staff, implemented a medical records program, and wrote all of the healthcare policies, procedures, and protocols.

A MODERN-DAY FLORENCE NIGHTINGALE: HOLLIE'S STORY

by Sally A. Sample

Strolling along the beach in Maine with her twins, Hollie had her first awakening to the threats to the planet where she and her children live. As they splashed through the tidal waves, she felt something hitting her ankle in the water. She found a foam soda cover with "Hollywood, Florida" imprinted on it, a place where she had grown up as a child. She almost had tears in her eyes as she wondered what would happen to the beautiful beaches over the next 20 years. Further on, she noticed syringes and other debris floating up on the beach. From that point on, Hollie began a personal crusade to reduce waste, recycle, and compost to preserve the environment.

Hollie is a registered nurse; a 1976 associate degree graduate, who began a mission in the '90s about the importance of recycling of waste. She started by encouraging the administration of Fletcher Allen Health Care System in Burlington, Vermont, to consider waste recycling. Hollie had been a nurse at Fletcher Allen since 1978 in diverse positions. She held positions in critical care, dialysis, post-anesthesia, and the resource pool, working mostly on the night shift as she balanced the responsibilities of a single, divorced mom with twins.

The second significant moment of truth came on a busy night in the post-anesthesia area. She remembers four multiple trauma patients who were admitted to the hospital. After care was provided and the patients were comfortable, she noted the waste containers on the unit were overflowing with trash on the floor. All she could think about was, "What if my kids could see this mess after I have preached to them about recycling." It dawned on her that there must be a better way to deal with hospital waste.

At that moment, Hollie made a conscious decision to find a way to deal with the waste and to do so by setting up a research project and finding a source of funding. She was successful. She spent six months with a community partner, who operated the REStore in a nearby town, setting up a research project called the MedCycle study, which was funded by the Vermont Department of Natural Resources. For a 30-day period, they collected the waste from 982 surgical procedures—waste that was generated BEFORE the surgical procedures began. Hollie influenced and cajoled her colleagues in the operating room to work with her in collecting the waste. This was quite a feat in itself. Following the 30-day collection phase, she

spent days in the hospital basement sorting the waste, while she continued to work full time, care for her children, and pursue a master's degree in administration. Somehow Hollie managed to keep it all together. Her commitment to the mission provided her with the energy and enthusiasm it takes to make a difference in the world.

Hollie discovered 34% of the waste was clean sterilization wrappers along with many items that had been removed from the operating room prior to surgery. Her finding indicated the entire system needed to be changed in terms of waste management, ways to create greater efficiencies, and how to recycle the tons of waste generated by the hospital.

After months of volunteer labor, Hollie gathered her facts and began the arduous task of convincing the hospital management that changes in waste management practices would be beneficial to the air breathed and create improved productivity. Management did not view this project as a priority, so Hollie had to educate them about the Vermont Act 78. This act mandated a 40% reduction of solid waste by the year 2000. To comply with this act, hospital management would have to reduce solid waste by over one ton a day. Hollie got their attention, wrote her own job description, and became the Clinical Waste Reduction Coordinator in the Environmental Services Division. She focused her efforts on changing the system and educating the staff, both of which she did with amazing success.

Hollie was now ready to tackle new horizons. With a new husband and partner, in 1991 she formed a consulting firm, CGH Environmental Strategies. The consulting firm helped hospital staff conduct waste audits and measure progress in waste reduction. As Hollie stated, "I was a trash specialist." Hollie reduced her hours at the hospital as a nurse in order to balance her diverse responsibilities as a business partner, consultant, and mother.

Hollie is a modern-day Florence Nightingale. All of her efforts are within the context of professional nursing, and like Miss Nightingale she uses assessment skills to investigate both old and new systems, organize data, conduct the research, and take strategic action. She has learned the nuances of seeking funding for her projects from such diverse organizations as the Ben and Jerry Foundation, Health Care Without Harm, and the John Merk Fund. Always a free spirit, Hollie has created a personal presence that allows her knowledge and expertise to make a difference.

From trash specialist to nursing advocate for the environment, Hollie has always believed she was practicing nursing. To reach out more directly to her nursing colleagues, Hollie determined she needed to create an organization that would bring her mission to life in a broader sense. She dreamed a lot of what the organization might be, researched the possibilities, and once again, made it happen. The Nightingale Institute for Healthcare and the Environment was established.

She recruited a board of directors from her network of colleagues to help her accomplish the mission of the organization. As one of those directors, I broke one of my own sacred pledges not to meet on the weekend for a board retreat. However, with Hollie at the helm, I could not say no. Hollie is able to gather people together, instill in them a vision, and create an enthusiasm that makes things happen. No one works harder to achieve her goals than Hollie. As the chief executive officer of the Nightingale Institute, Hollie was the sole energy force for the institute. She developed projects, raised money, and spoke in a variety of forums

The Nightingale Institute has its own Web site where nurses are inspired to become advocates of environmentally responsible healthcare. Hollie serves as a role model by demonstrating that nurses can make a difference in their practices as advocates for mercury-free care, PVC-free care, and latex-free care. She uses her creative talents to send a message to nurses that the products they use every day are dangerous and that they should become change agents in their workplaces.

Hollie's future has already begun to unfold. As a recognized expert in waste management in healthcare systems, she was recently appointed vice president of nursing in a small hospital in Vermont. I am certain Florence Nightingale would have been proud of Hollie!

ANGELS PASSING BY

by Debbie Downey Afasano

I N MEMORY OF MARY ODETTE AND ALL THE ANGELS WHO HAVE PASSED THROUGH OUR LIVES . . .

I work with nurse angels who are dedicated to a geriatric population. The staff members—*the angels*—work together to provide the best care for the older patients. They have developed and implemented an innovative end-of-life program known as "Angels Passing By."

In spring of 1999, one of our beloved, long-term residents was dying. Rita had lived in our facility for several years. We all knew that, although Rita was unique, there were many Ritas in all of our facilities. In a sense, all of our residents are Ritas.

We nurses were the extended family for Rita and her devoted husband, Curt. He knew every nurse's name and often brought chocolates and goodies to them. He also attended the facility events. When Rita was dying, the word spread throughout the facility. Staff from every discipline in the nursing home reacted to the news. Many questions were raised. "How do we help both Curt and Rita through the dying process?" "How do we support our staff as we prepare to say goodbye?" We wanted Rita to die with dignity, in comfort, and with a loved one at her side. Our response was to initiate a new program, "Angels Passing By."

The concept of "being with" takes team effort. Our first thought was to provide a visible and tangible presence at Rita's bedside, so we decided to place a journal at her bedside to record staff visitations. As staff members from all departments were assigned to care for her, they signed the book with their names and the date. Staff members also included words, prayers, or remembrances they wished to share with the family, Rita, Curt, or other staff. The journal strengthened the staff's presence at Rita's bedside and also became reinforcement for Curt. He knew we where there for both Rita and him. And he knew that Rita was not alone if he needed to leave her room.

Staff members wanted to eliminate the fear of Rita dying alone and the burden of guilt for Curt and the family. They wanted the family to know they did not have to be at the facility "all the time." Pam, a secretary in the nursing department, located two paper angels—one for the cover of the journal and another to be posted as a visual cue outside Rita's door. Angels represented the concept of nurses being "angels of mercy." The angels also reinforced the importance that all staff members could be visible angels—"passing by."

Staff members gathered their favorite music and put it at the bedside. They also put scented lotions and comfort items there. Everyone was educated about the use of voice, touch, music, support, pain management, and "end-of-life care." We were ready to embrace the concept of dying and put all of our learning into practice so Rita could die with dignity.

Curt was in full agreement to have "angels passing by" at the bedside. His confidence was boosted by the loving support of the staff, and we gained inner strength through the presence of co-workers! Nurse angels such as Karen, Shirley, Martha, and Angelica (what a perfect name for an angel!) reinforced the significance of love, support, and presence when caring for Rita.

Curt was encouraged to actively participate in Rita's care. The staff taught Curt how to warm lavender scented lotion between his hands and provide comforting strokes to Rita's arms and brow. He learned how to position Rita so that she could be comfortable. He was encouraged to share his love, feelings, and past memories with Rita.

The staff and Curt took a memory journey into the past. We asked Curt to tell us, "Where would you be if you could be somewhere else?" Without hesitation, he replied, "I would go to Holland and see the tulips like we did before she became ill." "Pack your bags," I told him, "we are going to Holland." We used this information to blend imagery with touch. Curt described the color of the flowers, the weather, and the paths of flowers. As we talked and envisioned walking through the tulip paths, Rita's breathing became calmer. Curt was present for her care and part of her comfort plan.

When Rita died, her journal was part of the church service. At her service, staff members realized the magnitude of their initiative. The minister reflected the importance of the statements of love from the staff. Our "what if" journal and bedside presence became a testimony to the relationships formed with Curt and Rita. It was a living tribute to her life and to her connection with our staff.

Curt made copies of the journal and sent it to family members all across the country. He wrote a letter to "all the angels of the wings of Bon Secours" and donated a memory fountain on the grounds of the facility. His letter validated the significance of the experience. A poem called *Angels Passing By* was inspired and written because of Rita's story. The poem has now become a part of all resident journals, as well as the name of the program that was developed to provide care to the dying.

The angel concept has grown and blossomed since our first angel initiative. We now have our own angel logo, designed by a member of our staff, for our door markers, journals, and stationery. The *Angels Passing By Program* has been instituted nationwide for Bon Secours Nursing Homes. The angel program now affects all the "Ritas" throughout the United States.

The angel journals are now pre-made and a part of an angel cart that is filled with comfort items and visual signs of caring for dying patients. The cart with comfort items is ready to go to a bedside at a moment's notice. The angels— the staff members—are the only items in the *Angels Passing By Program* that are not "pre-made." One daughter had the following to say about the care her mother received.

> *From the time her angel care was started, Mom was never without someone at her bedside regardless of whether the family was able to be by her side. Mom was the staff angels' full charge, and the care was so lovely—they would keep her comfortable as well as neat and clean. Mom's hair was stroked and her body caressed with lotion. She was talked to and prayed with. The angels also cared for us, the family.*

Space does not allow me to name all the angels, but I want them to know just how much I value their wonderful bedside ministry. The halls in many nursing homes are filled with angels in a variety of shapes and sizes. Angels are not restricted to any specific age, race, culture, or religious preference. The true measure of a nurse is not the degree held, but how nursing vows are sustained and an "angel of care" comes forth.

True nurse angels have similar qualities—their eyes are bright, focused, and compassionate. Their brows furrow as they therapeutically listen, and their mouths curve into smiles of warmth and acceptance. Their voices tell you that they are right there in the moment with you. Their faces are alert, attentive, and ready to respond to the moment.

ANGELS PASSING BY

by Debbie Afasano

Do not be afraid,
Kindness and caring live here.
We have come to your bedside,
God has beckoned us near.

In the night's quiet darkness,
And the morning's new glory . . .
Our Master has called us
To share your life's story.

We know no magic words,
But we know of God's grace.
We are all fellow travelers
Sent forth to a heavenly place.

Each of us has a journey . . .
Destiny links you and I.
We have stopped here to tell you,
We are angels passing by!

Our teardrops just remind us
That compassion is a gift to share.
God's common love will bind us
With hearts that love and care.

In the stillness of the night,
We are here to comfort you.
We are touched as we touch,
Midst the morning's new found dew.

We LISTEN for God's call,
To a glory beyond today's sky
'Til called to His presence . . .
We are angels passing by!

A NURSE WITH A MESSAGE AND A MISSION

by Judith S. Mitiguy

Countless children and adults across North Carolina and throughout the country have heard the words "stop, drop, and roll" and know these words as well as they know their own names. Why? Because they know the words of nurse Ernest Grant. There is no way to measure the burn injuries Ernest has helped to prevent or diminish, for the number might be in the thousands.

For example, one case involved a seven-year-old girl with Down's syndrome. She attended one of Ernest's "Learn Not to Burn" programs taught by a fire educator in rural North Carolina. This class provided the child with the skills to lead her panicky mother, sisters, and brothers to safety through their smoke-filled home. Ernest's voice resounded with satisfaction as he described the child's ability to save the family from an electrical fire.

Ernest has taught burn prevention since 1987. He has focused on caring for burn patients for nearly 20 years. When he first started working in the burn center, he was a licensed practical nurse (LPN). He now has both a bachelor's and a master's degree. His schedule includes full-time work in the burn center and many additional hours of volunteer work in the community. Ernest is committed to outreach programs like health fairs, schools, and other community venues that allow him the opportunity to spread the word regarding burn prevention. Ernest lives, breathes, and thinks burn prevention every day of his life.

Ernest was struck by the need for prevention. He remembers one toddler who was close in age to his own nephew. The child had been underfoot in the kitchen as his mother prepared a chicken dinner fried in a pot of hot oil. When she turned away for just a second, the child pulled the pot of hot grease down on top of herself and sustained life-threatening burns.

As a burn nurse, Ernest has met many patients like this little girl. He believes, with education, burns could be prevented, so burn prevention has become his mission and passion. Ernest will go to any extreme to carry the message of burn prevention to a group. When teaching kindergarteners and first-graders about burn prevention, Ernest dons a "Sparky the Fire Dog" costume. All 6 feet, 5.5 inches of him fits into the Sparky costume. Sparky just happens to be the mascot of the North Carolina Jaycee Burn Center.

Ernest believes there are many ways to prevent burns from happening. He lobbied the state legislature for a revision of the act to set the age of those who can buy fireworks. He also lobbied for the passage of a bill mandating hot water heaters be preset to 120 degrees and be labelled with information about how to prevent scalds. He also helped design the "Remembering When" program for senior citizens. This program is both a fall- and fire-prevention initiative that uses games and group work to teach safety to seniors. He also developed a long-term national burn awareness campaign that focuses on different burn prevention topics each year. Other examples include burn prevention when camping and preventing gasoline injuries.

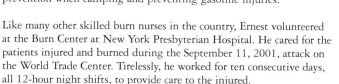

Like many other skilled burn nurses in the country, Ernest volunteered at the Burn Center at New York Presbyterian Hospital. He cared for the patients injured and burned during the September 11, 2001, attack on the World Trade Center. Tirelessly, he worked for ten consecutive days, all 12-hour night shifts, to provide care to the injured.

Ernest is well-known throughout many parts of the southeastern United States as Mr. Burn Center, and this title has been well-earned. Some say there is not a firefighter in North Carolina who does not know him. His communication skills and demeanor invite people to discuss and learn about the topic of burn prevention, a topic that most people do not discuss on their own.

Ernest has a full life. He is a nurse, a community leader, and an active member of his church. He is planning to go to law school. He loves being a nurse and may combine, in the future, his nursing skills with law and politics. Whatever the future holds, it is clear, Ernest will continue to make a difference in people's lives regarding burn prevention.

ARMY NURSES

by Janet Boivin

ajor Michael Sadler and Captain Brad West served six months with the Army's 250th Forward Surgical Team in Kandahar, Afghanistan. Sadler was the chief nurse. West was the chief nurse anesthetist. Both were serving in one of only two Afghanistan army teams that treated injured U.S. soldiers, allied Afghan soldiers, Al-Qaida and Taliban fighters. They went to Afghanistan in December 2001 after spending time in another Arabian Gulf country. Their team received the Combat Medical Badge because of their performance while providing medical care under enemy fire.

Their team was distinctly different from, yet eerily similar to, the nurses who served in the M.A.S.H. units during the Korean and Vietnam wars. West relays the story of treating a blast injury to a soldier's hand. An air attack was occurring at the Kandahar base, as West and his team was performing the hand treatment. All lights, with the exception of the lights close to the patient, were cut out during the attack. In the dark, West, Sadler, and their team heard loud explosions. Small arms fire was also occurring at the end of the airfield, which was near the medical compound. With little light and loud noises, and while small arms fire occurred, the team continued to perform the hand surgery. Sadler and West both recall, while the surgery was taking place inside the tent, medics and nurses were fighting outside the tent defending their location.

The medical team, including both West and Sadler, provided medical care as well as security for the wounded. When the firefight began, the tents had not yet been sandbagged. While the fighting positions were protected from projectiles, the surgical tent was not. West and Sadler, in the medical tent, did not see the flash of the weapons nor hear the whistle of the incoming rounds. They did not protect themselves with helmets and flak vests. Their 9 mm pistols on their hips were not for defending their position; they were for defending themselves and their patients while providing medical care.

West and Sadler spent much of their Afghanistan time treating patients in a green tent, just like the one on the television program "M.A.S.H." They treated gunshot wounds as well as other types of injuries, such as land mines, car accidents, and blasts, just like those in the TV show. The majority of injuries they treated tended to be of the extremities. The soldiers' thoracic regions were well-protected from injury by armor. Thus, the majority of injuries involved arms and legs.

Meals, just like those depicted in "M.A.S.H.," were the focus of their day. The 250th Airborne Division personnel brought the unit ready-to-eat meals and field kitchens made two hot meals a day.

Sadler and West feel special because they were trained by the Army Medical Centers to provide care in the war field. They did not have Special Forces training. In short order, they were airborne, qualified, and adapted to providing care in the war field environment. In the field, they both worked with experienced senior personnel. Both praise their teammates' clinical expertise, which rivalled that of any medical facility, military or civilian. Both West and Sadler agree that their medical team was comprised of the "right people at the right place at the right time."

The Army Forward Surgical Team consisted of 20-person units that included nurses, surgeons, medics, and an administrator. Nurse team members were in the Emergency Department, Intensive Care Unit, and Operating Room. There were also nurse anesthetists. In addition, the team had three licensed practical nurses (LPNs) working in the ICU.

The 250th Forward Surgical Team is an airborne unit. They are trained to parachute into an area to provide medical care. When in action, the Army Forward Surgical Team has two emergency room beds, two operating room beds, and four intensive care/recovery beds. West and Sadler are proud to have been part of this team.

While in Afghanistan, West witnessed the death of one U.S. soldier that he thought might have been prevented if the soldier had received blood as his first line of treatment. Because of this experience, West is currently working to expand the Air Force paramedics practice to include blood administration. West, in cooperation with an Air Force flight surgeon, developed a protocol that would allow medics to administer blood in the field. He also conducted a study that would help medics estimate blood loss. Both West and Sadler have a passion to save lives in the military war field, both through providing care and through changing policy.

Brad West, now an Army major, is in northern Iraq near the city of Kirkur. He and two other nurses from the 250th Forward Surgical Team made nursing history when they parachuted into Iraq with the 173rd Airborne Brigade about a week after the start of Operation Iraqi Freedom in March of 2003.

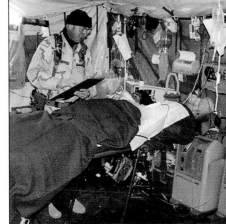

BEING A NURSE: THERESE C. MCGURKIN

by Mary Grace Tighe

Therese loved Mary's stories. Mary, a nurse and mother of eight children, volunteered at an inner city hospital. Mary's stories grabbed Therese's heart. The stories were about people living without running water, about families having no money to buy medicines, and about young mothers parenting children without a husband. The stories were about people who were too sick, too poor, and too alone. "I want to do something to help them. I want to wear a white uniform like Mary," thought Therese as she listened to Mary's stories.

By the time Therese was 14 years old, she was a volunteer at Wyncote Church Nursing Home. "This is what I want to do. I know for sure." By the time she was 18, Therese was a student at Saint Francis De Sales College of Nursing.

Therese, inspired by Mary's stories, decided to begin her career in the emergency department (ED) of an inner city hospital. "You need at least a year of medical/surgical experience before you can work in the ED," her supervisor said. It was on the general care unit on Christmas Eve when Therese cared for Mr. Smith. He was 19 and had lost his leg in an automobile accident. She was 21 and a new graduate nurse. "Morphine, please, for my leg pain. It's unbearable," he moaned. Therese felt helpless and confused because phantom pain was poorly understood. He couldn't be in pain—he had no leg. She withheld the morphine. Many years have passed, and she still thinks of him every Christmas Eve. Some patients influence nurses forever.

Working in the emergency department was everything Therese dreamed it would be. She quickly mastered all of the technical skills, but it was the emotional bonds that she formed with people that fed her passion for nursing. She often visited patients after they left the emergency department and were admitted to the hospital. Many times she stayed late, after her shift had ended, to accompany patients to the lab for their tests. Satisfaction came from being there for people when they were most vulnerable. And vulnerability was rampant in the ED. "It's the little things that comfort," Therese always believed. What others saw as "extras," she saw as nursing. Her behavior and passion to help patients earned her the respect of her colleagues. Therese had no formal title, no formal authority, yet she led by example.

Therese's career changed when her hemoglobin dropped to 4.9. Therese hadn't felt well for weeks. She had seen many physicians for her symptoms: a possible breast infection, a possible sinus infection,

and swollen knees from too much time standing. "Take these antibiotics and buy new shoes," she was told. She did as she was directed and continued to work. Unfortunately, a simple blood test led to a serious diagnosis of Acute Myelogenous Leukemia (AML).

After 18 years of caring for others, the tables turned. Therese was a patient. The good news was both her brother and sister were matches for a bone marrow transplant. The bad news, however, was dealing with the isolation, infections, fatigue, pain, anxiety, insomnia, a distraught husband, and a two-year-old son without his mother.

These and other memories continue to shape her practice, such as the nurse who put a towel on her pillow to catch her hair as it fell out and replaced it with a clean one every shift; the time she was incontinent, ashamed, and worried that she had inconvenienced her caregiver (she prays that none of her patients had ever felt that way); the nurses who introduced themselves, reassured her, and helped her fall asleep. It was the little things that provided comfort.

Therese was surrounded by proud family and admiring colleagues. She did not want to be honored for having survived AML. She wanted to be honored for her work in the ED and her current work conducting performance improvement projects to relieve pain (a lesson learned from Mr. Smith), prevent falls, and keep patients safe.

She can't go back to work in the ED or any other patient care unit. The transplant left her too vulnerable. That makes her sad and sometimes angry. She misses the physical aspects of care giving, but she thrives in her new role of championing performance improvement, teaching Catechism, coordinating Little League, and volunteering with a Bone Marrow Transplant Link Program. Her kindness, concern, and energy are welcomed everywhere. For Therese, that's what nursing is all about. For others, her image molds and informs the practice of nursing.

BRIDGING TWO WORLDS: JUDITH BLACK FEATHER

by Carol Ann Cavouras

Judith Black Feather bridges two worlds. She was born and raised in the northeastern United States to a family of middle-class privilege and wealth. Her mother was a Native American artist, and her father was an economics and statistics professor. She was educated in both private and parochial schools. Her family routinely entertained people of influence in government and international affairs. Her mother regularly produced commissioned works of art for congressional and business leaders. As a result of her family experiences, Judith describes herself as having the social skills to be comfortable and competent in interacting with people of many backgrounds.

Judith recognized at an early age that she was a child of two worlds. Not only was she comfortable in upper-middle-class society, but she also had the cultural heritage, background, and wisdom of her Native American roots. Her mother taught her to make traditional Native American foods and breads. Because her grandmother and aunts were healers, Judith was taught the importance of herbs and local remedies.

As a child, Judith was unsure about her future career. Physical education and health appealed to her. However, at the same time, she was attracted to preserving the environment as a forest ranger. Judith considered medicine, but felt it would be too demanding and would interfere with her hobby, dancing. After much thought, nursing became her chosen work.

As a junior in nursing school, Judith's future path became clear. She recognized the uniqueness of her background and saw an opportunity to "serve my people." She graduated with a Bachelor of Science Degree in Nursing from the University of Maryland. Soon after, she accepted her first clinical position in South Dakota. Judith describes living in a military bungalow with all of her personal belongings limited to what could fit in one trunk and a suitcase. Her role as a field nurse included making home visits and establishing clinics.

Judith's most memorable clinical experience occurred when she was driving a pregnant woman to a hospital 50 miles away . . . and not quite making it. Lois, a 9-pound baby girl, was delivered in the car on the side of the road. To add to the chaos of the situation, a strange dog showed up during the delivery and repeatedly attempted to get into the car. Judith was unable to deliver the placenta after the birth, so she drove to another health professional's home to get help. Mother and baby were eventually taken safely to the hospital, and the placenta was surgically removed.

Judith's career and personal life took her throughout the country. She married a Native American man (Sioux) and raised an extended family of eight children, two of which are her biological daughters. Her career took her to Arizona, Montana, Ohio, and North Carolina, where she received a master's degree from the University of North Carolina at Chapel Hill.

Judith's upbringing was most helpful in her work with the Indian Health Service, which provided many programs and financial support to people. Her social skills helped her to become well-connected in the political arena. Because she was comfortable with people from different backgrounds and had a grasp of the language, her messages were powerful and eloquent. She found it easy to make telephone calls to foundations or national leaders to obtain grants and resources in order to develop necessary programs to serve the healthcare needs of Native Americans.

Judith continues to live in multiple worlds. She and her husband reside in Arizona during the winter and raise buffalo in South Dakota in the summer months. Judith sits on several Native American community boards and lectures in university settings. She promotes the use of Western medicine with traditional Native American healing practices, using long-standing principles with contemporary technology. Judith, as a nurse, continues to serve people, bridging cultures, interweaving different *world*s, and always promoting healing.

CREATIVE THINKING: DOING WHAT IS RIGHT FOR PATIENTS

by Elizabeth Fredeboelling

Can you imagine how demoralizing it is to suffer from a mental illness, be without a home, wear used clothing donated through the generosity of others, and as a final insult, have no underwear? Or imagine being unaware of just how mentally ill you are, and the only underwear you have has been removed from you with scissors because it was soiled and you were not able to remove it yourself. This is the real world of psychiatric nursing, where problems like these are a daily occurrence. Who will advocate for you? Who will protect your right to have your most basic needs met, including being clothed? This is when Carol Kleinman, a nurse with humble beginnings and an interest in mental illness that would ultimately shape her career, enters the scene.

As a second-generation United States citizen whose grandparents had emigrated from Russia in the early part of the century, Carol was the first of her family to graduate from college. She worked and paid her own way through every level of higher education from an Associate Degree in Nursing (ADN) through a doctorate in psychology. Carol completed her undergraduate education in only three years with a 3.96 grade point average and received a National Institute of Mental Health Traineeship for full-time graduate study in psychiatric nursing.

Early in her career, despite the establishment of a thriving private psychotherapy practice in the earliest days of advanced practice roles for nurses, Carol developed an affinity for working with the most difficult of patients, the chronically mentally ill. What attracted Carol to working with this unique patient population was the challenge of working with individuals who were not in touch with reality. She liked the challenge of interpreting and deciphering, much like a detective, the elusive meaning behind patients' distorted communication and bizarre behavior. Successfully meeting this challenge and bridging the interpersonal distance created understanding, afforded the possibility of reality-based communication, and allowed the establishment of a therapeutic relationship on which healing could be based.

Patients who are not in touch with reality are the most challenging of all in mental healthcare. However, the rewards of reaching a withdrawn, isolated, confused, often delusional or hallucinating individual and helping that person return to the world of others created a level of gratification in an intensely personal, one-on-one manner that was unavailable to Carol in any other specialty. While consistently maintaining a private practice component in her career, Carol soon moved into managerial roles in mental health organizations where she could affect large numbers of psychiatric patients through her initiatives. This talent for administration quickly propelled her to executive levels.

To Carol, if patients needed underwear, the solution seemed straightforward. She would order it for the men and women of the inpatient psychiatric units who had none. In fact, she ordered a lot of underwear. It was cheaper in bulk and many would eventually benefit from the purchase, so Carol requested a minimal amount of money from her multi-million-dollar expense budget be allocated to the purchase of underwear through the creation of a new budgetary line item. This certainly seemed reasonable; however, the request was denied by the hospital administrator. Carol was told that it was too complicated for the accounting department to create a new line item for a new account for underwear. How was this possible? It was not a frivolous request. The patients, human beings in pain and in need, did not have underwear!

Many people donate clothes to charitable groups for people in need, which the mentally ill are qualified recipients. Carol worked hard to obtain clothing from these sources and from hospital-based clothing drives to provide garments for patients who often owned nothing more than the clothes with which they arrived on the unit. While many donate clothing to one of these groups, few donate *underwear.* Receiving new sets of clothes, albeit used ones, promoted the mentally ill patients' sense of self-esteem and improved their motivation to maintain personal hygiene. But this could not happen without undergarments.

To solve this problem, Carol had to think unconventionally and focus on the needs of patients as the first priority by not taking "no" for an answer; she needed to take a creative risk. So Carol took an unconventional approach to ordering underwear for patients who needed it. She knew there was an inordinate amount of money allocated for office supplies for her division. She decided she could do without some pens and stationery in order to protect patients' most basic needs. Believing creative risk-taking is calculated, not foolish, Carol simply purchased the underwear, charged them to the office supply account, and itemized the purchase as "paper clips." It came as no surprise to Carol that this purchase sailed through the accounting department without so much as a raised eyebrow. What was there to challenge? Paper clips were in the budget, underwear was not.

Carol currently directs graduate programs in health systems administration, disseminating to the next generation of nursing leaders the lessons of a lifetime of practice. This story is an example of her strong commitment, as a nurse, to preserve dignity. It is a constant reminder of the nurse's responsibility to protect and advocate for patients. The story also reminds her students to think creatively and unconventionally in the name of what is right for patients.

Carol's story highlights the need to push the traditional boundaries of convention far past what is considered "out of the box thinking" and, in doing so, opens up a world of opportunity for creative administrative thinking and patient advocacy that cannot be learned from any textbook. The decision she made on this relatively minor issue had a great impact on the personal dignity of those in her charge. The lesson was also communicated in a profound way as any

grand case study presented in the classroom. Carol is a model teacher and guide, and has become a mentor and a friend to many. She has taught her students that the small things are as important as the grand ones and that detail is as important as the vision.

This story is a reminder to do what is *just and right for patients,* even if it means bending the rules. The bottom line did not suffer, and patients were better served. Perhaps there were fewer "paper clips," but there was a great deal more sensitivity to the care and needs of patients. This is Carol's philosophy when providing care to patients.

ENGINEERING CHANGE

by Nancy Lynn Dextrom

I first met Sandy after she had graduated from nursing school. We were both working at a Veterans Administration Medical Center; she was a new nurse and I was the nurse educator. She worked nights in the intensive care unit meeting the needs of critically ill veterans. For a new graduate, she quickly established a very capable and reliable reputation as a charge nurse. In this role, Sandy served many times as a mentor to other new staff members. She had a knack for teaching all the "little things" that were important in caring for the veterans.

Over the next few years, we both changed jobs and once again found ourselves working together in another hospital. She was working as a part-time evening rehabilitative nurse, and I was functioning as a medical/surgical nursing director. I didn't see Sandy very much, because we worked different shifts, but I always kept informed of her professional practice.

In 1995, Sandy relocated to the northern part of the state and started working in a free-standing rehabilitation hospital. In 1997, I moved to the same organization as executive director. In three different organizations, at three different moments in time, I had the opportunity to see Sandy take care of patients. And what did I see?

I saw a nurse who is passionate about rehabilitation nursing. As I would walk down the hallway, I would overhear her explain the basics of rehabilitative care to a new occupational therapist, always sharing the rationale and explaining the "why." When talking to family members, Sandy would engage them in the active "what-iffing" to test their problem-solving ability. When Sandy developed short- or long-term patient goals with the rehabilitation team, she was proactive and queried other team members about the patient's potential. She also gave back rubs to all her patients. She believes back rubs are a standard of care, as opposed to a luxury.

As I have watched her professional nursing practice over the years, Sandy has always been proud of "being at the bedside." Sandy once tried a management role. In that role, she did not feel as "good" as when she was providing care to patients. "Right now . . . nursing feels good, and this is what I was meant to do," Sandy says.

Sandy's brother strongly encouraged her to become an engineer early in her career. Both brothers were working in a nuclear power plant and recognized Sandy's skill in mathematics and sciences was a good building block for engineering. When Sandy was studying engineering, her thoughts toward nursing waxed and waned. Finally, believing that she would like working with people rather than computers or technology, she dropped out of school.

Sandy tested out her hypothesis about wanting to be a nurse, by taking an adult nurse assistant course. Sandy had her first job with *real patients.* "I started working in home health, focusing on ensuring that patients were taking their medications correctly and getting their grooming, bathing, and dressing needs met. It really felt right, so I changed my major to nursing."

Her passion for rehabilitation nursing was fueled when caring for patients in their homes. "That is when rehab nursing really hit me! It was when I took care of a ventilator-dependent patient that I realized people lived, worked, and survived outside of the hospital. I learned patients and families coped with all sorts of problems—ones I hadn't even imagined!"

Sandy's patients taught her how to succeed as a rehabilitative nurse. She learned that if patients wanted something bad enough, they would figure out how to get it. Her patients taught her that if they had a strong desire to regain quality of life, they actually had a chance to meet that goal. She no longer tells patients what they have to do. Instead, she inquires, "What do you want to accomplish? And how can I help you?"

Whether with patients or family, Sandy's philosophy of helping people reach their goals is evident. Sandy remembers helping her brother, who was in a full-length leg cast, into the back seat of a Volkswagen (after she removed the front passenger seat). She also has family photos showing her brother floating in a swimming pool with his leg in the cast totally protected. She said, "I never told him he couldn't do it! And he wanted to swim!"

Sandy says, "It's ironic that my brother and I have kind of gone full circle. My brother's stepdaughter has a spinal cord injury, which is very unfortunate. Yet, we have taken this adverse life event and used it for inspiration. My brother's stepdaughter is in college, working on a bachelor's degree in business. "And she'll do it." Sandy's brother (yes, the one who encouraged her to go into engineering), at the age of 51, is enrolled in a nursing program. His goal is to become a flight nurse in a helicopter. "And he'll do it!"

Throughout her career, Sandy has taught healthcare and nursing skills in her community. Sandy has maintained her certification in rehabilitation nursing as well as pursued other education through professional associations. Sandy doesn't feel that she's different from any of her peers. However, I've been watching—and she is definitely different.

About a year ago, I asked Sandy to consider working the day shift. I wanted Sandy's expertise to be more visible to the team. I wanted this experienced nurse to mentor others. I wanted her professional practice to impact all of us. She agreed to work days. I am appreciative of having a nurse who practices the "let's put our heads together" philosophy—and who believes that she can make a difference in people's lives and help them reach their goals.

FILLING EACH DAY WITH CARE: DONNA MAE JENSEN—NURSE EXTRAORDINAIRE!

by Linda L. Chlan

Intensive care units (ICUs) are stark, noisy, crowded, and frightening places. They reflect "high tech" science. Donna Mae is a confident, knowledgeable critical care nurse who works in the Intensive Care Unit (4C) at Fairview-University Medical Center, in Minneapolis. Donna's goal is to calm ICU patients by *humanizing* the technology. Donna incorporates knowledge and skills from the best of two worlds—expertly caring for a patient receiving a "high-tech" intervention, like an intra-aortic balloon pump, while incorporating "low-tech," non-pharmacological interventions, like imagery and distraction. Her goal is to calm anxious patients by using a minimal amount of sedatives.

Comfort interventions are a large part of Donna's nursing repertoire. She enhances the "frightening ICU experience" by manipulating the lights and/or playing the patient's favorite music. A typical 12-hour shift on "4C" begins by Donna asking her patients, "How can I make today a good day?"

Donna believes her professional responsibility is to make the environment better for her patients. Donna's obligations to her patients are paramount. For example, Donna was caring for one particular woman who was not going to live. The woman talked to Donna about her wish to die. The patient was adamant that she wanted to die at home surrounded by loved ones, not in 4C! Donna felt a professional obligation to honor the patient's wishes. On her day off, Donna arranged for hospice care and supplies, which enabled the patient to leave the hospital and go home. Once home, the patient was extubated, received pain medications, and talked with family before drifting off to sleep and a peaceful death.

Why did Donna work so hard to help this patient attain her goal to die at home? Why did Donna take actions that were certainly "above and beyond" the call of duty for an ICU nurse? Donna simply explained, "Because I care and I had the ability to help my patient attain her wish of dying at home." Donna was willing to take risks, use her knowledge and skills to plan, trouble shoot, and coordinate the move so the patient could die at home. The patient's family members recognized Donna's efforts by giving her an "angel pin" as a token of their appreciation. The local American Association of Critical-Care Nurses also recognized Donna and, in 1999, named her "Critical Care Nurse of the Year."

Donna's nursing career has not always been smooth. Donna's career path was somewhat arduous. Initially, Donna was a chemistry major at the University of Minnesota. Later, she changed to anthropology. While in school, Donna worked nights as a nursing home assistant. After graduating with a Bachelor's degree, she decided to become a nurse. She attended a local, hospital-based diploma program. Donna did not have a "good fit" with the school or the faculty and subsequently left the program. She changed paths and obtained a Master's Degree in Public Health. The "call" to be a nurse continued to "nag" her, so she enrolled in another diploma program. This time at Fairview Deaconess Hospital, in Minneapolis, Donna flourished in the nurturing school environment and was amazed at what nursing could be like.

As luck would have it, Donna became a registered nurse during the early 1980s, a time of nurse abundance, and couldn't find a job. She eventually became a community hospital medical/surgical nurse in a small Wisconsin town. The time at that hospital and the subsequent time living in a town far away from her support system were very difficult for Donna.

The hospital leadership decided to have an all-RN staff. To accomplish this goal, approximately 90% of the new nurses hired came from the outlying areas. Licensed practical nurses (LPNs) lost their jobs and the local townsfolk, as well as the newspaper, referred to the RNs like Donna as "transients" taking jobs from the local citizens. Donna did some serious "soul searching" to determine whether she would stay in the town and stay working as a nurse.

Donna did stay working in the hospital for two more years before moving back to the Twin Cities area. There she accepted a position at the University of Minnesota Hospital and Clinics, which later became Fairview-University Medical Center. As fate would have it, the only opening was on 4C, a medical intensive care unit. Kathy Wilde was the nurse manager and became an important mentor to Donna. She saw Donna's value and potential as a nurse. Donna credits Kathy with keeping her in the nursing profession. Donna vowed then to never make nurses feel uncomfortable, like she felt in her first job. In fact, Donna has become a proactive encourager of other nurses.

Donna takes great pride in referring to the unit and her colleagues as "my unit." Donna deeply cares about the people she works with. She wants her colleagues and the unit to be successful. Donna believes, "You are directly responsible for the success or failure of the person next to you." She serves on many hospital and unit commit-

tees, mentors others, and is an invaluable resource to her fellow nurse colleagues. Regardless of the various peaks and valleys that have occurred in her life, Donna insists that her core values and beliefs are based on *attitude*. "I make the choice to go to work with a good attitude."

Donna has been an ICU nurse, in a fast-paced unit, for 15 years. She has never "burned out." Her prescription for resisting burnout is to stay engaged with unit activities, participate in ongoing professional growth, and develop skills as a critical care nurse. Donna believes, "Burnout has nothing to do with the amount of work you do, but rather, whether you like what you do."

At several points in her life, Donna could have chosen to leave nursing. The profession is fortunate and many are grateful that she chose to stay. "I have never done anything the normal, routine, and easy way. I'll do what I have to do—someone's got to do it—and I will make the difference. If I don't do it, who will?" Donna certainly has made a difference in her nurse teammates' lives as well as her patients' lives. She believes she is accountable for shaping her own life, and helping to shape the lives of other nurses and the lives of the patients she cares for.

GOING HOME AGAIN

by Geraldine Kelly-Mancuso

Janet Quinones grew up in the Longwood section of the South Bronx. She lived in an apartment building at 894 Prospect Avenue. It was September of 1976 when her family lost their home because of a fire that destroyed the building. After the fire, they found themselves living in a number of homeless shelters, including one on Fox Street, where she lived with her mother and three siblings. Her most vivid memories of the shelter are of brightly colored metal bunk beds, large rats, and water bugs that infested the apartment. It was almost six months before they were placed in the Soundview projects on Seward Avenue.

Janet began her nursing education at Dodge Vocational High School in September of 1978. Her first job as a licensed practical nurse (LPN) was as a residential camp nurse for the Catholic Youth Organization. She later worked for the Jewish Home and Hospital for the Aged. While working as an LPN, Janet attended Pace University, earning her Associate Degree in Nursing (ADN), RN license, and later her Bachelor of Science in Nursing (BSN) degree.

After a year of OB/GYN at New York Hospital in Manhattan, Janet continued her career at the Montefiore Medical Center. She worked in a general pediatrics unit for several years before transferring to a pediatric setting in her old neighborhood. The South Bronx Children's Health Center at 911 Longwood Avenue, a part of the Montefiore system, had just opened. This site was to serve as a hub for mobile medical units providing services for the medically underserved area. The big blue vans of the Children's Health Fund, created by Paul Simon and Dr. Irwin Redlener, provided a medical home for the children of New York City's shelter population. Montefiore and the New York Children's Health Project could now utilize a storefront and one of the Children's Health Fund's vans as a permanent site for care.

While renovation of the storefront was underway, Janet and the medical providers offered care in the mobile unit, which had limited exam space and storage. Ten-minute lunches and a sense of claustrophobia were the norm. After a while, no one noticed the van always listed slightly toward the curbside.

With an ever-growing population and the opening of the first section of the storefront, Janet juggled the intake of patients, discharges, immunizations, and blood work, not noticing the rain as she went from van to storefront. She served both patients and physicians. Even when the record snowfall of 17 inches left small mountains in the street, Janet was providing care.

Janet's job description was fluid and ever-expanding. She placed warehouse orders, updated equipment needs, obtained adequate vaccine supplies, and provided nursing care. Janet had a hand in everything, and it seemed she never got sick or even went to the bathroom.

Janet, a certified childbirth instructor, began giving childbirth classes on Friday mornings at the site. The classes were important to the young mothers-to-be, since travel to the hospitals to attend classes was just not practical. Janet made these young women comfortable, eased their fears, and treated them with respect, something often missing when people are financially and emotionally struggling.

Janet's unfailing compassion makes her special. She told me that her greatest source of satisfaction comes from helping new families. Typically, her new families have no insurance and hop from clinic to clinic. Janet enables families to receive the medical continuity that the clinic provides, regardless of their ability to pay. She not only identifies eligible benefits for the patients, she also helps them apply for the benefits.

Janet believes her job is all about building relationships between the clinic and families so they will trust what they are told. An example is when Janet hears a child, with no history of asthma, wheezing. She makes sure the child receives the needed medical treatment and education. Janet has the ability to calmly judge a medical or social situation and then take the appropriate action. For her, job and reward are one and the same.

Each clinic family "feels" Janet's respect for them. To Janet, people are truly equal. This feeling is also extended to the staff. Janet was my mentor when I was a young "eager to learn" nurse. As a mentor, Janet took the time and made the effort to reduce my brashness, halt my overly rapid tongue, and guide me in my efforts to improve both my nursing and personal skills. I still hope "to be Janet" when I grow up, always hoping to emulate her kindness automatically. Janet personifies team spirit and encourages camaraderie. But you can't tell Janet that she is someone extraordinary—it's just how she does her job. For Janet, her job and life are always about *giving back*.

HANDS-ON CARE: SISTER HELEN WATKINS

by Sister Mary Stephen Brueggeman

H elen's mother did not anticipate her insistence that Helen be trained by nuns would influence her to enter the convent. Helen's mother wanted her daughter to become a nurse. Her mother thought the nuns would make Helen "a good nurse." Helen, however, really dreamed of being a math teacher because she was such a whiz in math. It was not until Helen read the book *Sue Barton: Student Nurse* that she thought nursing might "work out for her." Helen believed she could become a math teacher later in life, after she became a nurse.

Helen became a nurse and a nun. She entered the convent just one year after finishing nurses' "training." Helen became a nursing supervisor after she completed the novitiate or "the period of being a novice."

Helen believes, somehow, the attire of a nun conveyed instant status with the physicians. Before becoming a nun, Helen had to rise when physicians came to the desk. She also remembers deferring to doctors regarding patient care. The "nun dress" changed all that for Helen. In her "nun uniform," physicians had a different respect for her knowledge regarding patient care. They actually listened to her recommendations on patient care. Helen welcomed the change in physician behavior. As a nun she had the ability to persuade physicians to provide the best patient care based on information from a nurse.

Helen began the practice of nursing when hospitals had "fiefdoms." The orthopedic floor, the surgical floor, and the medical floor were each unique with individual supervisors who did things "their own way" thinking "their way" was best. These were also the days of decentralization. At meal time, the food was brought from the kitchen in heated carts. The supervisor and nurses "dished out" meals according to their understanding of patients' illnesses and appetites.

Helen recalls patient treatments were also different. There are certain treatments, which she provided, that no longer exist or have drastically changed. She remembers turpentine stapes, the early sulfanilamides, and the administration, three and four times during the day and night, of the newly discovered penicillin. Nurses would even wake patients for their penicillin treatments. Nurses also hoped the penicillin would not solidify in the syringe prior to being given to patients. Nurses did everything during this era in addition to providing patient care. Nurses

supervised housekeepers and did the entire clerical and supply inventory work. There were no ward clerks or supply clerks. The treatments, tasks, and other work (like cleaning and sterilization of syringes) kept Helen hopping.

Sister Helen recalls hospitals changed after World War II. She noticed some progress in hospital care but also noticed limitations and challenges. Patient hospital stays dropped from an average of 14 days to 5 days. The shortened stay created nursing challenges because nurses did not have enough time to get to know their patients. Insurance premiums, new methods of diagnoses and treatment, and increases in the complexity and size of hospitals were other changes. Sister Helen looked at some of the changes with dismay, but she also addressed some of the changes as an administrator.

Sister Helen's love for direct contact with patients, coupled with the slowness of bureaucratic hospitals, led her back to the bedside. Sister Helen embarked on the emerging career of a clinical nurse practitioner. As expected, these early days as a clinical healthcare practitioner were challenging and not always appreciated by the medical community.

Sister Helen volunteered to serve with the United States Public Health Service assisting Vietnam nurses in the updating of their practice and skills. She experienced some of the rigors and dangers of war. She remembers having a bag packed at all times, just in case of an evacuation. She also recalls diving under the covers, and sometimes under the bed, when artillery shelling occurred.

Following Helen's time in Vietnam, she became a home healthcare nurse. This career did not last long because she was called to be a consultant in Cambodia. Catholic Relief Services had appealed to the religious communities to help care for displaced children and families due to Cambodia killings. Sister Helen and 12 other nurses and social workers went to Thailand to help these families and their children.

After returning from Thailand, Sister Helen became a parish nurse. She provided nursing care for the elderly in their homes. She taught the elderly about proper nutrition, deciphered their physicians' orders, and explained their medications. Sister Helen also got involved with Ancilla HealthCare System and HUD in the building of housing for the elderly.

Finally, after three decades, physicians began to accept and even welcome the role of clinical nurse practitioner. Physicians were under the pressure of a busy practice and needed nursing assistance. Sister Helen took a refresher course, relied on her past clinical experience, and became a nurse practitioner. She was eager to work side by side with family practice physicians. Her role of clinical nurse practitioner was exactly as she had envisioned some 30 years earlier. Sister Helen was now using her "brushed-up skills," volunteering with a busy family physician who served a low-income clientele.

Today, after nearly 50 years in nursing, Sister Helen is again working at patients' bedsides in a free clinic She is working with volunteer physicians providing healthcare to patients who fall between the cracks, having no Medicare, Medicaid, or other sources of healthcare funding.

Sister Helen is still teaching physicians about communicating with patients. Physicians ask her to see the "difficult" patients who don't seem to understand their medical treatments. Sister Helen talks to patients about their treatments in simple words they understand. Both doctors and patients admire her endless patience and teaching abilities. Sister Helen believes all her nursing experiences have led her to this niche, her niche of providing hands-on care. Hands-on care is what Helen loves and intends to do as long as she can.

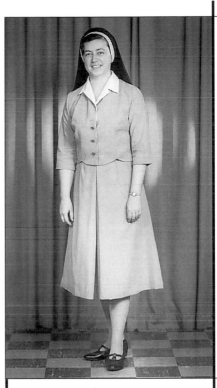

IN, OF, AND FROM THE NEIGHBORHOOD: MICHELLE KNAPP

by Mary Ann McDermott

Michelle was baptized, married, and plans to be buried from one of two churches; the very same churches where she has served as a parish nurse for the last 14 years. With her warm smile, she says, "I was always preparing for my parish nurse role." Michelle says this with a smile because parish nursing was not part of her nursing education nor was it a recognized role when she graduated from Evanston Hospital School of Nursing.

Michelle is very committed to the community where she lives, worships, and practices parish nursing. Her community is of Swedish heritage. She was raised in this neighborhood with four younger sisters. Michelle can often be found in the local Swedish restaurant with friends, with family, or with her morning walking group from the church. Her Aunt Cora Swanson, also from the neighborhood, has been a great influence on Michelle and has served as the role model for her nursing career.

Michelle and her family had a very significant twist of fate in the community, as well as within the church. Granger Westberg, the Lutheran minister who initiated the parish nurse program for the community in the mid-1980s, had also played a role in her family in prior years. Granger was not only the pastor who initiated the parish nurse program where Michelle is the nurse, but the pastor who performed the wedding of her godparents. Michelle is very thankful that she was able to tell Granger the "family story" before he passed away.

Michelle held several nursing positions before coming to the parish-nursing program. One of those positions involved working in a pediatric office caring for children. She credits the pediatricians for honing in on her communication skills, especially listening. The pediatric staff modeled holistic care. She learned how to listen to the stories of the children and those of their parents. She uses the same skill today, treating the whole patient and the whole family. Truly being with people, walking with people on their journeys, and being able to share their stories is one of Michelle's greatest satisfactions as a parish nurse in the community.

Michelle speaks easily about her motivation for caring for others and the social concerns she addresses using the gospel. As a nurse, she cares for two Lutheran congregations, which consist of 500 families. She connects the needs of her patients with medical care, spiritual care, and community resources.

Several mornings each week, Michelle coordinates a "together" group. The program provides services of music and storytelling activities to at least 75 preschoolers and their parents or caregivers. The purpose of this group is to help the participants give support to each other in their parenting roles and to provide health education and first aid. Michelle has had some influence in the group, as one of the students eventually chose nursing as her career. The ongoing relationships of the "together" group create "huge" parishioner/client/patient charts. These "huge" charts also represent "huge" relationships that have meaning to the participants.

Sundays often represent a workday for Michelle. She offers blood pressure screening after morning services along with other rituals such as "laying on of hands in a blessing." Michelle is with many individuals at the end of their lives. The congregation she serves has a large number of elderly who need assistance. Long-time friends of these elderly have died and quite often family members are not in the area. One memorable 93-year-old parishioner lived in a neighborhood that experienced "urban gentrification." The woman was displaced when her apartment, her home for 63 years, was sold to a condominium developer. The challenge of facilitating the move was difficult, yet Michelle managed to become the woman's advocate and found her another home in the same community that meant so much to her.

Michelle will always remember the day when Charlotte entered her congregation, her community, and her own life. Charlotte was born with cerebral palsy but had the most beautiful smile. Her mother was a social worker who made sure that Charlotte felt a part of the community and recognized the need to contribute to society. Despite a variety of chronic illnesses (stroke, heart attack, and diabetes), Charlotte was independent for a majority of her adult life. Some say her smile helped a lot. One of Charlotte's wishes was to visit her mother's gravesite. Michelle and Charlotte, hand in hand on a snowy November day, ventured together to the cemetery. Eventually, they found the grave and prayed. They later went off to K-Mart because Charlotte always had "one more thing to do," and Michelle always wanted to help.

A troubling sore on Charlotte's foot never quite healed. The community hospital was changing and Charlotte had to be admitted to an unfamiliar hospital. Michelle brought Charlotte her favorite music tapes to ease the unfamiliarity and was with her when she took her last breath, smiling the same beautiful smile as when Michelle first met her. However, that was not Charlotte's final smile. During her funeral service, her favorite cross was missing. It was delivered to Michelle two months after the service, and, once again, Michelle saw Charlotte's great smile.

Michelle meets monthly with six other parish nurses and a chaplain to "refill her cup" so that she can continue to nourish others. The purpose of the group is to reflect. Each nurse presents a client from his or her congregation and examines the client's care in light of the gospel. The nurses also gather together for prayer and support.

The births of Michelle's two sons, now 22 and 29, are her most memorable experiences. Parish nursing has provided Michelle with the opportunity to examine her own outlook on life, family, community, and nursing. She has had the opportunity to question and affirm her beliefs. Health ministry and parish nursing have empowered Michelle to bring her faith to nursing, to the community in which she lives and serves, and to her own family.

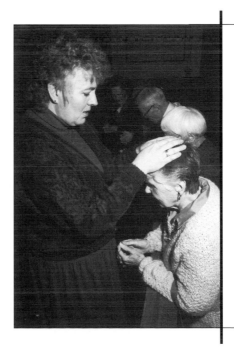

JOAN'S JOURNEY

by Jackie L. Sallade

s a young girl in St. John, Barbados, Joanava McDaniel dreamed of being a teacher. She loved learning new things and sharing her knowledge. She bored easily and was always learning to do two things at the same time. However, when Joan, as she was called by some of her family, was 15 years old, her life would be changed by a serious illness.

Joan had to stay in the hospital, and for the first time she was exposed to the world of nursing. Joan witnessed the compassion, caring, and knowledge a nurse needs to do her job. She saw nurses absolutely make a difference in someone's life. It was this experience that changed the course of her life.

A desire for a nursing education took Joan to England. However, she did not limit her studies to nursing. She remained that girl so easily bored. While in England, Joan studied cosmetology, hair care, and sewing, all vocations that would come into great use later in her career.

Joan began her nursing career in public health and eventually moved to the United States. She started her home care career 21 years ago. As she was establishing herself professionally, Joan always made time for her spiritual life and was involved with her church. However, in 1994, fate would again enter her life, just as it did when she was a teenager. A missionary to Haiti came to her church and gave a talk on the dire needs of Haitian children. As Joan remembers, "It was as if she were speaking directly to me." She heard stories of rejected children, hunger, disease, illiteracy, and lack of healthcare and basic hygiene. The missionary said she needed trained individuals to come and help improve the lives of these children. Joan heard the call and was ready.

Joan intended to make just one trip to Haiti. But that first visit revealed extreme poverty, total lack of basic sanitation, much disease, and the need for basic education in simple hygiene practices. Joan knew this was to be her life's pursuit, to try and improve the lives of the Haitian children.

Photography by Sue Tramontana

The preparation for each mission trip takes months. She has learned to carry everything she is taking. She packs donated suitcases and, at times, wears layers of clothing. All but the clothes she wears home on her back are left in Haiti. The suitcases are given to the many people in Haiti who keep all their belongings in them because they have no dressers or bedroom furniture. Donations of toiletries, clothes, shoes, and suitcases are always welcome. Items that we all take for granted are very special to the Haitian children. For example, Joan collects condiments from fast food restaurants, and when the children see the ketchup or mustard they think it is a treat!

Toothbrushes and soap are always in short supply. At the orphanage, all the toothbrushes were kept in one container, and the children used the first brush they grabbed. Some of the children were HIV positive yet their caregivers had no idea of the danger in shared toothbrushes.

Parasites, skin rashes, and malnutrition are three of the major health issues missionaries must address. Teaching basic hygiene is a priority. In eight years, Joan and her missionary teams, led by a Haitian physician, have helped to establish a cleaner, healthier orphanage and a school with an enrollment of 166 children holding two classes a day. Joan has taught the local people proper hygiene practices so they can teach others in order to maintain a standard of cleanliness. Thanks to the missionary team, there is a clinic, prenatal teaching, and blood pressure screening.

The mission also has a 35-bed hospital. Unlike U.S. hospitals, the patient's family must provide sheets, food, plates, and cups. The electricity and the water run at the discretion of the government and can stop at any time. Yet, the work goes on. Joan and her missionary teammates have helped to establish Christian children's groups, women's groups, and men's groups led by local leaders to carry on the gospel and improve the quality of life.

Joan taught hair care and skin care and brought fabrics for people to make clothing. Little did she know that when that bored young woman learned these trades in England she would be using them to help people on an island in the Caribbean.

Traveling in Haiti can be dangerous. Aside from the small, old outboard motorboats they use to travel to different villages, the practice of voodoo sometimes poses a threat. In many places, missionaries are not welcome. In fact, political unrest and threats of violence have forced many churches to end their missionary work in Haiti.

Yet, with all of the problems and dangers, Joan continues to go to Haiti every year, at her own expense. When she isn't in Haiti, she is thinking about the people of Haiti, their healthcare needs, their spiritual needs, and her next Haitian trip. It is apparent Joan never really gave up her dream of being a teacher. She is a teacher to everyone she meets. Joan just happens to be a teacher with RN after her name.

JUDI'S STORY

by Vicki Keough

Judi, I need your help. My daughter, Nikki, needs a kidney transplant. They tell me she will die soon if she doesn't get the surgery. I can't lose my baby. The doctors here are not equipped to do this type of surgery. I have no insurance, and I have no money. What can I do? Can you help me?

These are the kind of questions that send Nurse Judi Jennrich into action. For her entire career, which spans over 30 years, Judi has been there for her patients, her friends, her students, her colleagues, and her family. How can one person do so much for so many? A review of her story is a story of an ordinary nurse who continues to do extraordinary things.

The first time I met Judi, I was a graduate student at Loyola University Chicago's Neihoff School of Nursing. She was my professor. I didn't trust her. She seemed too nice to be a faculty person. No teacher I had ever met seemed to care as much for her students as Dr. J. In each class, she would hand out articles. They were not articles for the class but articles for individual students that provided the latest information or the latest update or seminar on their specific areas of interest. She often brought students news of job openings in their fields of interest.

Why would she do this? Why would she spend hours reading and clipping articles for students? I really didn't understand. In fact, I truly didn't understand until years later. The reason she did this was because she cared for each and every student. And as for the students who would never appreciate her warmth and the breadth of her love for them, she cared for them the most.

The first nurse to influence Judi early in her teens was her New Trier High School nurse, Hannah Wilson. Judi talks of how she would work on projects with Hannah and listen to Hannah's stories about nursing. But Judi was not sure she wanted to become a nurse. Even though she volunteered during high school at Cook County and Evanston Hospitals in the pediatric units, when the time came to choose a career, she was not ready to make the commitment to nursing. Judi went to college to become a teacher. After Judi's first year at Adrian College, she needed knee surgery. While recovering from her surgery, she walked the halls of the hospital at night talking with nurses on the unit. She really enjoyed her time with the nurses and

was inspired by their work. It was after this experience that Judi made the decision to leave college to become a nurse.

One of the things that makes Judi such a unique nurse is that she came to be a nurse from humble beginnings, not humble in a socioeconomic manner but humble in the academic sense. Judi laughs as she relates her rocky course of training at Mt. Sinai School of Nursing. She was admitted on probation because of her grades, and she remained on probation throughout her studies. She had a very difficult time with the hard sciences and, to this day, I believe this academic struggle is what gives Judi the compassion for her students. Just as someone believed in Judi enough to help her through her program, Judi believes in her students and gives them the confidence to continue with their education.

After graduation, Judi went on to work at Mt. Sinai Hospital where her area of interest was critical care. She spent many years as a staff nurse and head nurse, working full time in the critical care unit while completing courses at the University of Illinois for a Bachelor of Science Degree in Nursing. She then went on to obtain a Master of Science in Nursing degree and a PhD from Loyola University Chicago (LUC) School of Nursing. This was the beginning of a long relationship with LUC School of Nursing. For the past 26 years, Judi has been a faculty member at LUC and has been influencing students for over a quarter of a century. Judi says her teaching career has given her great satisfaction.

Judi's greatest pleasure comes from the successes of her students. She brags that her students are now some of the greatest leaders in nursing. She doesn't hesitate to name some very successful nurses, and her eyes light up as she talks about the intelligence and creativity of her students. She believes that her gift, her purpose in life, is to help young men and women succeed in their desire to expand their nursing careers. Her students give her a reason for living, they justify her existence, and they have not let her down.

Ten years ago, Judi went to Belize, Central America, with other Loyola faculty to seek international experiences for nursing students. That one trip began a long relationship with healthcare workers in a country with very little money and few resources, but a wealth of love and beauty that Judi shares with her students every year. Judi says her greatest joy in the Belize experience is to witness the changes in the hearts of nursing students as they render care to the residents of Belize. Her heart is warmed as she sees the students touch the children, treat the elderly, and work with the Belizean nurses. Judi believes that, with each visit to Belize, the Americans return with so much more than they could ever give. Students return humble and touched. Most students say it was one of the most heart-warming experiences they have ever had. Judi knows that this experience cannot be delivered lecture-style in a classroom in Chicago.

Judi says it is in Belize that she feels most like a nurse. She takes her students to deliver care in clinics where there are often no physicians but many patients who need care. She talks of being there for the birth of babies and sitting with elderly or injured patients as they face death. She talks of being challenged to deliver the best care possible under less than ideal circumstances. She is constantly looking for resources, challenging the students to look inside themselves for what they can offer the patients.

A typical day in Belize begins at about 5:00 a.m., when Judi begins to gather supplies for the students to bring to the villages, clinics, schools, or hospitals. But Judi says it is the end of the day, when the students gather for a post-clinical conference to relate their stories of the day that brings her the greatest joy. This is when she begins to see the transformation of the students. When the Belizeans say to the students, "Thank you . . . when are you coming back?" the students relate how these words touch their lives. This is what makes it all worthwhile for Judi and the students.

In Belize, they call her Sister Judi, and they know that she is there for them. She treasures these friendships. Judi is constantly soliciting donations throughout the year and ships medical supplies, computers, books, magazines, and clothing to her friends in the schools, clinics, and hospitals in Belize. In fact, there is a hospital library in Belize named after Judi, since most of the books in the library have come from her donations.

Remember that little girl, Nikki, who needed the kidney transplant? Nikki lived in Belize and received the transplant in the U.S. with the help of many generous people including Judi and her students, who held fund-raisers and donated necessary medications to help prevent transplant rejection. Judi continues to support this family through donations. Many Belizeans have received medical care, equipment, and medications through the support of Judi and her current and former students. The students know, when Judi calls, it is never for herself, but for someone who needs help.

There is an old Belizean proverb, "If you drink our water, you will always return." Judi has had the water and knows that Belize will always be a part of her life. The ability to be able to offer this experience to students each year is a highlight of her career.

Judi has another career marker of which she is very proud. She was one of two faculty members who, in 1993, began the first Acute Care Nurse Practitioner Program in Illinois at LUC. The program has graduated over 60 nurses who practice as acute care nurse practitioners (ACNP) throughout the country. The experiences of developing the program and going back to the clinical setting to gain the expertise and hours required to sit for the certification exam were some of the most memorable experiences of her life. The ACNP program continues to expand and thrive at LUC and has a solid national reputation.

Judi knows that she has been blessed. She has a career that blends the best of all worlds—caring for patients, caring for students, and constantly being on the cutting edge of new knowledge and technology. The people who actually have been blessed are the people who have been touched by Judi. If Judi has one fault, it is that she cares so much. The baby, Nikki, now an active 6-year-old attending elementary school, is a living example of how Judi, an ordinary nurse, has touched so many lives.

lotilde Bruner, the daughter of Peter and Clotilde Elder Bruner, was born in Breckenridge County, Kentucky, in November of 1820. Clotilde's family was deeply rooted in Catholicism. Her grandparents had come to America at a time when the Roman Catholics were not welcome in England. It was in her mother's home that the first mass was offered in Kentucky. The bishop of Natchez, Mississippi, W.J. Elder, was one of Clotilde's uncles who later became the archbishop of Cincinnati.

Clotilde was a frail, delicate child, and many feared that she "would go into consumption." If this were not a recorded fact, it would be hard to believe because in later years she was an extremely large, healthy woman, weighing between 250 and 300 pounds. As a child, Clotilde was entranced by the Indian stories in the far West. One of her aunts was even taken captive by the Indians for a number of years. Clotilde never tired of telling how she and her little brother felt when the aunt returned home, listening to the stories of her captivity (The Historical Development of the Health Care Ministry of the Sisters of Charity of Leavenworth, 1984).

Clotilde's family had been wool weavers in England. Even though the family lost their factory, they were still able to live the life consistent with "well-to-do" people. Clotilde was noble, simple in her manners, domestic, and had exquisite taste. She wore dresses of linsey-wool with velvet collars and cuffs. The material was cut, corded, spun, woven, and made at home. As the daughter of a "well-to-do family," Clotilde was a refined lady who enjoyed nice things.

Clotilde's sensitivity and love of her family was evident. One evening in 1876, she stood on a doorstep of her home where she had been sewing. She lingered, admiring the inexpressible beauty and charm of the setting sun as it cast a bewitching peach-bloom tinge over the Black Hills. Tears ran down her cheeks as she said, "The

peach-bloom tinge is so vivid I can recall the days of my happy childhood and can fancy myself in my 'old Kentucky home' on my father's peach orchard." She continued, "When the orchard was in full bloom, it was the admiration of all the neighbors for miles around; it was such a beauty and when the peaches were ripe it was even more attractive" (The Historical Development of the Health Care Ministry of the Sisters of Charity of Leavenworth, 1984, p. 63).

Clotilde entered the Sisters of Charity of Nazareth but not without obstacles. She later discussed her entrance into the novitiate by remarking, "I had a hard time, but like John the Baptist, I got up and came of mine own accord." She was given the name of Sister Joanna Bruner.

Over the years, Sister Joanna proved to be habitually kind, yet maintained her own opinion. When she was convinced of being wrong, she graciously yielded. The problem was trying to convince her she was wrong in the first place! Some of the sisters referred to her as the "warrior." Sister Joanna always strenuously defended what she felt was right (The Historical Development of the Health Care Ministry of the Sisters of Charity of Leavenworth, 1984, p. 63).

In 1848, she volunteered to nurse the sick and care for those dying from cholera. After this experience, she repeated this phrase, "The love of my life is the care of the sick" (The Historical Development of the Health Care Ministry of the Sisters of Charity of Leavenworth, 1984, p. 63).

Sister Joanna left the Sisters of Nazareth community to establish and become part of a ministry in Kansas. From the time of her arrival in Kansas, she gave willingly of herself by serving in many roles in this small but steadily growing community. Her strong, undaunted spirit set the pattern for other Sisters in healthcare.

Sister Joanna Bruner was one of the pioneers who played a major role in the development of the healthcare ministry of the Sisters of Charity of Leavenworth. She was a woman of deep faith with above average business acumen and good judgment. Sister Joanna was good-natured, kind, and respected by the Sisters. She was appointed the first Sister Servant of St. John's Hospital in Leavenworth, Kansas in 1864. She was the first woman to serve in such a capacity in the

*Note: Excerpts with permission from *The Historical Development of the Health Care Ministry of the Sisters of Charity of Leavenworth* (1984).

The history/story of Sister Joanna Bruner was first presented in the dissertation of Sister Mary Carol Conroy SCL. Sister Mary Carol Conroy passed away December 2002, the month her story was being rewritten. Thus this story is dedicated to Sister Mary Carol Conroy.

western territory and also was the first qualified nurse in Kansas (The Historical Development of the Health Care Ministry of the Sisters of Charity of Leavenworth, 1984, p. 61).

She constantly devoted herself to making the hospital a real home for the sick. She instructed other nuns who did not have previous nursing experience at the bedside. Sister Joanna developed the apprenticeship method of teaching the art of nursing (The Historical Development of the Health Care Ministry of the Sisters of Charity of Leavenworth, 1984, p. 64).

The first patients Sister Joanna accepted in the hospital were poor refugees from Alabama. They were patients before the hospital building was completed and opened. They were suffering from cold, hunger, and neglect. Following several months of care by Sister Joanna and other nuns, the patients became healthy and were able to return to their homes.

One cold November morning, while the Sisters were dusting and sweeping the hospital, they were distracted by a large lumber wagon. A man was lifted from the "deep bed" of the wagon and laid on the pavement. Then four more men were lifted from the wagon. The Sisters stood in amazement. Without any explanation, the man in the wagon began to return to his perch. The Sisters called from their window asking the man what he was doing. He responded, "Just what I was told to do. A man at the depot hired me to bring them (the men) here and so I have done that. They are men caught in the last blizzard while hunting buffalo near Fort Hacker. Their names I do not know" (The Historical Development of the Health Care Ministry of the Sisters of Charity of Leavenworth, 1984, p. 65). Passers-by were startled by the most unusual sight of five men on the pavement and promptly offered to help transport the men inside the hospital. It was at this time that the community started donating money to the Sisters. Two men who donated $50 each came to the hospital and said, "It is our duty to help you, and it is a pleasure for us to perform the duty" (p. 65).

Services for the transient population of the frontier town were available at St. John's Hospital. As patients became more numerous, care became hard to get because of the scarcity of finances. Sister Joanna suggested a festival be held to benefit the hospital. However, the festival was unsuccessful as a fund-raiser. Consequently, without notifying the Sisters, the ladies in town planned a gala ball to support the Sisters. They even raffled off articles not sold at the festival. The event was very successful; however, a priest told Sister Joanna that she had to refuse money obtained in this manner, so she did as she was told and refused the money.

A few days later, a grocery wagon came to the hospital and delivered a large quantity of groceries. Sister Joanna was astonished and asked who ordered the goods. The delivery driver said, "A man from Ireland." Other items came to the hospital, such as new carpeting and washstands. Sister Joanna never realized that the proceeds of the ball were financing these "fringe benefits for the hospital" (The Historical Development of the Health Care Ministry of the Sisters of Charity of Leavenworth, 1984, p. 66).

It was not unusual for Sister Joanna to remain up all night caring for the sick. It was during a cold, bitter winter that she became the recipient of a warm "Balmoral skirt." Sister was given the skirt by a friend, who was confident she would never dream of purchasing such a fine, warm garment. Delighted, Sister Joanna accepted the gift, wishing that each Sister might have such a warm garment (The Historical Development of the Health Care Ministry of the Sisters of Charity of Leavenworth, 1984, p. 66). Dr. M.S. Thomas had worn the skirt at a masquerade ball and, after the party, gave the skirt away to a friend of Sister Joanna. When providing medical care to Sister Joanna, Dr. Thomas saw his masquerade ball skirt being worn by her and was very surprised.

In 1875, Sister Joanna and other nuns from Sisters of Charity of Leavenworth arrived in Laramie City to start a hospital. Laramie was a real "Wild West" town where real robberies were common. It was in Laramie that Sister saw three men hanging from a lamppost. While distressed, she did not get discouraged. Her job was to renovate an old hospital and gather supplies for a 24-bed hospital. Sister Joanna and the other nuns went as far away as 50 miles to seek funding for the hospital. "Habits and head dresses could be seen on the rail handcar as the Sisters traveled to railroad or mining camps to secure the funding." The Sisters were noted for begging for hospital funds (The Historical Development of the Health Care Ministry of the Sisters of Charity of Leavenworth, 1984, p. 76).

Sister Joanna encouraged the "Society for Hospital Care" to provide hospital care wherever the Union Pacific laborers were working. She made this recommendation after a boiler in one of the Union Pacific mills exploded, killing four men and injuring 11 others. These men needed nursing care. The Society of Hospital Care collected 50 cents a month per worker for potential nursing care and service requirements in the event of illness or injury. This was a forerunner of United States healthcare insurance.

More than 100 years later, Laramie recognized Sister Joanna as part of its history. In 1981, the county commissioners named a street "Bruner Drive." Bruner Drive is the first street in Laramie to be named after a woman and certainly the first street in Laramie to be named after a nun (The Historical Development of the Health Care Ministry of the Sisters of Charity of Leavenworth, 1984, p. 78).

Sister Joanna was truly a pioneer in the Wild West. She taught nursing staff at the bedside, she focused on providing care to the poor, she used fund raising as a way to raise money for the poor and build hospitals, and she developed an employer pre-payment system as a type of insurance for workers who might become injured or sick.

MARY FRANCES MURPHY

by Marie Duffy

Mary Frances knew at the age of four that she wanted to be a nurse. However, when she was a high school senior, she dabbled with the idea of being an artist. She carefully gathered her portfolio and applied to several art schools. She also applied to several nursing schools, "just in case." Several months later, she was accepted at both and had to make a decision. She literally flipped a coin, heads for art school, tails for nursing school. Tails came up three times. Now, 20 years later, this wife, mother, and critical care nurse has taken a lead role in preparing the staff of New Jersey's Bon Secours Hospitals for bioterrorist attacks.

In 1998, Mary Frances attended a weapons of mass destruction course sponsored by the Department of Defense. It was there that she and other staff members saw the need to prepare for events ranging from chemical spills to sarin gas attacks. They quickly realized their 20-bed emergency department was not built or equipped for such an event. Many costly physical changes and much staff in-service education would be necessary so the facility and the staff would be ready to adequately respond to such an emergency.

In 1999, Mary Frances was recognized as a leader at St. Mary Hospital's Emergency Department. Shortly thereafter, the Metropolitan Medical Response System (MMRS) was formed in Hudson County, and Mary Frances was asked to join in an effort to write a disaster plan for the entire county. She worked with public safety and health agency personnel in the system and co-chaired the Pharmaceutical Stockpiling and Decontamination committees.

On September 11, 2001, the nearly completed Disaster Plan was prematurely tested. Because of the September 11, 2001, ("9/11") attack, 10,000 people on the city's mile-square waterfront in New York City were decontaminated. Some 2,000 people were triaged at a makeshift staging area near the Hoboken train station. Many more were treated at all the Hudson County hospitals, as thousands of people fled from Manhattan. Her own husband, Harry, a Jersey City police officer, was recalled to duty. Hudson County employees worked tirelessly under a universal plan to help its crippled New York neighbors.

On any given day, you might find Mary Frances doing a dozen different things, like preparing special themed cupcakes for her three children, getting the next staff schedule ready, or even "popping up" a decontamination tent. She is heavily invested in the future, not in the past. This is one nurse who doesn't regret putting aside her brushes and oil paints to practice the "art" of emergency nursing.

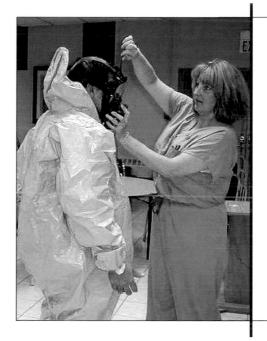

MEMORY CATCHER: DOLORES' MEMORABILIA

by Pat Mezzina

Nurses' Week at St. Mary Hospital in Hoboken, New Jersey, is a special time for celebration, and Dolores Heinzmann will always be found heading up the festivities. As a graduate of St. Mary Hospital School of Nursing, Dolores has remained a dedicated and respected member of the nursing staff. She demonstrates nursing excellence at the bedside as well as by her participation on nursing department committees. Some of the committees she has served on include the Professional Practice, Pain Management, and Nursing Recruitment and Retention committees. Dolores has focused on committees that affect people, whether they are patients or staff.

Dolores, when not at work, holds various regional and district offices. She is a charter member of the National Association of Orthopedic Nurses (NAON) and an active member of the American Association for the History of Nursing (AAHN). She now focuses much of her efforts and free time collecting important nursing history items.

On a daily basis, Dolores is viewed by her colleagues as one who is devoted to a traditional model of nursing, the art of caring. Dolores credits her initial career interest in nursing to an experience as a child. Her younger sister had suffered an acute appendicitis, and when she returned home from the hospital Dolores helped care for her. Dolores' mother commented on her seemingly natural affinity to provide comfort and foster healing while changing her sister's dressings. As fate would have it, Dolores became a nurse and her brother a physician. Dolores models her practice after Dorothea Orem, a patient advocate who fosters self-care and has a deep-rooted commitment to the very traditional ideals of Florence Nightingale.

Dolores attributes her interest in nursing history to the first head nurse with whom she worked, Mrs. Winters. "I find that I've always gravitated toward older nurse practitioners because they always were able to give advice based on experience and their history. Mrs. Winters was a Cadet Nurse and she would share stories with me about nursing then and now."

Dolores enjoys being part of St. Mary Hospital's nursing history. Since graduation, she was also involved with the school alumni until they stopped meeting. Dolores spearheaded the resurrection of the alumni group in 1988 during the hospital's 125-year anniversary celebration. She has been the chairperson ever since.

Over the years, Dolores' interest in nursing history has blossomed into an extensive collection of nursing memorabilia. One of her favorite collection pieces is a letter written and signed by Clara Barton of the American Red Cross. Her most recent addition to the collection is a Royal Doulton limited edition statue of Florence Nightingale. The collection includes several original, handmade, one-of-a-kind nurse items, such as "nurse" dolls, plates, bells, pictures, advertisements, stamps, mugs, teapots, puzzles, and ornaments. Her memorabilia collection is a favorite display at the St. Mary Hospital Nurses' Day celebrations. Her collections have also been shown at the Emergency Nurses Association convention.

Dolores' latest endeavor is being a member of the nurse newsletter committee, which focuses on promoting and recognizing the diverse talents of nurses. Dolores knows today's nurse stories will become tomorrow's nursing history at St. Mary Hospital.

NEITHER RAIN, NOR SLEET, NOR SNOW. . .

by Susan Randall

It was a day several years ago, prior to cell phones being everywhere and certainly prior to the global positioning systems being used in cars. It would have been an ordinary winter's day if we were in New York, Ohio, or Massachusetts. But we weren't in those states, we were in northern Virginia and it was anything but ordinary.

Overnight, there had been a modest snowfall, five to seven inches, which, in the metropolitan Washington, D.C., area, counts as a major winter storm. The day dawned bright and icy cold. The day was forecasted to stay icy cold. There would be no melting or warm-up. Schools were closed and kids headed out with their sleds for a rare Virginia treat. The news shows extended their newscasts with live, on-the-scene reporting of snowfall totals and fender-benders. An announcement from the postal service stated mail delivery would resume when mailboxes were cleared and carriers could get to work.

At the Visiting Nurses Association, the day was anything but a *treat.* Snow days are one of the most hectic events in our business. In our area, we don't get too many opportunities to practice snow-day activities. Our patients, regardless of the snow, need to be triaged, called, shuffled, and rescheduled.

Betsey, the manager, was already in the office when I arrived 30 minutes late. I was filling in for one of the coordinators, who had the day scheduled off. The first order of the day was to determine which nurses were coming to work and which nurses were not able to come to work. The calls from the nurses began to come in. Some nurses could not make it to work because their children were not in school, and they did not have childcare. Others nurses reported being delayed until their cars were shoveled out of the snow. Some nurses had already called their patients and rescheduled visits; other nurses were giving medical and treatment instructions to patients and family members over the phone. In the office, we worried not only about this *snow day,* but also about the next days because so many patients were rescheduled for their visits.

Together, Betsey and I looked over the patient visits that needed to occur on the snow day. We were concerned about the diabetic patients, patients with complex dressing changes, and the oncology patients who needed cassette changes for their pain pumps. At mid-morning, the manager and I finally were able to take a few minutes to compare notes about patients and nursing staff. This was when we realized we had heard from every nurse except one, Jean.

Jean is a low-key, easy-going case manager, who marches to her own drummer. We called her house, but got no answer. We paged her, but did not receive a call back. Jean had her daily schedule of patient visits planned; however, Jean had not given the schedule to the office. We were unsure which patients Jean was planning to visit. There was no choice but to start calling Jean's entire patient caseload.

Betsey and I divided the list and started calling her patients. Responses we received from Jean's patients included: "No, we haven't seen her." "No, she's not due until next week." "No," "No," "No." As only nurses can worry, we began to worry that something had happened to Jean . . . that her car had slid off the road, that she was stuck by another car—or worse, we worried that Jean had been injured. We continued to make calls to Jean's patients. Finally, we got good news, "She was here, but she's gone now," the patient's daughter said. We kept making other calls. "She just left." And then, "She just called to say that she was on her way." Finally! We left a message to have Jean call the office when she got to her next patient. We waited to hear from her.

Betsey got the call. Jean was out seeing her patients, on skis! On skis? "Well, yes," Jean told Betsey. "I heard the weather report last night and as a precaution, I put my skis in the car—just in case. Patients had to be seen, snow or no snow, so I wanted to be prepared. I parked my car in a central location, strapped on a backpack and the skis, and took off for my patients' home visits. No big deal. I was just taking care of my patients. Is anything wrong?" No, she was assured, everything was just fine.

We were amazed! The post office and schools were closed because of the snow, but a home health nurse, Jean, was skiing around northern Virginia making home visits, taking care of her patients. We were amazed and proud!

NEW GRADUATE, MASTER TEACHER: LAURA DIFIGLIO KLINK

by Jorie Moberley

I recently learned that a drunk driver killed one of my former students, Laura Difiglio Klink. The news of her death struck a devastating blow to me, the nursing profession, and indeed, our planet. Laura was one of the finest individuals I've ever had the pleasure of knowing. The impact of her death prompted me to evaluate why I was so heartbroken over losing someone I knew for only a short while. That required only brief reflection. It was the way that Laura made me feel about myself and about others. Laura, herself, was such a captivating individual. In fact, when I was her instructor, I found myself in somewhat of a unique role reversal; the teacher learning valuable life lessons from the student.

Laura was a student in an accelerated bachelor of science in nursing program at the Niehoff School of Nursing at Loyola University in Chicago. After almost 10 years as a CPA, she decided to pursue a career in nursing. Because Laura was older and more experienced, she was clearly focused on her nursing education. It was a pleasure teaching her because she would sit with rapt attention, taking in every piece of information I had to offer.

Often times, students are less than enthusiastic about taking a course they're not interested in, but they see it as a means to an end and muddle through the course work simply to get it out of the way. That was not my experience with Laura. She made me feel like everything I had to say and offer was worthwhile. No aspect of her education was a waste of time. I think that was a large part of her appeal. As a new teacher, I often felt unsure of myself, but her enthusiasm to learn made me want to be a better teacher.

The thing I admired the most about Laura was her kindness. I can honestly say that I never heard her utter one unkind word about anyone. I find that an incredible feat considering the cynical world we live in, but it is an achievement to which I now aspire. Laura treated everyone the same, regardless of rank or status. She had a unique way of making people feel valued and actively sought out opportunities to connect with those around her. Laura possessed these qualities even as a student. Upon the completion of patient care, when other students huddled around the nurses' station, Laura could be found engaged in a conversation with one of her patients. The topic of conversation was irrelevant, simply sought to convey a sense of caring and concern, and she was successful every time.

After Laura graduated, she called me a couple of times to ask for letters of recommendation. Each time I spoke with her, she would ask me how my family was or how work was going. She made me feel like she was less interested in the letter than she was in hearing about me. That may have been her way of getting a good letter, but her thoughtfulness was too sincere to be contrived.

I also admired the way Laura cared for her patients. She was completely devoted to them and provided the best care she knew how to give. No task was too menial, no request too big. Laura enjoyed her work because she found gratification in every aspect of the job. I'm saddened that Laura will no longer be able to make a contribution to the healthcare profession, and that people will miss out on the wonderful care she was able to give.

Laura described her commitment to service in a speech she composed for the honors and pinning ceremony that was held just prior to graduation. She described in detail how she and her husband came upon a man lying face down in the middle of the road as they were driving to a party. Although she was afraid of what she might find, she was compelled to help. Before she even realized it, she found herself racing toward the injured man. Laura described how people gathered around but failed to help the man in need. Despite her novice status, Laura performed like a seasoned professional as she completed a head-to-toe assessment of the gentleman and told others around her how they could help. Outside of the hospital setting, where equipment and technology aren't readily available, experienced professionals might be intimidated by the stranger Laura encountered. Yet, even as a student, Laura acted with courage and resolve and instinctively offered a helping hand.

I mourn Laura's loss because of the person she was and for the person she had the potential to be. It was a pleasure and a privilege to know Laura Difiglio Klink, and I am grateful for the opportunity to share my thoughts and feelings about this extraordinary individual. Although she lived only a short while, her time on this earth was not unnoticed. I know that she left an indelible mark on my life, and I am a better person for having known her. Laura was the model for nursing qualities we so much admire and need when providing patient care. She was also a truly incredible person and a model for others.

NIGHT SHIFT ON THE BUS

by Alicia Pufundt

The sun was just starting to set when the bus pulled over to the curb. Approximately 60 people were lined up, anxiously waiting for the bus. The staff emerged from the bus and started to assemble a food table for hot dogs, chips, pretzels, and lemonade. They encouraged the crowd to move back from the bus door and to stay in an orderly line. Eating dinner was the crowd's top priority. After everyone in the crowd had received food, some returned for "seconds," which were carefully put in a bag or container for later. As they received their food, almost everyone said, "Thank you." Matt walked through the crowd, greeting people he knew and asking how they were feeling. Matt was dressed in a tee shirt and jeans with a stethoscope around his neck. His name tag simply read, Matt—Nurse.

Patients served by Matthew Sorenson are people of all ages who are unable to receive conventional food and healthcare. They are the homeless, the working poor, and the mentally ill. Most of the people know the Night Ministry bus schedule. Most arrive on foot, a few by bikes. Some push shopping carts with all their worldly possessions piled high. Their faces reflect the difficult lives they lead; their clothes are not new. Some look shy and embarrassed to be at the Night Ministry bus, while others appear comfortable. A few people bring folding chairs so that they can sit, eat dinner, and chat. Others leave immediately after they finish eating.

When most are done eating, Matt makes rounds through the crowd, giving advice and asking about follow-up healthcare. He discusses medical problems while other staff hand out dental referral information. Some of the people seek Matt out, others are brought into the bus for medical assessment, testing, and counseling. Matt kneels next to an elderly woman to discuss her arthritis and asks how she is feeling. Then the staff begins to "pack up." Most of the people are gone; some have to be at their neighborhood shelters by 8 p.m. Others say good-bye till the next time the bus comes. It's been a good night; Matt assessed several people and gave others referrals for follow-up healthcare. The Night Ministry bus drives off in the darkness to the next stop because another group of people are waiting for food and healthcare.

Matt calls it a "relaxed kind of nursing." Matt has been a Night Ministry volunteer for the last four years. He works for the ministry one or two nights a week. He considers Night Ministry work a lot of fun. Matt is deeply committed to community nursing. He believes nursing should focus on the following question: "What can we, as nurses, do to help people make more positive changes?" This type of nursing requires patience and persistence, and relationships have to be established and trust must be earned. The Night Ministry has been serving the community for many years and has created trusting relationships with many of the "regulars."

This unique setting allows Matt to perform the type of nursing that really makes a difference. He strongly believes that nurses have a professional responsibility to provide the necessary resources by educating people so they can change *their own* behavior. Matt provides the patients with educational information and referrals to community resources. Matt knows that it's ultimately the patients' decision and responsibility to change their behavior. Night Ministry nursing allows Matt to reach a patient population whose needs are not met by the conventional healthcare system.

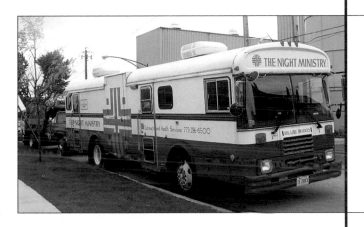

Matt enjoys being a nurse in the Night Ministry. It allows him to use his community and psychiatric nursing education, as well as his previous paramedic experience. For example, there are times when he assesses clients and calls 911 because of cardiac arrhythmias caused by drug abuse and/or respiratory problems secondary to heroin use. He recalls having to persuade his client's girlfriend to go to the emergency department after a fight with her boyfriend. She had a fractured clavicle and initially refused to go to the hospital.

Matt laughs as he recalls his most memorable experience with the Night Ministry. He was driving the bus on the west side of a Chicago neighborhood. He was driving carefully at 20 mph when he heard tires squealing and saw a car speeding erratically, in reverse, toward the bus. The car came to a screeching halt in front of the bus. Two women exited the car and came to the bus explaining that they *really* needed some of the free condoms the Night Ministry distributes. After receiving the condoms, they proceeded to drive away but this time in the right direction!

In his other life, Matt is working on postdoctoral research to determine whether stress is linked to multiple sclerosis exacerbations. He hopes to prove that increased stress affects the severity of multiple sclerosis symptoms. How can someone be so passionate and committed to two totally different types of nursing? However, Matt does not think these two types of nursing are different. Matt believes the nurse's role is to provide care and teach patients so they can change *their own* behavior to become more healthy. In the case of multiple sclerosis, if patients have better coping and stress management skills, they can positively impact their own health. Like the Night Ministry, Matt believes when patients understand their community resources and are provided with health education, they can change their behavior in a positive way to become healthier.

NURSE JOSIE
by Lori Fewster

"Good morning, Nurse Josie," shouts a pint-sized patient to the nurse as she makes her morning rounds. Nurse Josie greets each small patient on her 26-bed unit every morning, and each child greets her. She calls everyone by name, asks the older ones how they are feeling, and asks parents how their child slept. Josie poses these questions because she cares and listens carefully to the answers. She lets each patient know that "she is just around the corner" if anything is needed. Josie's individual attention makes each patient and family feel special and well cared for.

As a teenager, Josie watched as her father died in her arms at home because of a heart attack. She didn't understand what was happening at the time and was rendered helpless. At that moment, she vowed that no one else should have to watch a family member die and not understand what was going on. So she decided to become a nurse. A neighbor from down the street worked at a hospital and Josie asked whether she could tag along while she worked. The neighbor agreed, but it meant that Josie would have to wait by the side of the road every Saturday morning in the dark until the woman drove by to pick her up so they both could go to work.

Josie has touched so many patient's lives in her 28 years at the children's hospital. A day does not pass that she doesn't have a child or two on her lap while she is trying to do her paperwork. She talks on the telephone, holds one child, and feeds another all at the same time. Josie has made multi-tasking an art form.

Josie has seen most of her patients get better. She has also seen some of them die. Whether living or dying, Josie has always been at their bedsides because she cares and because she remembers her experience with her father. She likes the challenge of being there for her patients. Josie is so good at providing care for her patients they request her day after day. She is the nurse you would want to care for your children if they were in the hospital.

To Josie, the best part of nursing is watching one of "her kids" get better and go home. The worst part is watching one of them die. She feels a personal loss when children die, because they are the ones with whom she has spent the most time. She held them, bathed them, and helped them eat or drink.

The children become like family to Josie, and she does whatever she can to make them feel even the slightest bit better. Due to the chronic nature of some patients' illnesses, the children and parents feel as though they really are her family and ask Josie to be present while they die. At these times, the only thing Josie can do is hold a hand and let them know that they are not alone.

Although Josie is a wonderful teacher, there are some attributes that cannot be taught. These attributes are present in some people just as they are in her. The magnitude of her compassion knows no bounds. Her passion for being a nurse shines through each day. She goes quietly about her work each day, expecting no thanks, just enjoying what she does.

Josie and her husband often think about retiring and opening a bed and breakfast. Then reality sets in and Josie realizes the bed and breakfast would have to be near a hospital so she could be a nurse. Why would she continue this work after 35 or 40 years? Because being a nurse is who she is and always will be.

NURSING THE COMMUNITY: ELLEN BARTON

by JoEllen Wilbur

Her course was not that of a young woman who entered nursing because of an interest in the caring aspect of healthcare or because of restricted career options. She was of the new generation of women. The woman's movement, the war on poverty, and an unpopular Vietnam War influenced these women and her. This direction and focus provide the historical backdrop for Ellen Barton as she grew up in a suburban community of Chicago. Ellen began her 1972 college years in the business school at the Champaign campus of the University of Illinois. Ellen had a keen sense of social justice. Ellen's major was economics. She focused on the economics of poverty, rather than on the corporate world.

Armed with a college degree, she became a VISTA volunteer in impoverished, predominantly African-American migrant communities in Washington state. Ellen wrote grants, raised funds, fought for tenant rights, and worked in migrant clinics. Ellen began to experience how social justice and healthcare intertwined. She later worked with emotionally disturbed teens at a nursing home and in a dialysis clinic. Both experiences exposed Ellen to the human suffering and lack of preventive care experienced by the underserved.

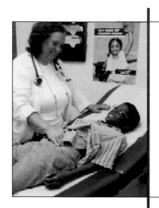

As Ellen's activist spirit grew, she sought a career that would further furnish her with the tools to address the healthcare needs of both individuals and their communities. For Ellen, public health nursing made sense. As a public health nurse, she could have interpersonal interaction with patients and the community, as well as implement her passion for social change.

Ellen obtained a second bachelor's degree, this time in nursing at the University of Illinois at Chicago. With barely a pause, she received a master's degree, specializing as a nurse practitioner and community nurse specialist. For over a decade, Ellen has selflessly dedicated her time and energy to working in a community healthcare center. The center is in a Chicago community that ranks among the highest for individuals living below the poverty level, teenage pregnancies, cardiovascular disease, and crime.

Ellen is clear as to why she provides nursing care in this community. She serves and learns from the people. Ellen does not push an agenda of her own. Her agenda is that of the people and the community she serves. Each patient encounter begins with a question, "What can I do to help you?" She responds to patients' needs by using language that is understandable, thus taking the mystery out of healthcare. Her co-workers report Ellen's patients are known for "pushing the system." This is directly attributable to Ellen's advocacy and the empowerment she instills in her patients.

On a typical day, Ellen can be seen at the clinic juggling many issues and patient problems at once. She always has a welcoming smile, and it is obvious that she loves her work. Her work embodies family care, and she cares for all extended family members, including aunts, uncles, and cousins of her caseload. Ellen fondly speaks of a 22-year-old African-American woman she followed and cared for 10 years ago. The woman periodically calls Ellen, just to check in and let her know how she is doing. Ellen's patients know she is there to help them celebrate accomplishments and to support them in difficult times.

Ellen's talents and advocacy are widely known among community and university leaders. They call upon Ellen to serve on task forces and advisory boards related to the care of the underserved on Chicago's west side. Examples include diabetes panels, asthma care committees, sexually transmitted disease initiatives, and health-promotion committees. Ellen likes to be involved in intervention programs that make a difference. Ellen values her ability to facilitate necessary connections to get healthcare projects "off the ground" and actually implemented in the community. Ellen serves as a role model and preceptor to community members wanting to gain exposure to healthcare careers, as well as to undergraduate and graduate students in nursing, public health, and medicine.

Central to Ellen's life is her husband, 13-year-old daughter, and 10-year-old son. Ellen's family lives, works, and goes to school in the racially integrated community. Her husband's job is to provide computer support for the local high school. Ellen and her husband chose this community because they are committed to fostering social justice for their children. From infancy, the children have accompanied Ellen to community health fairs and to the food depositories. They are now following in their parents' footsteps. Ellen's children are always the first to give money to a homeless person. A true spirit of shared responsibility allows both Ellen and her husband to blend family life with work through community service. Ellen truly *nurses* the community.

(Photography by Mark Meshon)

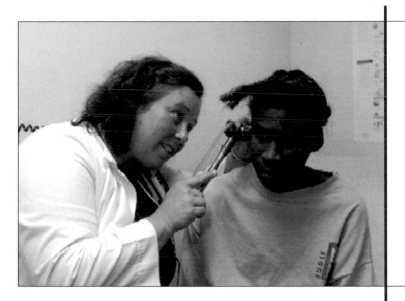

Ellen is clear as to why she provides nursing care in this community. She serves and learns from the people. Ellen does not push an agenda of her own. Her agenda is that of the people and the community she serves.

OLD SCHOOL: MISS MARY JANE MORRIS

by Elizabeth Burn Joosten

She wasn't our idea of today's nurse. If anything, we would pass her in the hospital and be amazed there were any nurses still around like her. Seeing her walking erectly down the halls of the University of Virginia Medical Center, we considered her a throwback, the nurse of yesteryear who seemed to us novices to be out of place in the modern world of medicine where we now worked.

It wasn't just the way she looked, although that was part of it. She was tall, thin, and walked the halls with a poised air, head held high, shoulders squared, back erect, just like you were supposed to look having been schooled with a book on your head. Her dress was even more distinguished. Her bright white hair was pulled back and neatly tucked under her pristine nurse's cap. Her white geriatric nursing shoes were always polished. She wore a crisply starched, white cotton uniform that hit her mid-calf. That's where the true sign that she was from another era was observed. There, running up the back of her white stocking legs, were the seams, straight as an arrow.

She was as particular about patient care as she was about her dress. She was in charge of training the nursing assistants, a job we thought appropriate for one seemingly so removed from the high-tech nursing we practiced. She would spend endless hours ensuring they learned how to make a proper bed, give a relaxing back rub, and patiently feed an elderly patient. We thought it was nice, but not really nursing.

We doubted that she comprehended the complex technology we used daily. We wondered how someone could have survived in such a vacuum. How could she not laud the technological feats we mastered daily? How could she remain so serenely confident and happy, teaching and doing the menial nursing tasks that she did daily and at her age?

And then one day, I was on a gurney being rolled back to my room after having had a tonsillectomy. She passed me, turned around, and escorted me back to my room. She changed me immediately out of the hospital gown into my flannel nightgown. She fluffed my pillows. She spooned me ice chips. She made sure I had some pain medication. She adjusted the lighting so that it wasn't too bright. In that half hour, she taught me about the art of nursing. She also made me a believer in and a practitioner of the special "art" of nursing.

PHONE CONVERSATIONS

by Frances R. Vlasses

Ida returned from a meeting with a little scrap of paper that had an e-mail address on it. She was as pleased as punch. "I found the perfect nurse for your book! We met and talked on an airplane, and you must call her," said Ida. And she was right. Colleen Kelly Redeker is full of incredible, amazing, happy, and sad stories. She is a raconteur, a storyteller whose stories inspire and instruct. Her career spans 15 years with stories about nurses taking care of children and adults with neurological problems. Through the stories, she shares the wisdom, enthusiasm, and peace that she finds in her privileged position of caring for others during their critical life passages.

Early in her career, Colleen worked at the Chicago Institute of Neurosurgery and Neuroresearch. "The brain fascinated me," she says. "For all that we've advanced in the sciences, we still know little about the spinal cord and brain." This motivated her. A short, unsatisfying stint as a travel nurse forged her patient advocacy skills and confirmed her commitment to neurological nursing. She enjoys the intellectual stimulation and support she finds in high-tech university settings. Of course, this means that she works with the most challenging situations.

Colleen tells of a four-year-old who was admitted to the intensive care unit, where she worked, after the sudden onset of a severe illness. This child earned the unfortunate title of being "the sickest child I took care of in my career." Ten days later, as she was caring for this child and cradling him like a baby, he woke and said to her, "I'm not a baby." She says, "There is no greater joy than to watch this type of recovery." She also tearfully remembers a handsome young man with severe brain injury from a motorcycle accident. Her only connection to him was to help his friends say "good-bye."

The first child that she "lost" was a healthy little boy who fell at the park. He was supposed to live. "I was so shocked! I was like the family." But she calls this patient her turning point. "This patient changed me. It was then that I knew I really liked neuro and realized what an honor it is to be a part of these special times with families."

She participated in the Head Injury Support Group for six years. "It was a humbling experience for me. The group really altered my opinion of what they *should* be doing and/or *could* be doing with their lives.

She comforted a woman with a 20-year history of drug abuse whose family never bothered to call her during her Gamma Knife treatment. "Thank you for being so nice to me," she said, "a lot of people are not very nice to me." "I didn't think I was being overly nice to her, I was just being her nurse."

As the stories roll out, a good listener begins to hear the concepts Colleen values. She is teaching about caring for others with joy and peace. Each lesson is connected to a very personal experience with one of her patients. She shows us nursing practice knowledge at its best. Here is what she taught me:

On personalized care: No two neurological patients are the same; everyone's story is different, regardless of the outcome. People need to be cared for. Individuals with brain injuries are often disregarded. They must be treated with patience and respect. I try to determine what the brain tumor is doing to the person versus what the treatment is doing.

On how we serve: As a nurse, you want to "fix everything." Many times, we can't "fix" things, they just happen.

On prognosis: We can't judge, and we can't take away hope. There is so much that we do not know.

On coping: My lifeline is being able to care for patients and families—being involved, being present.

On politics and bureaucracy: The patient always comes first.

Colleen's commitment to neurological nursing is strong. She actively works to educate people about neurological disorders and Gamma Knife intervention. Although her career has included some major leadership accomplishments, she finds her joy in taking care of patients. In her current position at the University of Washington Gamma Knife Center at Harborview, Colleen works with many individuals with end-stage disease and various types of vascular malfunction. She is working to improve quality of life. She develops extremely intense relationships in the eight hours she spends with each patient. "It's amazing," she says in describing her patients, "they are the kindest, most compassionate, and warmest people to work with. Their perspective is different."

She sees emotional pain more than physical pain in her patients. Her interventions are about comfort. In her extremely high-tech, ultra-modern environment, she calls up the armamentarium of her most powerful interventions from the fundamentals of practice, gentle touch, eye contact, explanation, respect, listening, and warm baths. Her goal is to help people journey beyond what illness brought them by hearing their stories, to remind them that they are interesting people, not diseases, and to affirm them as unique individuals.

During my conversations with Colleen, I was struck by her thoughtful reflection, her presence, her passion to learn from each patient. She shows us the interior aspects of a nurse's thoughts and how she builds the foundations within herself to continue to serve others. Difficult work, yes, but for Colleen, the only kind.

POETRY IN NURSING

by Mary Beth Williams

There is nothing ordinary about Hollye Harrington Jacobs, a nurse with a passion for life and palliative care. Of course, few nurses are ordinary, and Hollye is definitely no exception. Florence Nightingale wrote that nursing is "the finest of the fine arts." Of all the fine arts, nursing, to me, is poetry. Poetry's great power is its ability to take a moment, an experience, a feeling and to hold it and communicate it before it is understood. It is a communication from one soul to another. Langston Hughes (1998) may have said it best when he said,

> POETRY IS THE HUMAN SOUL ENTIRE.
> SQUEEZED LIKE A LEMON OR A LIME,
> DROP BY DROP, INTO ATOMIC WORDS (P. 34).

There is a compelling poetry to Hollye's nursing practice as a pediatric nurse in palliative care. She embodies moments of grace as she accompanies children and their families into that foreign and terrifying world of illness, fear, suffering, death, and grief.

Hollye's strength is her ability to be with and stay with family members wherever they need to journey during their experience. Hollye exhibits the art of simply being with someone in a difficult moment. Her artistry is reflected in her sensing and then being able to find the words and actions families need to hear and feel to support them.

Hollye's character is exposed in her inclusion of others within the interdisciplinary team in the journey. She may be leading the way, but she does not control the process. Hollye expands the space around the family to assure that there is room for all members of the team and that the family is the true focus.

Is this poetry in action? Listening and experiencing the way Hollye engages, connects, and collaborates with families and colleagues, one is struck by her genuine caring. Families, patients, and staff see Hollye's search for rhythm and meaning when working with her. Hollye's poetry generates focus on what "really matters and is meaningful" to the child, family, and staff.

Hollye Jacobs came to the University of Chicago Children's Hospital with a passion and a hope that she could improve the lives of kids and their families who were faced with diseases or conditions that do not have a therapy or cure readily available. As a fellow in medical ethics, she focused her energy on understanding the complexities when resolving ethical dilemmas. Now, Hollye combines her medical ethics knowledge with her ability to serve as an advocate for children. Hollye explores with the family and the child what they define as quality of life when faced with life-threatening diseases. She makes sure families and the children understand their medical and life options when they make difficult life and death decisions.

With a captivating curiosity and energy, Hollye studied pediatric palliative care programs across the United States and Ireland. Her goal was to understand and quantify best practices. Hollye reached out to staff in all the units, departments, and disciplines to share the knowledge she gained from this research. She also openly shared the practices and tools that she collected and developed. Hollye created a palliative care curriculum and conducts classes to assure full access of her knowledge to all interested.

With equal impact, she has made herself available to families during the tough times of sadness, pain, and yes, anger. She never avoids the family and the child during their challenging times and decisions. Hollye places herself next to the family and the labyrinth of complex feelings that they hold in their hearts and spirits. She does not waiver, no matter how difficult it may be. Hollye assures that the poetry of life is not denied a child or family even when in the final phase of life.

There are many nurses at the University of Chicago Children's Hospital who inspire me with their character and spirit, along with their professional commitment. They squeeze poetry out of life's toughest moments. This is what inspires me as I work with and learn from Hollye Jacobs. She is extraordinary. She is a poet.

Nurses in the Chicago community have taught me so much about the poetry that is expressed through nursing. A few of my nursing muses include:

- *Margie Wisniewski,* who illuminated the best in nursing practice in the middle of the night as she does now in the daylight.
- *Karen Freehill,* who frames hope for others in their darkest moments.
- *Jamie O'Malley,* who leads nurses, like no other, into full poetic expression in their practices.
- *Lisa Krammer* and *Judy Paice,* who understand suffering and the power that words backed by knowledge and wisdom have to relieve it.
- *Dawn Baddeley,* who exudes integrity and honor in the difficult moments as well as the easy ones.
- *Kathryn Clarke,* who has the gift of a poet's voice as well as the depth.
- *Sharon Jackson Barton,* who is the finest poet within the nursing profession.

As William Butler Yeats (1938) once wrote:

THINK WHERE MAN'S GLORY MOST BEGINS AND ENDS
AND SAY MY GLORY WAS I HAD SUCH FRIENDS (P. 123).

Hughes, L. (1998). *The best American poetry.* New York, NY: Scribner.
Yeats, W.B. (1938). *New poems.* Dublin: Ireland: Cuala Press.

SECOND TIME AROUND

by Susan Randall

Tom always moves through the nursing unit with confidence. His peers consider him one of the best nurses in the hospital. His graying hair exposes his experience and comforts patients. Physicians and Tom collaborate respectfully on patient care issues. In less than one month, Tom will celebrate his first anniversary as a nurse.

Tom started out with dreams and the best intentions. He was smart and after high school was interested in the world around him. Tom went to college to study science. Four years later, he graduated with a degree in biology. However, by then the world had changed and presented the facts of life to him. With the Vietnam War raging, he felt lucky to have finished college at all. Tom had a high draft number so he did not get called to serve in the military.

Facing difficulty finding a job and making a living with a science degree, Tom looked beyond laboratory work and teaching. He found a job in a pet store where he could combine his science degree with business. At this time, most pet stores were independently owned and operated. He was young and eager and was rewarded for his hard work. After a few years, Tom had learned enough about the business and saved enough to buy his own pet store. He married and began a family.

Tom read in *Time* magazine about out-of-work steelworkers in Pittsburgh cross-training into other fields so they could support their families. "How interesting," he thought. It seemed so out of character, especially the picture of the burly man with large hands and thick forearms lifting a tiny preemie from its incubator. It seemed like a strange twisting of roles. The brawny man, accustomed to hard, physical labor, changing his course in mid-life to pursue a nursing career as a caregiver and healer. This memorable picture stuck in Tom's mind, as he continued to run his pet business.

For 20 years, the pet store business was very good for Tom and his family. However, as the pet store industry evolved, the small, independent pet stores faced insurmountable competition from the large chain stores. Tom was forced to liquidate his business in 1998. With a family to support, Tom weighed his options. He liked people, liked helping, and wanted to use his science background. Another of Tom's desires was to have a job where he didn't have to sit down all day. Tom remembered the picture of the burly steelworker who had become a nurse.

Tom's mother was a nurse, so he had a favorable view of the profession and a realistic idea of what it took to be a good nurse. After careful consideration and family consultation, Tom enrolled in Northern Virginia Community College. In June of 2001, he graduated with an Associate Degree in Nursing and embarked on his second career.

Barely three months into his new career, the September 11 events occurred. It was Tom's day off, but as soon as he heard about the Pentagon tragedy, he called the hospital for instructions as to how he could help, wondering what he was in for. It was hours later before he and his peers realized there would be few patients to care for, because most were dead. This experience helped solidify some of Tom's deeply held beliefs, especially about service and patriotism. His philosophy is that the sheer act of being a nurse is, in itself, patriotic, because nurses do *good* for society.

With conviction, Tom believes more young men should choose nursing as a primary career. He believes nursing provides a good salary to support a family and provides possibilities for advancements. He also believes there are many misconceptions about the work of nursing. He thinks people look at nurses as service workers whose job it is to "bring people things and keep them happy." Tom believes the public does not see nurses as consultants and associates to physicians, thus devaluing the standing of the profession. He believes the public views other careers as more exciting or glamorous; thus, men do not seek nursing as a career.

Based on Tom's own personal experience, he believes there are many similarities between a business career and a nursing career, such as the need and use of problem solving, decision making, customer satisfaction, and communication, to name a few. Unlike business, however, Tom believes nursing is one of the most respected and trusted professions. He believes nursing provides immense personal satisfaction. One of the most satisfying aspects of Tom's job is knowing that no matter how hard he works during the day, at the end of his shift, he turns his patients over to a competent, caring colleague. Tom also finds it very rewarding to go home, after working as a nurse, knowing he made a difference.

Tom has learned a lot as a nurse, such as hard work pays off. You can do anything if you put your mind to it, and profound opportunities arise out of adversity. "It doesn't get any better than this," he says. Tom is a true advocate for nurses and feels fortunate he can receive so many rewards from nursing.

One of the most satisfying aspects of Tom's job is knowing that no matter how hard he works during the day, at the end of his shift, he turns his patients over to a competent, caring colleague. Tom also finds it very rewarding to go home, after working as a nurse, knowing he made a difference.

SISTER SHEILA MURPHY

by Carol Hutelmyer and Peggy Daly

heila Murphy entered the Sisters of Mercy in 1961. She initially taught elementary school children and later in 1970 earned an Associate's Degree in Nursing at Gwynedd-Mercy College. Sheila's nursing career began in a medical surgical unit at Misericordia Hospital, an inner-city hospital (presently Mercy Hospital of Philadelphia). Throughout her nursing career, Sheila carried out the mission of the Sisters of Mercy by providing care and help to the neediest of the needy.

Sister Sheila volunteered to go to Peru to work with the poor. She taught the people very basic health procedures, such as hand washing, boiling water, and other aspects of hygiene and nutrition. Her journey in Peru lasted 8 1/2 years. Upon returning from Peru, Sister Sheila accepted a new challenge as a nurse at Calcutta House in North Philadelphia, a non-denominational residence/hospice. The Calcutta House had 18 residents who received care for HIV. As director of resident care, Sheila's primary goal was to create a home for people who have never known one. Residents came to this special place for several reasons. Some hoped to get their lives back together; others who had become disabled by their disease had no place to live, and still others needed hospice care because they were dying.

When asked directly what she did with and for the residents at Calcutta House, Sheila simply says, "I was there with them." Despite this seemingly limited description, Sheila identified her goals as creating a home for the residents, stabilizing the disease process, and assisting people to use available resources to manage their illnesses. Her other goals for the residents at Calcutta House were to help them learn social interaction skills and self-care skills and to modify existing behaviors. Sister Sheila wanted to ensure each resident the best possible results. Sheila spent time with each individual and tried to foster an environment of love and caring. While Sheila talked little about what she did, she spoke freely about the people with whom she worked.

Sheila identified some special moments of her time at Calcutta House. Love blossomed for one couple, and the newlyweds now live in an apartment at Calcutta House while learning to manage finances (deal with a bank and budgeting), cooking, and other life skills. A person with a brain tumor wanted to walk again. Sheila supported his hopes and dreams by arranging evaluations and physical therapy at a rehabilitation center. While reality may limit his

final outcome, maintaining hope is an essential element of his care. A blind man received attention and love from the staff. A transgender person found acceptance in the Calcutta House.

The atmosphere at Calcutta House is casual. The professional staff is comprised of a number of disciplines, such as nursing, social work, and occupational and physical therapy, to name a few. To accomplish the best care for patients, Sister Sheila provides guidance to and participates in a multidisciplinary approach. Tensions could and do arise among the disciplines and/or residents over such issues as how to support a demented person with inappropriate behavior or when to apply "tough love" to deal with the behaviors of a person with an addiction. Conflicts are resolved with an eye for what is fair to all the residents. The approach to the issues is decided at multidisciplinary staff meetings and weekly resident meetings. At Calcutta House, the approach is holistic because the residents are valued as whole persons.

The gift Sister Sheila received while at Calcutta House was the ability to listen to the longings of the human heart as a nurse and to develop a great appreciation for those life concerns identified by the residents. For example: a wheelchair-dependent person who was receiving dialysis desired only to return to his home and his children; an individual married to a drug addict is admitted to hospice, and his sole desire was to be present for his little girl, the center of his life. Sheila considers the frequent conversations she had about these very personal concerns as gifts and made sure that the care goals reflected these concerns as gifts—to improve the quality of future life or to experience peace-filled end-of-life care. Sister Sheila returned to Peru in August of 2002 after 5 1/2 years at Calcutta House. She is much loved and is greatly missed.

THE ART OF BENDING WITH THE WIND

by Deb Gauldin

ife takes some unexpected turns. But these are a whole lot easier to navigate when you have faith that you are being divinely guided. When your heart is open and your intuition is calling, it's like a branch in springtime, like a tree that simply cannot *not* bud. So it is for Certified Nurse Midwife Therese Doyle.

Therese is a woman of remarkable strength and determination, whose guiding principle is staying true to herself and the plan that God unfolds, one day at a time. Professionally, that plan includes having earned an advanced practice nursing degree and establishing her own Chicago-area business, Midwest Midwifery. Since 1996, Therese's business has provided women with the compassionate care and dignity they deserve.

Therese is a wife of 21 years and the mother of three daughters. She is as adept at running a busy household as she is at delivering newborns. Therese will tell you staying flexible and *bending with the wind* serves her best. This piece of wisdom, she says, comes after years of balancing drive and idealism with exhaustion and reality. With maturity has come the ability to accept that sometimes she has done simply "all she can do."

And then there are those times she is led to do more, much more. In 1990, when she saw the "20/20" television report revealing the unfathomable suffering of orphaned and abandoned Romanian children, Therese knew there would be no end to the lengths she and her husband would go to help. The first order of business was to pull out an encyclopedia to discover just where Romania was situated. Seventeen months and many challenges later, they returned from Eastern Europe and with tears of joy, they introduced Shannon, eight, and Megan, five, to their new little sister. To this day Christina, a delightful 11-year-old, full of whimsy, is a reminder to Therese to never second guess her instincts, doubt her faith, or fail to do what she feels must be done.

Therese is only rigid when it comes to accepting the limitations placed on nurses by others. Because she is an avid learner, bright, and self-assured, she takes advantage of many opportunities. Therese works hard to bridge the gaps that often separate nurses, physicians, and administrators.

Therese has witnessed success firsthand. While celebrating her success, she has also had to address challenges. In spite of each new challenge, her practice gathered momentum as more women opted for midwifery care. Through it all, Therese stayed true to her convictions and mission. She ultimately forged a path making it easier for future nurse midwives to follow.

Therese's profound respect for the nursing profession was rekindled when she was forced to deal with the healthcare system as a wife. Her physically fit, affable husband was recently diagnosed with multiple sclerosis. In the midst of the initial crisis, Therese found herself sitting in a hotel room outside a renowned clinic turning to the most basic tenets of nursing theory. Surrounded by specialists attending to lesions and organs, no one seemed to be looking at the whole person. Therese instinctively penned a nursing care plan that was a holistic look at her husband and the many facets of his care.

"I have never been so aware of the differences in nursing and medicine as I was when Jack became sick," Therese reflects. "There were times when the physicians didn't even ask our names or why we were there. We were never asked how we were doing as a family or why we traveled so many miles." But nurses did ask these questions!

The family has found the most comfort, not surprisingly, from nursing specialists, who acknowledged what a shock this diagnosis created. Therese has met nurses who aren't afraid of tending to a patient's spirit and nurses who aren't afraid to share a tear. This experience has moved Therese to encourage young women and men to consider a career in nursing. She is determined to keep chipping away at the barriers and stereotypes that taint the profession and to see nurses receive the credit they deserve.

How will Therese handle the challenges ahead? Probably in the same way that she did in Romania. The same way she fought for midwifery practice. The same way she has always responded to human suffering, with an open heart, with unwavering faith, taking one day at a time, and with flexibility . . . *bending with the wind.*

THE GIFT

by Susan Randall

Think for a minute about something *bad* that happened to you, then think about the *worst* thing that ever happened to you. Imagine you are a young housewife with three young children and a spouse. One of your children is born with multiple disabilities, but your family is coping with the stress, and your son is doing well. Your husband, a career military man, receives a dream assignment in Hawaii. Your family is excited about living in paradise, even if it is far away from the support of family and friends. Then, your disabled child gets very sick and needs specialized care. What would you do?

When Matthew, their son, became ill, the family was transferred by the military to Washington, D.C., so he could have specialized care. Laura learned all she could about her son's care needs, both in the hospital and at home. She learned how to use the equipment Matthew needed, and she became proficient in the very complex care skills Matthew needed. The home health nurses were a great support for the family and in teaching Laura skills. Laura appreciated what she was taught; however, she most of all appreciated being encouraged to care for Matthew with *motherly love.* With the continued teaching and support from nurses, Laura and her family were able to care for Matthew until his death at eight years of age.

There are few events as painful as the loss of a child. Grief is a physical sensation. Every part of the body aches, the inside and outside of the skin seem painful. The brain is numbed, and the heart feels as though it will split in two or more pieces. How could Laura possibly go on? She didn't think she could, but somehow in spite of everything, she did go on. The daily routine of life provided structure and comfort for Laura during her grief.

Time passed and each day was a little less painful for Laura and her family. She often thought of the nurses who helped her get through the nightmare. Some had become close friends. Laura was profoundly grateful for the support and care she received from the nurses during the family's ordeal and wanted to repay the kindness in some way. When her husband retired from the military, Laura began to consider going back to school. As she considered career options, Laura asked one of Matthew's nurses about nursing school. She also asked the nurse whether she thought Laura "had what it takes" to be

a nurse. "I know you as a mom and a person, and I know how well you cared for your son. I think you will be a great nurse," she told Laura.

So began Laura's professional career path of nursing. It was a career borne out of tribute to both her son and to his nurses. It was a career rooted in service to others and in the desire to care for the whole family experiencing the illness of a child. Laura knew right from the start that she wanted to work in pediatric acute care. Laura used her connections to get a job interview and subsequent employment as a pediatric nurse.

Laura is able to see the care environment from both sides, from a nurse's perspective and from a parent's perspective. She works hard in maintaining healthy boundaries with families and seldom shares her story of Matthew with families and colleagues. Laura believes she has been given a gift, the ability to anticipate parental concerns and needs as well as see the situation from the family's perspective.

She aims to make the transition from hospital to home occur as smoothly as possible for her patients. Laura makes sure families are knowledgeable about continuing care needs and are capable of providing the care the child needs.

Looking back on her life, Laura is glad she has been able to help so many families with sick children. She is thankful that she has been able to give back and return the favor to the profession, the same favor that helped her and her family when Matthew was sick and required home care and mothering. "Knowing I've made such a difference," she says, "is the best *gift* of all."

THE MILLION-DOLLAR SECRET: SCHOOL NURSING

by Phyllis Powell Pelt

The collective financial impact of "lost school days" could amount to at least one million dollars during the career of one school nurse. Lost school days are due to pregnancies, injuries, infections, stress, sleeplessness, low academic productivity, lack of day care, and law suits. To date, no study has been conducted to actually document the financial impact of the school nurse. However, school nurses like Debbie Koppelman are testimony to the fact that professional school health services positively impact the health, wellness, and achievement of students while saving lots of money over time.

Debbie had surgery for thyroid cancer at the age of seven, and that is when she decided she wanted to be a nurse. Like many nurses, after graduating from the University of Illinois in 1968, Debbie searched for a nurse specialty in which she could make a difference. Debbie became a public health nurse in Washington, D.C., for VISTA. When Debbie returned to Chicago, there were no openings for public health nurses. Not easily discouraged, Debbie recognized she could use her public health skills as a school nurse at Evanston Township High School. Today, Debbie is the head nurse of Student Health Services. "School nursing is the only real job I have ever had where I use my skills by teasing out health issues that impact life and learning." At first, other school personnel did not see how Deb fit in the school system, but now they seek her out whenever there is a question about the impact of health on students and on their learning.

Debbie reflects on some of her most critical and pivotal contributions related to support of student achievement. Her school health practice includes numerous examples of the impact of her involvement on the lives of the students and programs offered because she thoughtfully "challenged the process and system." As a school nurse, Deb has been in a position to maximize *teachable moments* by serving as a catalyst to resolve health issues of students and by supplying needed and effective resources. For example, when a student was raped at the school, Deb, a member of the student service team, was able to arrange for the widely acclaimed Sol Gordon to talk to students and staff. His presentation on teen sexuality had a powerful effect on the students and helped refocus the response of the rape crisis.

Another *teachable moment* involved working with a student who had a congenital bladder problem that created an offensive body odor. The student performed self-catheterization daily in the health office. The student had no friends and said she did not need friends. School Nurse Deb, knowledgeable in growth and development, became involved, which improved the quality of this student's life. Deb had multiple conferences with the student and her teacher, family, and psychiatrist. Together, they helped the student tell her peers about her medical condition. At the end of her presentation, students and faculty were crying, and she was given a standing ovation. This was a turning point in the student's life. She developed friends and continues to receive support from School Nurse Deb.

Debbie was an "early adopter" of the school-based clinic at Evanston Township. She was able to articulate the impact of a partnership between school nursing and a school-based clinic. She was not threatened by the opening of a clinic. Her school nurse team provided assessments for the school-based clinic, which actually decreased the number of students missing school and/or being treated in a hospital. Early detection and treatment of health problems, along with increasing the time students spent in the learning environment, is yet another cost savings that impacted the partnership between school nursing and a student clinic.

Over 15,000 students visit the high school health services annually. Debbie and her team have become very adept at assessment and referral. "A large percentage of the students do not have an organic problem." Panic attacks, anxiety issues, school phobia, and abuse are some of the problems that often are woven into the physical complaints. Debbie's conversations with students and parents help her discover the "real" source of the student's physical complaints.

Debbie is proud of an updated process developed by the student health team that assists students who have a history of substance abuse. She was an original facilitator and liaison for students with substance abuse. Now there is a full-time, certified addiction counselor at the school site.

Debbie returned to the University of Illinois at Chicago to pursue a Master of Science degree in Nursing. After that, she was a preceptor for school nurse interns and students from other disciplines. She also continues to be innovative in her approaches to challenges and passionate about supporting students and staff so they can become effective health consumers. Her legacy is the development of a safer, *healthier school community* and preparing students to navigate healthcare systems in their adult lives. Ultimately, Debbie hopes she has played a positive role in helping students become mentally and physically healthy and thus more productive citizens, an investment clearly worth more than a *million dollars*.

THE QUIET SOLDIER: RUTH SMITH

by Sharon Brody Heath

three-year-old little girl once sat in a hospital bed for ten days. She didn't remember any of the illness, only that she wanted to be a nurse. Never changing the goal of her career, she knew it was her destiny; she was meant to be a nurse.

Right after high school, she attended nursing school in a three-year hospital diploma program. After three years of hard work and long hours, she started her career in a small community hospital, working on a medical-surgical unit. Quickly, thirty years passed. Many nurses have worked beside her and learned from her. No one has ever had a negative thought about her, just great admiration and respect.

Eight years after she started her career, at the age of 29, something was not physically right for her. She was having difficulty with dizziness, extreme fatigue, right leg parasthesia, and numbness and tingling of her left leg. She was diagnosed with multiple sclerosis, a disease that attacks the brain cells, causing weakness to muscles and the body. Being treated by doctors and hospitalized when needed, Ruthy could not be stopped. She insisted on working. She never complained or asked, "Why me?" Some nights, by the end of the shift, she could barely walk the long nursing hallways. She never asked for extra help, and she never accepted a lighter load than her co-workers. For Ruthy, things had to be equal and fair. There is no easy road for her. She never sat when there was work to be done.

Through the years, Ruthy learned, in order to do nursing work, she had to pace herself. On days off, she conserves her energy in order to keep up with the hectic pace of nursing shifts. "I have to set small goals and have rest periods in order to have energy for my workday." Setting short-term goals allows her to follow through with any obligation she accepts.

Ruthy says, "Being diagnosed with MS has taught me life's priorities. I learned that family and friends are important. Being a nurse and doing the best I can on a daily basis is what I try to do. There are so many negatives in life—we need to look for the good things." Ruthy's greatest satisfaction comes from making an impact on someone's life. She enjoys helping a patient understand the doctor's explanations, teaching patients about their diseases, watching the health progress of patients and their families, and being able to follow through from the beginning to end with a patient and the family, whether it be happy or sad, a healthy situation or even a terminal one. In all cases, Ruthy shares a smile to make someone feel good. These values and actions form Ruthy's unique signature.

Being a role model was not in Ruthy's plan. "It must be something that just happened; it wasn't something I set out to do." She can't believe people look up to her and respect her. "I never knew people saw me that way. I just try to do the best I can, to look for the good things and to give positive feedback. Just to hear a patient say 'thank you' or 'you have helped me understand,' that's what it means to be a nurse."

Emergencies happen all the time; things become very busy, sometimes to the point where chaos prevails. Patients need beds and a nurse to care for them and have questions that need to be answered. Remaining cool, calm, and collected can be very difficult, but not for Ruthy. She handles every problem/situation calmly and slowly, giving time, energy, and compassion to patients and families without missing a beat. She puts the staff, the patients, and their families at ease, bringing a smile and kindness with her at all times. Ruthy is the quiet soldier.

THE WHOLE IS GREATER THAN THE SUM OF THE PARTS: A TEAM OF NURSES

by Janie Lea Gawrys and Mary Beth Williams

I n the midst of challenging times, there are often individuals who will step forward and distinguish themselves among all of the others. Much more unusual is when a group of individuals is able to come together during a time of adversity and form a team united in focus and commitment.

This is a story of just such a group of individuals; this is the story of six staff nurses and two nurse educators. These nurses initially came together as an education steering committee. In the process of working to achieve its goals, the group evolved into an extraordinary team, a team that was a powerful force for change, a team that gave new definition to the concept of colleagueship in the Pediatric Intensive Care Unit (PICU) at the University of Chicago Children's Hospital.

This partnership among nurses began in September of 2001, after a pediatric intensive care nursing focus group identified priorities for improvements that were needed for both patient care and staff satisfaction. At the time, the pediatric intensive care unit was faced with complex and long-standing challenges, making the retention of experienced nurses very difficult. With a razor-sharp eye focused on quality and a commitment to excellence in caring for kids and families, this group of staff nurses stepped forward and volunteered to look honestly and directly at the standards and care practices in the nursing unit.

The nurses looked into the problems, challenges, and potential solutions that existed in the nursing unit. They took significant risks as they asked the hard questions and brought to the surface the clinical, educational, and leadership flaws that existed. However, instead of receding back into the safety zone of neutrality, something incredible began to grow within this group. The nurses began to move out of the traditional roles of fellow committee members and into a dynamic and cohesive team, a team committed to action and excellence. The relationships among this team of diverse individuals confirmed the adage that "the whole is greater than the sum of the individual parts."

As a team, they showed an ability to function seamlessly together and achieve outcomes that were previously considered nearly, if not totally, impossible. Educational initiatives took root and staff support and recognition efforts were undertaken. Collaborative relationships with nursing and medical colleagues, as well as with all of the other disciplines, became the expectation. The unit began to achieve the goals and dreams so many nurses had deserved and desired for such a long time.

Who are the faces and what is the story of these courageous nurses who stepped forward to create quality and excellent care during challenging times? *Mary Strenski* is one of the original nurses who provided leadership for the education team/committee. She is amazing and never ceases to amaze others with her talents and personality. Mary is a charismatic nurse who is well recognized for her superior clinical skills, her status as a senior nurse, and her understanding and sensitivity to families under stress. Mary is honest in the most wonderful way. She can be counted on to tell you the "full and accurate truth" about a difficult situation. However, while telling you the truth, she maintains your dignity and that of others in the process. Mary's gift of humor lightens the heaviness of the message she communicates, but it does not diminish the accuracy or importance of the message she is conveying. She was a natural leader for this team and the challenges it undertook.

Families and colleagues trust *Annabel Bedoya.* She has the ability and willingness to give you "the straight scoop." If a difficult decision lies ahead for a family, Annabel is the one person families will request to provide their care because she can be counted upon to stay with them through all of the difficult questions and times. These skills made her a natural for the education team. The same commitment and talents she exhibits in her care with kids and families were and continue to be transferred to her work with colleagues. Her respect for others combined with her high standards make for a powerful combination.

Nilsa Campos is a nurse who is a perfect example of "still waters run deep." Everybody feels her quiet strength as she serves as a compass for others. She is often identified as a "thinker." She never jumps to quick conclusions, but systematically lays out the bigger picture and context for situations. Like her team members, honesty is one of her hallmarks as is her ability to hear a confidence and maintain it "like a vault."

Amanda Wulff might be considered a junior nurse by standards of longevity. However, after only three years, she has jumped forward into an informal role of staff advocate in her work on the committee and within the daily operations of the pediatric intensive care unit. Amanda has spearheaded multiple initiatives. Her efforts communicate, in a sophisticated and meaningful way, invaluable support for staff members when they are doing their important work of caring for children and their families. At heart, Amanda is a risk taker with a passion for the truth.

Gloria Sandoval is the quintessential team player. As a nurse, she maintains confidences and communicates respect to all fellow nurses, physicians, or housekeepers. Gloria does not discriminate based upon position or status. Gloria demands no credit be given but simply commands the respect and admiration of all team members. She has a keen wit that balances the serious nature of others. Gloria is someone you can count on with important matters.

Michele Rosado, although a nurse, is a teacher at heart. She has an uncanny ability to remember information, rationales, and clinical experiences. She brings these memories and facts together in a meaningful and most natural way. Michele has no false pride, and if she doesn't understand something, she is the first to "look for the information" and bring the knowledge back to others. Michele's wisdom is a strength that enhances her role within the team as she brings her past knowledge and experience to the team members as they seek to learn and improve care.

Melanie Sojka and *Chris Schindler* are the two nurse educators who first brought this team together. Together, they set out to create the path to excellence. Melanie and Chris had a vision of how change could occur on the unit. Through staff-driven educational initiatives, the quality and comprehensiveness of care would stretch upward. Their vision was to include and support staff reaching for and providing the standards of care the children and families deserve. It was through their exemplar facilitation, mentoring, and trust that Chris and Melanie quickly instilled the same vision in the committee members. Chris and Melanie's leadership enabled the group to transform from a traditional committee into a cohesive, dynamic, and results-oriented team.

Was it Melanie's talent in connecting the uniqueness of each individual member that was most influential, or was it her stellar initiative as a professional? Was it Chris' integrity and conceptual skills that were most responsible for the development of this team? If you listen to the team members, they will say that it was the vision, commitment, and courage that Chris and Melanie demonstrated that helped transform the committee into a dynamic team. It was their commitment and vision that empowered the individuals and thrust them into the cohesive team; truly *"the team as a whole was greater than the sum of the individual members of the team."*

Interactions with this phenomenal team suggest there is no one nurse hero. In fact, the members of the team have collectively achieved that which is most difficult. They have blended their talents, both personal and professional, into a cohesive and seamless whole. They have balanced each other in honest and committed dialogue, supporting each other through some very challenging landscape.

The team can be credited for improving all aspects of patient care. They are altering the experience of their nursing colleagues. The team gives hope to nurses committed to excellence. They are creating a practice environment for nurses to provide the excellence in care that families have entrusted nurses to provide to their children.

When books are written about what it takes to be a particularly dynamic and effective team, I suspect the authors are merely describing in words the characteristics and activities of this group. Clearly, when nurses work together like this team, they form a powerful chemistry and hence, a force for impressive change and excellence!

WEATHERING THE STORM: JANICE MARSHALL

by Judy Lau Carino

Although Janice has been a nurse for 21 years, she cannot recall choosing nursing as a career. Janice truthfully admits she became a nurse because nursing was going to exist forever and nurses would always be in demand. She knew nursing was a job she could step into and feel secure. However, getting through nursing school was a rough road for Janice. While other college students got A's and B's, Janice struggled, studying endless hours just to pass. Janice finally earned a degree in nursing, receiving the security she desired. To her surprise, she became passionate about nursing. Janice began nursing on a general medicine floor at Loyola University Medical Center, outside Chicago, and currently works in the telemetry and surgical cardiovascular unit. Janice is a nurturing and caring single parent of Ashley and Michael.

Janice has learned she really enjoys working with people and being a patient advocate. She makes the voices and needs of her patients heard. Janice simply wants to make a difference in people's lives. She has always felt "blessed" to be healthy and to be "out of the bed" as a caretaker. However, while Janice values the importance of taking care of herself, for 17 years she knew she had fibroid tumors in her right breast. She always monitored the tumors with appropriate screening. In January of 2000, Janice noticed that the lumps in her right breast were growing larger. The follow-up mammogram and biopsy revealed a malignancy.

Janice does not remember hearing anything after the word malignancy. She doesn't remember being angry or in denial. She does remember fear settling in. A wave of shock spread throughout her entire body. How were the bills going to get paid? Who would take care of the children? These were only a few of the many questions traveling through her mind. Janice thought her life was over.

The day after this shocking news, Janice arrived at the altar of her other home and family, her church. As a "born again" Christian, she dropped to her knees and asked God, "Please give me something so I know that I can make it through." She knew *He* had plans for her and she would continue to spread *His* word. In the silence of her prayer, Janice heard, "I will never leave you." At that moment, Janice knew she was going to make it.

Janice was luckily placed on disability leave from work, which ensured that her bills would be paid. Janice had surgery, and her

children were strong and believed their mother would get well as they took care of her. The children's father, Peter, as well as Janice's mother helped care for Janice and her children. Janice's mother was there when she received the news of her diagnosis, was there for the surgery, and took Janice to and from chemotherapy for eight weeks and then for her radiation treatments. Janice lost her hair, was nauseated and couldn't eat, and battled anemia. Janice fondly remembers being placed under "house arrest" because she was so immuno-compromised. Her mother stood by her from the start and she is grateful.

Janice is in remission from cancer. What does this all mean to her? It means that life is short, and the little things that used to bother her don't anymore. Janice feels she has received another "chance" at life. She feels she has received another chance to give to others as a nurse. For a year after her surgery, Janice took time to heal. She volunteered at church and provided prayer services to help others. Janice always looked forward to "going back to normal." She returned to nursing 14 months after her illness.

Janice never reveals her own personal experience battling breast cancer. Janice reaffirms her calling as a nurse every day. Janice sets out to do the best she can in every role she occupies. She instills a sense of hope in her patients and encourages them not to give up when facing tough life battles. Janice can do such patient magic because of her own strength—strength gained from her past experiences with breast cancer, strength from her family, and strength and faith in God. Others who know Janice gain strength by learning about *how* she coped with her illness using faith, hope, and perseverance. No matter how frustrating life gets, Janice never complains. Janice simply loves life and lives it to the fullest. Her personality, demeanor, and integrity have filled many hearts with admiration and inspiration. Janice lives her life, *weathering the storms,* with grace and dignity.

WHERE NURSING LEADS: MARY VERGERA

by Diane Henley Peters

ary Vergera is a registered nurse at Thomas Jefferson University Hospital in Philadelphia. She has experienced an "extraordinary" nursing journey, complete with several mountain passages. Mary was introduced to the world of nursing when her oldest daughter, Liz, became a registered nurse in 1988. Liz brought home many stories about the treatment and "cure" of open-heart patients. Mary loved hearing the stories and would frequently bring lunch to her daughter's unit to be part of this exciting world. Mary decided to become a nurse in order to help others and gain the sense of satisfaction these young nurses felt.

Mary entered Burlington County College in 1988, 23 years after she graduated from high school. While caring for children at home, teaching CCD classes at church, being a room mom, and being a member of the executive committee of the PTA, Mary became a student. Mary soon became a leader in her class, as the class vice president and graduation chairperson. During her final school year, Mary became a part-time nurse extern at Thomas Jefferson University Hospital.

Upon graduation, Mary accepted a nurse position in the telemetry unit. Mary brought the same enthusiasm to her nursing role as she had to her mother and community leader roles. Her first love is working with people, and she quickly bonded with her peers and patients. She describes her most meaningful experience in this way:

"Hazel was a sweet 76-year-old woman who I believe changed my life." Hazel had reached the terminal phase of her life, and her family had requested termination of life support. Mary advocated for both Hazel and the family. She spent many hours working with the hospital ethics committee and the family to assure that Hazel and the family's needs were met. Ultimately, Hazel was taken off of life support. She lived three weeks. Mary cared for Hazel every day that she was on duty. When the end came, Mary attended the funeral and grieved with the family. It was during this experience that Mary learned what it meant to be a nurse.

However, nothing could have prepared Mary for her next event. Mary had decided to return to school to obtain her BSN and was well on her way to meeting that goal when she was suddenly confronted with the diagnosis of her middle daughter. Rachel had a malignant brain tumor. Mary advocated for Rachel as completely as she had for Hazel. She never gave up hope and saw each day as a new opportunity. Mary continued to work full time, caring for patients daily, while she saw Rachel through surgery, chemotherapy, and radiation therapy. Mary remained positive and optimistic until the end. Rachel died in 2000.

After her daughter's death, Mary did not want Rachel forgotten so she started a scholarship to support Rachel's dream of becoming a pediatric nurse. She raised money to award an annual scholarship to nursing students who excelled in pediatric care. When the money for the scholarship fund was exhausted, Mary began fund-raising events to support the scholarship.

Mary continually learns from the challenges she faces. The final life experience that has shaped Mary is providing nursing care to an elderly ailing Roman Catholic cardinal. When the cardinal returned home, Mary took on the role of visiting nurse.

Mary also constructed a memory garden for Rachel. Mary wanted a place for family, friends, and neighbors to remember Rachel. She planted a garden and built a beautiful stone wall around it. Friends and neighbors have contributed items for the garden that are reminiscent of Rachel. This garden is a place for annual gatherings for the scholarship fund and other charities. Mary is growing her hair to donate for children's wigs through the American Brain Tumor Association. She feels that it is important to help others who have cancer.

Mary has a remarkable ability to use her personal trials to help others. Mary continually learns from the challenges she faces. The final life experience that has shaped Mary is providing nursing care to an elderly ailing Roman Catholic cardinal. When the cardinal returned home, Mary took on the role of visiting nurse. She visited him twice a month, making sure he was in compliance with his medical regime. Mary checked his blood pressure and sat with him regularly.

One of Mary's sweet memories relates to a time when the cardinal's cardiac status was decompensating, and his physician requested he return to the hospital. The cardinal declined. He was then told, "Well, your nurse, Mary, also recommends that you go to the hospital." At that point, the cardinal agreed to return to the hospital with Mary. She accompanied him to the hospital, protected his identity, and was his advocate. Mary was with the cardinal when he died. She was invited to his prayer mass and funeral. She still thinks about him regularly and has retained a standing ashtray that was given to her in his memory. Mary is on an extraordinary journey helping others whether it is to sustain life or experience a dignified death.

PART II

FAMILIES KNOWING THAT THEIR NURSE'S STORY IS SPECIAL

ADA

by Helen Jean Talbot-Bond

"Little Ada" was petite, feisty, redheaded, and freckled. Ada was a loving and dedicated daughter, sister, and wife and a fiercely protective mother and grandmother. Ada, a pianist, was also a lover of dancing, Hershey bars with almonds, and "I Love Lucy." Ada, a Sunday school teacher, was also an advocate for children and a staunch supporter of Planned Parenthood. Ada, a nurse, was a gentle spirit and "guardian angel" for many grateful recovery room patients and staff.

Niagara-on-the-Lake, Ontario, 30 miles across the lake from Toronto, was Ada's home. Our mom, Ada, was only 16 when she completed her high school studies at Niagara. Mom was too young to begin nursing studies. When she was old enough, she studied at the Mark Training School in St. Catherine's, Ontario. Mark Training School was one of the first nursing schools on the North American continent. I remember Mom telling us that a representative from Mark had visited her high school at Niagara. It made quite an impression on her. In those years, vocations for women were pretty much limited to nursing, teaching, clerking, or secretarial work. Nursing seemed a natural choice for Mom, who was a bright, caring, and motivated woman.

Mom told us about the rules and how strenuous the requirements were and what long hours the student nurses had to work. Nurses scrubbed floors, changed beds, and did many of the menial jobs unheard of in nursing today. Student nurses had to do most of their studying during "off duty" hours, which often meant late at night or on weekends.

Student nurses followed rigorous rules of conduct. When "allowed" to leave their residence, student nurses had strict dress codes; they wore black stockings, capes, hats, and gloves. There were strict rules about visitors. No males in the students' rooms. There was a curfew too. Mom and Dad (who were courting at the time) made numerous frantic trips back to the residence, worrying about being late because the Welland Canal Bridge might be up and delay them. The school had very strict rules against students marrying or even being engaged, so when Dad and Mom were courting and eventually became engaged, Mom wore her engagement ring on a chain around her neck inside her uniform.

Nursing was a grueling pace. Mom had rheumatic fever during her training, yet she persevered the pace as she always did. Once Mom had set her mind to something, she was a force to deal with. Although she was "no bigger than a minute," Mom sure had pluck! She was gentle, kind, and quiet, but watch out if she felt that an injustice had been done. Remember she had red hair and freckles! Especially where her family was concerned, Mom could really go into action. If one of her family were ill, Mom's dedication, resourcefulness, and nursing really went into high gear.

Mom was always taking care of someone or dedicating herself to some noble cause, such as the study of nutrition, which was very futuristic at the time. She wanted to improve the health of her family. We had whole wheat bread and plenty of fresh fruit and vegetables. I don't recall ever tasting white bread until I attended a friend's birthday party when I was in the fifth or sixth grade. Our meals began with salads, vegetables, and then fish, chicken, or lean meat. Sometimes our meals were strictly vegetarian. Along with fresh-squeezed orange juice, we had wheat germ on our oatmeal for breakfast. When our grandmother, who lived with us, had serious

ADA CATHERINE IRVINE TALBOT, 1911 TO 1998

She was the epitome of excellence in nursing and motherhood.

problems with her eyes, Mom purchased a juice machine and made fresh juice every day. The juice included California carrots, celery, beets, parsley, and a variety of fruits; I bet we were the only family in the city who had a juicer in the cellar. During World War II, Mom worked part time but increased her hours to help pay for our grandmother's medical bills.

As devoted as Mom was to her nursing, she valued her family more. Never was there a more devoted mother. Because she chose to spend summers with us at our cottage in Niagara-on- the-Lake, she had to forego the benefits and status of being a full-time staff nurse. Those days at the lake, in the cottage, were some of the very best years of our lives. I know that my brother and sister would agree. Mother finally went on staff at Niagara Falls Memorial Hospital after we were beyond childhood and our grandmother had died.

Our mom was always taking care of someone. As a child, I remember going to homes with Mom where she would take care of patients who could not afford the expense of continuing nursing care. One of Mom's private patients, who had been in a serious car accident, was on a Stryker frame and was paralyzed from the neck down. She was living with her elderly parents. Mom cared for the woman on a regular basis and always after work. I know Mom never took any money for the care she provided this patient. I know Mom was always gracious and generous with her nursing skills and her time.

Our parents were devoted to each other for more than 50 years. Mom became so ill that she had to be placed in a nursing home. Our father died exactly 30 days later. I think his heart was broken.

As I remember our mom, I think that she could very well have been a beloved and respected character in the Bible, because her life exemplified everything that was selfless, honorable, righteous, and good. She was the epitome of excellence in nursing and motherhood. The world was certainly a better place for *"Ada having lived here!"*

At Mom's memorial service, my childhood dance instructor told me how sweet and kind Mom had been to her when she awakened in the recovery room after surgery. She said she'd never forget Mom's voice saying, "Jeannie, it's time to wake up now, dear." Jeannie said she thought she'd gone to heaven and that Mom was surely an angel.

ALL IN THE FAMILY

by Kathleen Archibald Simon

f there's a gene for the nursing profession, it must run in my family. To put it more accurately, certain qualities that make for good nurses, such as compassion, leadership, and creativity, to name a few, seem to be dominant family traits.

My family has a history of a long line of callings, such as nuns, priests, and nurses. In fact, there are several generations of nurses in my family. Two nurses, in particular, stand out in my mind. My Aunts Dorothy Szymanski and Mike Grzonka. Both are my mother's sisters and both are nurses.

I can't really say either one of them chose nursing, but both agreed they did have a calling early in life. My grandfather facilitated the process for them. A person ahead of his time, another characteristic that seems to run in the family, he decided in the midst of the Depression that it was important for his oldest daughters to have a profession.

Dorothy graduated from St. Mary of Nazareth School of Nursing in Chicago in 1932. Within a few months of passing the state licensing test, she became night supervisor of the Labor and Delivery Department at St. Mary of Nazareth Hospital. The position gave her a great deal of autonomy and responsibility, which was unusual for a woman in those days. Dorothy worked tirelessly to improve procedures and simplify routines in the Labor and Delivery Department. The physicians relied on her judgment, and she came to relish her independence.

Dorothy did not marry, so St. Mary's Hospital was her family. She presided over night-shift in the Labor and Delivery Department for almost half a century. More than once, she delivered the babies of young women she had cared for some 20 years before.

In 1962, the Chicago Hospital Council singled out Dorothy as "Employee of the Year." This was quite an honor as she was chosen from among all the council's member hospitals. The citation honored her with phrases such as "sympathy and kindness." To her, there is no such thing as eight hours of work. Her day is not complete unless she knows all is well. Always ready to help the needy, her spirit of generosity became synonymous with her every act.

Dorothy was also an educator, yet another quality that seems to run in the family. She taught several generations of student nurses, including one of her younger sisters, Michaline. She also took the time to teach me, her niece.

Michaline graduated from St. Mary of Nazareth in 1942. She, too, took charge of a department as soon as she passed the nurse licensing exam. Michaline supervised postpartum care at St. Mary of Nazareth. She was providing care to moms and babies during the height of the baby boom. To this day, Michaline recalls her feelings about work. "We literally had to run to keep up with all the needs of the newborns and moms."

Michaline shared her sister's abilities as a leader, educator, and collaborator with physicians and patients to form healing partnerships.

She developed a program to teach first-time mothers what they needed to know about how to care for a new baby. Today, parent education is commonplace, but in those days new mothers often left the hospital with very little information about how to take care of an infant, unless, of course, Aunt Mike was their nurse.

Michaline was also an inventor and created a quality-assurance process for making infant formula in the nursery. After a brief stint as a nurse in Texas, where her husband was stationed, Michaline returned to Chicago. She also returned to postpartum nursing. She took the position of director of the postpartum care unit at St. Elizabeth's Hospital and remained in that role until she retired in 1967.

I was one of the baby boomers born during the time my two aunts provided nursing for women in labor, delivery, and postpartum in Chicago's near northwest side. Whether it was our family genes or their influence or both, there was never a time I did not want to be a nurse. I graduated from St. Mary's in 1970.

Once my aunts had mastered nursing care for labor, delivery, and postpartum patients, the next natural phase for them was providing nursing care for children. Thus it was natural for me to be attracted to a pediatric population and also to leadership. Therefore, I went straight from graduation to Northwest Hospital in Chicago (now Our Lady of the Resurrection). My role was to open the hospital's first pediatric unit.

During my years at Northwest, I read *The Wizard of Oz* to many young patients. The story helped teach the sick children the value of courage, brains, and heart. The story also helped teach me to appreciate those same qualities that were so obvious in my aunts. Reflecting on my aunts' qualities and experiences helped me cultivate the same qualities of courage, brains, and heart in my own nursing career.

While providing nursing care to children, I developed a strong interest in preventing disease and promoting health, hardly a radical idea today, but forward-thinking at that time. This interest and my abilities as a teacher, which I had learned from Dorothy and

Michaline, took to me my next position in occupational health. I joined Commonwealth Edison and had a career unlike any I could have received in a traditional clinical setting. It set the stage for the rest of my work life. Commitment in jobs is another characteristic that runs in our family.

In the 1970s, the field of occupational health focused primarily on conventional treatments and approaches to workplace issues/problems. My energy and interest were on education, prevention, and workplace safety for employees. Like my aunts before me, I started to envision and develop programs. The programs were based on my passion for integrating a holistic paradigm with current health services. Over the next decade, I worked with national health organizations and for other large and small employers developing workplace health education programs. The early 1980s were days of spiraling healthcare costs. I took on special assignments, working with unions and management, to control costs through prevention and to teach employees how to navigate the difficult managed care system. I developed an advocacy program with a major insurer establishing a nurse-managed health benefits hot line, one of the first in the nation.

As the long shadow of HIV spread across the workplace, I collaborated with medical schools about how to educate physicians and with corporations about how to talk to employees about the disease. I also urged benefit managers to treat HIV like any other chronic illness. My aunts had always fought for patients who were vulnerable and voiceless, and I was proud to follow in their footsteps.

Dorothy and Michaline were women of faith who intuitively understood the connections of mind, body, and spirit. I also spent much of the '90s developing and implementing a holistic model of workplace health. Today, I work and advocate for fully collaborative healthcare where all practitioners are advocates for patients, not their specialties.

Though the nursing profession led Dorothy, Michaline, and me down separate career paths, our "family genes" united us and our calling kept each one of us involved in nursing, not only in our careers but also in our lives. What an honor!

A PATTERN FOR A NURSING QUILT

by Angela Renee Starkweather

Donna L. Fuhlman never received any awards for saving the life of an infant on a summer day at the lake. However, at the age of sixteen, she was a hero in the eyes of two parents. Donna had seen the young boy struggling to swim as the water began to pull him under. On instinct, she swam out to him and pulled him back to shore. The look of gratitude in the parents' eyes was enough to change the course of her life. In the top 10 percent of her high school graduation class, Donna could have chosen many paths. The feeling of being a part of something larger, of performing a good deed, of saving a life, never left her. Donna entered nursing school to continue this conquest.

As a farm girl from a small community and the oldest of four daughters, making the move to Seattle, Washington, to enter the University of Washington's nursing school was a huge endeavor that she never regretted. As a new graduate caring for her first patient, she experienced the loss of a life. A young boy who had been sledding down a hill had a massive head injury. In contrast to her earlier experience, this time she was the one who had to tell the parents, "There was nothing left to do for your son." Instead of handing back a breathing boy, full of life and vigor, she was only able to lead them to the bedside and let them hold their son's hands as he took his last breath.

Every patient encounter has the potential to leave someone a changed person, especially when the patient is a husband. In 1973, Donna's husband was diagnosed with Hodgkin's disease. With two children to take care of and the potential of losing her husband, Donna took on a new perspective. A church attendee since childhood, suddenly *knowing* about Jesus changed to *friendship* with Jesus. Her friendship with God gave Donna strength, meaning, and joy in each new day. Facing her own mortality, Donna decided to make the most of every day. Her husband survived his disease. He is a daily reminder of the commitment she made to herself and to Jesus Christ, the commitment to make the most of every situation.

In 1982, Donna moved her family back to Yakima, Washington, near the farm where she grew up. She has been working as a nurse in a family practice for over 20 years now. Every patient she meets is a unique individual, valued and worthy of her genuine love. Each interaction with a patient or family is a chance to have an impact on them, whether it is teaching healthy behaviors, giving social support, or providing resources. She describes these encounters as the most precious part of being a nurse.

Donna brings more than nursing care to people around the world. Four years ago, Donna traveled with a medical team to Haiti to serve the poor and destitute. For two weeks, she provided medical attention to hundreds of patients who had walked two to three days and waited in lines that stretched for blocks to receive care. Visiting a third-world country was also a life-changing event for her. Donna looks forward to the day when she can "visit the trenches" again as a missionary and give assistance to those with medical and spiritual needs.

Donna has always been active in her local church. She is part of the church choir and has toured Europe and experienced the joy of bringing music to those living halfway across the world.

As Donna looks back on her life, she identifies life's treasures as those short but precious moments with family and friends. When her children were young, she took up downhill skiing so they could spend weekends together. Looking up at the bunny hill for the first time was quite an intimidating experience, but she managed to learn the rope-tow and became a great skier. She often planned family camping vacations in the Cascade Mountains, Mount Rainier, and other national parks. Her children acquired their appreciation for nature and being outdoors from her.

Her love for the outdoors is evident in her garden, a beautifully serene refuge that has been nurtured with much knowledge and care. Her daughter chose to be wed in her garden because, to her, it is a reflection of true love. Donna's yard sits at the basin of Yakima Valley, a large desert complete with rattlesnakes and sagebrush. Her garden would not survive without continuous attention and devotion and a commitment to keep it healthy and alive, the same qualities that Donna uses when caring for patients and family.

Donna has always cherished family gatherings and continues to make them memorable experiences for everyone. For instance, every Thanksgiving each member of the family tells what they are thankful for that year. At Christmas, she devises a unique way of telling the Christmas story, through skits, pictures, movies, or reading. "It's those few precious moments that are so rich in meaning that create what life is really all about."

Donna's latest endeavor has been quilting. Although she has been a seamstress her whole life, quilting provides a whole new creative process. Her love for this art has given her a new freedom of expression, one that she readily shares with others. She has made quilts for all of her family members and, on special occasions, for friends. Quilting provides her a way to give something solely of herself to another person, a theme very similar to what nursing has meant to her throughout her career.

Each patient is part of a larger picture, and every encounter provides an instance where Donna can play a part in that person's life. Arranging each piece of the quilt reminds her of the process of providing nursing care, fitting each unique square to make a whole, beautiful pattern. Donna's love for improving the lives of her patients is very evident in her practice—similar to the process of *making a quilt;* she approaches both with care, patience, and creativity.

AND NOW THERE ARE FOUR
by Cheryl Vajdik

Lillian, my mother, is the sixth child of eight. She enjoys sharing stories with us about growing up with her two brothers and five sisters. Even as a small girl, she looked for ways to be helpful. She liked helping her mother with household chores. Cooking for their large family has always been an important part of her life.

When asked why she became interested in nursing, Lillian said, "I have always wanted to help people. I knew if I became a nurse, I could help take care of all family members, friends, or neighbors if and when they became ill."

Lillian attended high school during World War II. One of her school bus stops was at a neighborhood hospital where she saw several nurses disembarking to go to work. Lillian admired their professional appearance—the starched white uniforms, the crisp-looking caps, and the navy blue capes. Most of all, she admired them for all their "good deeds."

After graduating high school, she took the challenge of her dreams. She entered the diploma program of nursing at Englewood Hospital where her older sister was a student. Lillian visited her sister at school many times, she knew everyone by name at both the hospital and school and they knew her. She had suddenly become part of a "second large family." She became part of a "nursing family."

During the war years, the hospital was extremely short of help, so the dedication and hard work of the students really made a difference in the hospital's ability to deliver quality care. Lillian loves to share stories about her nursing school experiences. She tells of times when she would attend classes all day and then be assigned an eight-hour shift either in the evening or night. She gets a certain glow when she reminisces about her student experiences, about being in charge of a medical/surgical floor, supervising the nursing assistants, or helping patients who were suffering with an illness or dying. She met, as well as cherished, those challenges.

While Lillian was a student nurse, her father was admitted to the same hospital where she and her sister were students. For a number of years her father had suffered from progressive complications of diabetes. But during this particular hospitalization, his condition quickly deteriorated. Despite the dedicated nursing care that Lillian and the rest of her family provided, he passed away. It was a difficult time for the entire family. Lillian, being the strong one, helped the family cope with this great loss.

Lillian graduated from nursing school in 1945. Her dream had come true; she was a registered nurse. Now she would wear the starched white uniform, the crisp-looking cap, and the navy blue cape, just like the nurses she admired at the bus stop when she was in high school. Her first job as a registered nurse was on the medical surgical floor at the same hospital where she trained. She knew the patients and the nurses really needed her. She had so much to offer her patients; she had a special ability to encourage patients and helped them get through their tough times.

Lillian was also a private duty nurse. She gained great personal satisfaction from giving excellent patient care. She loved providing patient care and helping them feel better, and her patients loved her. Lillian was always kind, caring, and willing to go "the extra mile" to put the patients' needs first. Many of her private duty cases and their families became Lillian's friends.

After Lillian married and had a family, she continued to practice nursing. She worked part time in the evenings while her children were growing up. She chose to work in a community hospital near her home in case her family needed her. Once again, Lillian became part of a "second family" at the community hospital where she worked. Everyone knew and respected her for her excellent clinical skills and great sense of caring.

During these years, Lillian enjoyed raising her family. She had always been a great cook, and every holiday there was a large family gathering with large festive meals and homemade desserts. Lillian's husband played the piano, and during the holidays, the family would gather around the piano and sing together. Having a large extended family meant big gatherings and big fun!

When Lillian's children were older, her mother suffered a stroke. Her mother lost her vision and mobility. She had had hearing problems for years so these additional sensory losses were devastating. Lillian ordered a hospital bed, put it in a spare room, and lovingly cared for her mother. For two years she dedicated 24 hours a day to her mother. Lillian wanted her mother to live with dignity, receive the type of care that "money could not buy," and have care that only

patient's behavior was psychotic. Lillian told the resident the patient seemed to be experiencing hypoglycemia and stated she would check the patient's blood sugar. Sure enough, the patient was hypoglycemic. The patient was treated and recovered. Both the nursing supervisor and the resident commended Lillian for her astute observations and quick actions.

One of the hospital's leading neurosurgeons always requested Lillian take care of his patients. He recognized she was an outstanding nurse. He said his patients were in the *best hands* when they were in *Lillian's hands.*

Lillian's organizational skills were always outstanding. She could come to work, find the unit in chaos, and get it organized and running smoothly like no one else could. Both supervisors and staff respected her organizational skills. If other units were in chaos at the beginning of a shift, the nursing supervisor would send Lillian to get things organized.

Lillian still carries on the family traditions of big meals and large family gatherings during the holidays. She still helps take care of sick members of the family. Lillian is still the sixth child of eight but only four are still alive.

Lillian could provide. Lillian gave her mother excellent care. Her mother, bedridden for two years, did not have one bedsore. Lillian's mother suffered a second stoke and was admitted to the hospital. Lillian continued to provide nursing care and nutrition to her mother. Her mother died while being treated for the second stoke.

Lillian was extremely close to her mother, so her death was a most difficult time. Her children were older now, so Lillian decided it was time to return to nursing on a full-time basis. She returned to work in the community hospital as a full-time night nurse. Because of her excellent clinical, organizational, and leadership skills, she was soon designated the charge nurse on the medical/surgical floor. As in the past, all respected her. The night nursing supervisor would ask Lillian to start intravenous treatment on patients with difficult veins. Lillian was an outstanding resource for patient care.

One night around 2:00 a.m., a patient was yelling, restless, combative, confused, and diaphoretic. The new resident thought the

Lillian has been retired from nursing for over ten years. She is a widow and lives with one of her daughters and two grandchildren. She is still proud of being a nurse and continues to read about current trends in the profession. Family gatherings provide the stage for the dynasty of nurses in the family to reminisce and share their nursing experiences. In addition to Lillian, there are four other nurses in the family: a sister, two nieces, and a daughter. Nursing is and will always be part of tradition of Lillian's family.

Lillian's love of family and her pride in nursing continue to be sustaining factors in her life. Her compassion, caring, and inspiration continue to touch the lives of those around her. Lillian became a nurse to help family, friends, and neighbors in need and this is what she did. Nursing gave her the tools to care for others. Nursing also gave her and me a special bond . . . the bond of being a nurse, for we are both registered nurses. Each day I am grateful for my mother's love and support, I am also grateful for our special bond, the bond of nursing.

CADET NURSE BY DREAM: THE ART OF POSSIBILITIES

by Carolyn Hope Smeltzer

n the 1930s, a little girl on the south side of Chicago could always be found "fixing up" baby dolls. The dolls had broken legs or arms, headaches, or stomach aches. The dolls always had Band-Aids on them and were given loving care in a doll buggy. The little girl herself was sick, weak, and often in a wheelchair. She was a middle child, very quiet, caring, and yet sometimes forgotten. It may never be known whether she treated the dolls as sick children because she was sick or because she just had a knack for nurturing.

Since the time Mary cared for the dolls, she always felt the urge and need to be a nurse. A number of other events reinforced her desire to be a nurse. For instance, when Mary was a teenager, her parents had two more children, both boys. She took care of them and she also worked in an orphanage caring for the many children who were sick. However, it may have been a war poster of a young girl with blues eyes that really impressed Mary and drew her closer to a nursing career. The young girl in the poster was "urging women to play a part in the war and become a cadet, to become a nurse." After seeing this poster and in light of her other caring experiences, Mary completed the cadet application, continued to work in the orphanage, and finished her high school education.

It was during this same time period that Mary met a sailor preparing to fight in World War II. They met at a local roller skating rink while he was stationed at Navy Pier and Great Lakes. At the same time, Mary's father did not return from work one day. He died while working on the Chicago streetcars. He died at work doing his job. Mary's mother was left to care for five children, two being under the age of three.

There was one more major event in Mary's teenage years that affected her decision to be a nurse. When a letter of acceptance arrived from the Nurse Cadet Corps, reality quickly set in as Mary's sister pointed out the impossibility of their mother caring for five children without Mary's salary. Even though Mary was prepared to go into the Cadet Corps, she unpacked her bags because she knew "Ma could not support the family without my salary." She needed to support her family so she put her own dreams on hold.

Years later, when her younger brothers were teenagers, she married the sailor who had gone off to war. She also raised three children and three dogs and worked in the family television repair business. On her days off, Saturday and Sunday, she would work in the local hospital as a nurses' aide. The hospital was thrilled to have someone requesting only weekend work. Her patients liked being taken care of by her, and her co-workers became her friends. Mary saw a lot of the young nurses' aides become nurses, including her own daughter. Mary watched when her own daughter was "capped" and received her nursing pin. She was also there when her daughter opened the letter stating that she had passed the state boards. She took a photo of that moment.

While Mary was waiting to reach her own dream of being a nurse, she accepted another huge challenge. Mary was always afraid of the water. Having light skin, she never really took advantage of Lake Michigan for swimming or sunning. However, at the age of 40, she decided to overcome her fear of water and learn to swim. She accomplished her goal and to this day she swims at least three times a week.

Mary never forgot her dreams of becoming a nurse. When her last child was nearly through high school, Mary enrolled in nursing school. She studied on weekends and in the evenings, after the family business hours were ended. Since most of the students in her class were recent high school graduates and prepared for nursing school, Mary, who was in her 50s, had to brush up on basic issues, such as math, writing, and the sciences.

Mary was a nurse for nearly 20 years before she retired. Perhaps she was a nurse forever if you count "fixing up dolls." I can still remember how proud Mary was to shop for crisp, white nursing uniforms and supportive nursing shoes. She always wore her nursing cap, because she earned it and it represented her dream. I still remember her coming home from the hospital with patient stories and, of course, doctor stories. Being an older nurse, she had the wisdom other nurses, patients, and doctors admired and listened to. She would always tell it "as it was."

The visualization of Mary reaching her dreams of becoming a great nurse will always be forefront in my mind. The little boys she stayed home to care for when she was a teenager are my uncles, Jimmy, Kenny, and Danny. The sailor she married is my father. One of the dolls she cared for, who just happens to be missing a leg, is on my bookshelf. The cadet poster of the girl urging young women to do their part and become a cadet, to become a nurse, is hanging on my bedroom wall. Mary's acceptance letter from the Cadet Corps is taped behind the original poster. Mary, the nurse, is my mother. Mary, my mom, taught me *the art of possibilities.*

This story was the commencement speech for the nursing graduates of Marcella Niehoff School of Nursing, Loyola University Chicago, May 11, 2002.

Hope, Dreams and Possibilities

Bonnie V. Custen, RN
(for Niehoff School of Nursing Graduates Loyola University Chicago
May 11, 2002)

Bursting with pride for our graduates today
Your futures are bright in every way
The Tin Man thought he found his heart
But had a true one from the start

Nurses have endless heart to share
Proven each day by how they care
How could the Lady have loved the Tramp?
Like we loved the "Lady with the Lamp"

Who'd think a scarecrow had a brain
So much hope and no disdain
Believing that a "Super-man" can fly
Careers will soar so very high

A graduate degree will take you far
Finding out who you really are
Although all of nursing cannot exceed demand
Give each day with full heart and hand

What you take away from this day
Is what you choose, come what may
On-going learning through your life
Will assure the least of any strife

Do not wonder why you are here
The world now holds a nurse so dear
Respect and love you will attain
Have the best of everything to gain

CENSUS OF ONE: STAFF OF FIVE

by Elizabeth (Betty) J. Corso Falter

arol and I made the decision. Our sister Sheila needed to be moved from the sofa to a hospital bed in the living room. Sheila shook her finger at me and said, "No!" She knew all too well what a hospital bed in the living room signified, sick people who *weren't* dying rested on the sofa. But I insisted and she let us move her. I tried to ease the transition by playing a CD of Civil War tunes. Sheila tapped her bony knees to *The Battle Hymn of the Republic* as I rolled her wheelchair across the room.

Sheila, a registered nurse for 35 years, was dying of pancreatic cancer. My sister Carol and I, also nurses with more than 30 years of experience, knew the perils of pancreatic cancer, and we knew we had to go to Sheila immediately. We met one day at Sheila's house in Maryland to help her husband take care of her. After a few days, Carol and I decided to give Sheila's husband and the other caregivers a break, so we sent for the other nurses in our family. My nieces, Rita and Anne Marie, represented the second generation of Corso nurses. They were thrilled to offer their services.

That clear, warm night in June, my sister Sheila became a census of one with a staff of five nurses: *Elizabeth Corso Falter, RN; Carol Corso Bodine, RN; Rita Bodine Meadows, RN;* and *Anne Marie Corso, RN* plus my daughter *Carol,* my sister's namesake. Our hospital consisted of Sheila in the living room, our sleeping quarters in the adjoining recreation room, and our nurses' station in the kitchen. The patient, who felt better because fluid had been drained from her lungs, decided to take charge. First, there was a birthday to celebrate; my daughter Carol turned 25 that day. Sheila had ordered Rita, the baker, to make a cake to surprise Carol. Rita arrived with a sheet cake with blue icing trim and decorated with items from her children's parties: candles, plastic balloons, clowns, turtles, and Power Rangers, 25 items in all. That cake looked like it had been made with only two hours' notice but we savored every bite.

Sheila appointed my sister as supervisor and me as hospital administrator. We went to the kitchen to devise a nursing care plan. Our diagnoses were standard: alteration in skin integrity, pain, fluid volume deficit, and alteration in respiratory status. Our care plan included full-body massage using balms that had been purchased by Anne Marie. Sheila suffered from pruritus, especially on her buttocks. As Anne Marie massaged Sheila's back, starting at the shoulders, Sheila instructed her to go lower and lower; the plan came to include what Sheila called "butt duty."

It was midnight when I reviewed our plan with Sheila and the full staff. After the brief review, Sheila, forever directing, told me that I should go to bed. As I drifted off in the recreation room, I heard the sounds of nurses carrying out their duties: the rustle of sheets as Sheila was turned, whispers about pain medication, "She won't take it, afraid to sleep."

Later that night, Sheila told Carol that she didn't want to die. Carol felt unprepared to receive this confidence, searched for a response, and remembered a rainy night when Sheila was 8 and Carol 10. Sheila had had a bad dream and Carol woke her, drew her into a hug, and said, "It will be okay." Now, decades later, how was one to respond to this very real nightmare? Carol hugged her, as she had when they were children. "I will do everything I can to help you live," she said. "But if I don't succeed, Dad will be waiting for you." Sheila said, "Okay," and then let herself fall asleep while Carol watched over her.

That clear, warm night in June, my sister Sheila became a census of one with a staff of five nurses: Elizabeth Corso Falter, RN; Carol Corso Bodine, RN; Rita Bodine Meadows, RN; *and* Anne Marie Corso, RN *plus my daughter Carol, my sister's namesake. Our hospital consisted of Sheila in the living room, our sleeping quarters in the adjoining recreation room, and our nurses' station in the kitchen. The patient, who felt better because fluid had been drained from her lungs, decided to take charge.*

At 6:00 a.m., I arose to check on our patient. I noticed that Carol had crawled into bed with me during the night. When I entered the living room, I saw Shelia, awake in her bed. She raised her finger to her mouth to shush me. Rita was asleep on the sofa, my daughter Carol in a chair, and Anne Marie across the bottom of Sheila's bed. Sheila had been awake for hours while the entire night shift slept.

Her health improved, briefly, after that night. She ate more and even took short car trips. Sheila's staff of five went back home, and her husband and other local family took over her care. She died in September. But during that night in June, we were able to deepen our already strong bonds as sisters, women, friends, and nurses. For that we are grateful.

So the next time someone asks me about the best staffing conditions, I'll tell them: a census of one and a staff of five. Midnight shift. A beautiful night in June.

Reprinted with permission from *American Journal of Nursing (2002), 102*(4), 25.

COMMUNITY OF FRIENDS
An addendum to Census of One: Staff of Five
by Carol Vandrey

"We'll take them out to dinner. You pick the restaurant. I'll send the invitations."

Thus began my first conversation with Sheila Mills, newly elected president of District 5 of the Maryland Nurses Association. We were planning her first board meeting and brainstorming about how to get very busy, over-scheduled, high-achieving nurses to give up precious free time to attend yet another meeting. After pricing dinners in several restaurants, it occurred to me I could prepare a home-cooked meal at a fraction of the cost. So I suggested we meet at my house. I would cook and Sheila would provide the ingredients.

Our first board meeting began with appetizers: cocktail shrimp on a bed of lettuce, salmon mousse with crackers, and crabmeat dip with French bread. The entrée was chicken salad. We had tomato aspic with cottage cheese, Waldorf salad, mini croissants, fresh strawberries, cheesecake, and chocolate mousse. Fifteen nurses responded to the dinner invitation and attended the first board meeting. While the food nourished our bodies, the hour of fellowship during the meal nourished our sense of community. Friendships evolved as we shared stories of our challenges at work, family illnesses, and other love and joy. We never got to an agenda at that first meeting because Sheila's agenda was "building community." Her agenda was reached. Her vision helped us grow from acquaintances, so worried about revisiting bylaws, to friends who cared deeply about each other.

Sheila was a role model of the essence of nursing, nurturing. She nurtured each of us as individuals and inspired us to sponsor educational offerings and support nursing bills at the state level, mentor nursing students, and plan a state convention where we celebrated a Century of Nursing. The governor of Maryland was the keynote speaker.

At the time of Sheila's death, there were 300 nurses in District 5 who all truly believed that Sheila Mills was their best friend.

COMFORT BY THE YARD: A SPECIAL NURSE AND NIECE

by Carolyn Hope Smeltzer

Nurses do more than conduct nursing assessments and prepare care plans. Nurses provide care that is based on a trusting relationship between the patients and themselves. Janice Kane fosters this trusting relationship between herself and her patients by making and giving away pillows.

The small pillows, less than 12 inches long, made by Janice and given to her patients represent hope and comfort. They create a warm environment for the patients and are useful as an armrest or neck support. These pillows are Janice's way of going beyond the nurse assessment and care plan for her patients; they are her way of providing care.

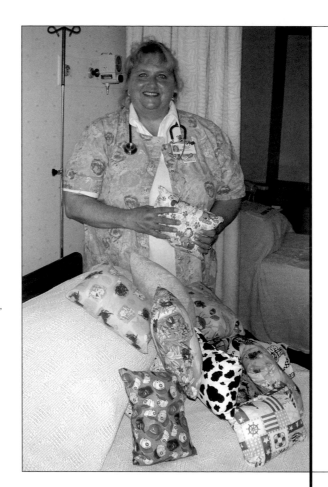

Janice has lovingly made over 8,000 pillows since her project began in February of 2001. She began making pillows after a very elderly woman patient asked for a pillow so she could clip her call bell to something. Janice clipped her call bell to a handmade pillow. The patient could easily reach down and find the pillow to press her call button and could now find comfort when calling for the nurse.

Janice believes these pillows make the nurse's job easier. "When we go into a patient's room for the first time, the pillow breaks the ice." The patients can also place the pillows underneath their necks or around their wounds. The "look" on an elderly visitor's or a young child's face, when given a pillow, is priceless. Janice believes she is fortunate because of her opportunity to provide one-on-one care to patients. She also feels lucky to be able to give patients the added comfort of a pillow.

Janice can make approximately 50 pillows in an hour. Her husband helps by turning them inside out and stuffing them. For patients, the pillows represent joy, comfort, and hope. For Janice, the pillows are a work stress-releaser. She currently has over 100 pillows in her sewing room. After making these pillows, she has to close them up and bag them for delivery to the hospital.

It is not unusual for Janice to make 150 pillows a week. She makes the pillows after commuting for many hours from Eugene, where she lives, to Corvallis (Heart of the Valley) Oregon, where the hospital is located, and after providing nursing care on units where nurses are on vacation or sick. The number of pillows Janice can make depends on her time, as well as her budget. She pays for the fabric for the pillows "out of her own pocket." Janice does not mind the expense because the pillows have such a great impact on patients and their families. She is quick to say the pillows are "not for sale." The pillows are for "give away" only.

Janice can make eight pillows from one yard of fabric. She has been known to make pillows to match patients' pajamas. The pillows are not only for the patients but also for family members. Janice urges patients/family to take as many pillows as they need to feel comfortable while in the hospital. Patients clutch the pillows to their chests when having pain or trying to cough; they also use the pillows to elevate an aching arm or leg. New mothers use the pillows to position the babies as they breast- or bottle-feed. Children as well as adults hug the pillows, bury their faces in the pillows, and sleep with the pillows. Patients keep the pillows close to them during their hospital stay, and returning patients say, "Where is my pillow?"

Janice says every pillow represents a patient and *tells* a story. She fondly remembers one patient who had post-traumatic stress after the September 11, 2001, attack. The simple act of giving the patient a pillow made all the difference. She had been ill and at "her wit's end." When handed the pillow, the patient stopped crying and just looked at the little heart pillow.

On one occasion, Janice was being interviewed about her nursing and the pillows. She handed the reporter a pillow and he said, "What am I to do with the pillow?" Janice replied, "Use it for comfort or *give* it to someone who may be in need of comfort." The reporter went on to his next assignment, an automobile accident. With pillow in hand, the reporter started comforting a young girl who had just lost her girlfriend in the accident. He gave his pillow to the girl who had just lost her friend. The young girl hung on to the pillow and used it to help deal with her loss.

Janice believes hospitals are too clinical, "cut and dry," and very mechanical, except for the caring. She says a nurse cannot be with a patient every time he or she needs comfort. On the other hand, a pillow certainly can be with a patient at all times. The pillow serves as a "nonhospital-like item, a comfort thing." Some patients are lonely; they never receive cards, flowers, or visitors. The gift of a bright pillow may be the only thing that can add comfort to a patient's day.

Janice reflects, on a daily basis, about how she would like to be treated if she were the patient. She does not just "provide the pills" for patients and walk away. She interacts with them and cares for them in the same manner she would want to be cared for. She gives them the gift of a pillow, and that makes all the difference.

Janice is now making pillows for the service men and women who were injured in Operation Iraqi Freedom. She has sent over 150 pillows to Walter Reed Hospital and is calling this project "Operation Pillow Comfort." She gives them *comfort by the yard.*

Ms. Eleanor Jagielski read about the book, *Ordinary People, Extraordinary Lives: Stories of Nurses,* in the *Chicago Sun-Times.* She learned the editors were looking for authors to write about "special nurses" to be featured in the book. Ms. Jagielski wrote Carolyn Smeltzer a letter, stating her niece and godchild, Janice, is a special and caring nurse. Ms. Jagielski, who was 82 and going through numerous medical treatments and was not up to writing, sent a newspaper article about her niece to Carolyn and asked her to write her niece's story.

GAYL — COMPOSING ONE LIFE, NURSING MANY OTHERS

by Kimberly A. McNally

ayl is my mother. She is also a nurse who has earned this tribute to her extraordinary caregiving. Borrowing from Margaret Bateson's work about composing a life, my mother has woven the practice of nursing into the composition of her life. Her nursing skills, both her clinical expertise and compassion, have left an indelible mark on my family as well as on countless neighbors, friends, pediatric patients, and families When I asked my mother what role nursing played in her life, she said, "Nursing taught me to be an advocate for myself and others around me, and not just for health matters."

My mother graduated from Children's Hospital School of Nursing in Boston in 1956. She worked on some of the first pediatric open-heart surgeries. Her dream was to work at the American Hospital in Paris. Meanwhile, her romance with my father was percolating. My father was transferred to Hawaii to serve with the Marine Corps Officer Training Program. The story told is my mother was tired of having the telephone charges reversed and decided to fly to Hawaii to get married.

A year later, I was born, and my four siblings followed over the next 16 years. My mother's nursing career outside the home included part-time work on the weekends after my father returned from his road work as a salesman. Although my mother didn't practice much, she always maintained her license and took a number of continuing education courses.

At home, her energies were directed to us as she tended to countless broken bones, cuts, bumps, bruises, earaches, bee stings, bouts with the flu, and a variety of emotional upsets. Her no-nonsense, efficient, calm, caring style always seemed to quicken our healing. She taught me the importance of good nutrition, infection control, and healthy habits. She had some "tried and true" treatment regimens. When one of my brothers had a scraped knee or jellyfish sting, she would take him to the ocean, have him stand in the waves and let the cura-tive effects of salt water take over. At the first signs of a cold, she would make us gargle with warm salt water.

When her children grew into adulthood, she continued to provide expert care to her grandchildren. She supported my siblings through some life-threatening health situations. She also provided long-dis-tance first-aid advice for a curious grandson experimenting with shaving while in an isolated vacation cabin and to a granddaughter wheezing from asthma.

After we were grown, she spent many hours volunteering at the art museum and conducting arts education programs for school chil-dren. Involvement in the arts nourished her spirit and provided a means of self-expression. She approached the arts voraciously, always on the lookout for an interesting show or art class.

About 15 years ago, my mother was visiting an older friend in the hospital. She started to reflect on the looming nursing shortage, and it ignited her passion to encourage nurses to return to the workforce. After being out of the workforce for almost 30 years, she went to speak to the chief nurse executive, intending to inquire about a recruiting position. To the contrary, she found herself enrolled in a ten-week refresher course.

As she began thinking about candidates to recruit, she heard her own voice saying, "You have to recruit yourself!" So, at 54 years of age, she took a position in pediatrics at Maine Medical Center, a position she held for eight years. The physical part of the job was especially challenging. She has juvenile onset rheumatoid arthritis, and after several consecutive shifts, she would be exhausted. Her personal success and engaging, positive personality influenced other older nurses to rejoin the workforce and make a dent in the nursing shortage. I was really proud of her for mastering the challenges of contemporary pediatric nursing practice, with all the new medications and equipment that did not even exist 30 years ago. I suspect her wisdom and rich life experiences made up for any rustiness in technical skills when she was dealing with dying children and their families.

Back at home, my mother was caring for her most challenging patient. My father had a myriad of chronic physical and mental health problems, and he often had complications and adverse drug reactions. My mother was vigilant in facilitating his care. I remember how indignant she was when the hospital staff didn't attend to his skin care needs as thoroughly as she did. She nursed his diabetic feet, post-operative incisions, and wounded soul day after day. She worked diligently to meet his physical and emotional needs.

After his death last year, I was cleaning out some drawers at their home. I found some notes my mother had written, detailing my father's complex health history. Her "nursing notes" were written on plain notepaper with all the necessary dates and details. Simple and straightforward, efficient and complete, she carried them with her and frequently gave a report to the healthcare team. When my father died, she made a final entry on the notes, acknowledging that his suffering was over.

While painting one afternoon, my mother was interrupted by a phone call from a neighbor who had an unrelenting bloody nose. She stayed with the neighbor for hours, packing her nose and offering her support and comfort. For years, I remember my mother being the neighborhood nurse. She informally operated a nurse call line. Neighbors and friends recount stories about my mother's quick mind, big heart, steady hands, and calm presence during medical emergencies, large and small. She is currently providing support and health advice to my brother who is dealing with an eye disease.

These days, she's moving through the grief process with grace and steadfastness. She has immersed herself in painting and has turned a spare room in her old Victorian home into a studio. Now she spends a peaceful afternoon mixing her paints and applying them to a fresh canvas. Although art has always been a source of renewal for my mother, her current work is particularly striking. She paints abstract representations of people and landscapes. The colors are bright, the strokes bold. Her life experiences are reflected on the canvases and hang in an orderly manner around the studio. My mother thinks about the connection between nursing and art and says, "Nursing and art are both about touch, physically and intellectually, both are tactile inside and outside."

My mother's life has been and continues to be composed of the act of extraordinary caregiving. As her life continues to unfold, I suspect caring skillfully for others will be on her palette and that many more extraordinary acts of nursing practice will be contributed to the world around her. With much love and gratitude, I salute my mother's life of caring for others.

HANDS OF GOLD

Story of Lillian Hedrick Falter Class of 1929, Saginaw General Hospital
by Elizabeth (Betty) J. Corso Falter

When I first arrived at my husband's hometown, Lillian, his mother, was coming home after working the night shift at Elmhurst Memorial Hospital. She was considering retirement after 35 years. Nine months later we needed Lillian.

Our first son was born and we were alone in New York. My sisters were nurses but had families of their own. They would visit and chat by phone, but Lillian was willing to come for those first few weeks after childbirth. I remember her at 2:00 a.m. encouraging our Michael to nurse or at 8:00 p.m. reassuring us that his colic would subside. It didn't matter what I knew as a nurse, as a new mother I needed my own nurse. Lillian was so good at helping me we had her come for the births of our next two children. Her important message to us each time was "the baby and you will be fine."

I had a melanoma at age 33. I knew what this meant, so once again we called Lillian, now 72 years of age. I would require much more than at-home postpartum care. Lillian would tend to the large dressings for my very difficult skin graft and encourage me to eat after being confined in a supine position for a week. My young family of three children and my husband also had needs. Although my family came from Maryland to visit, Lillian, my mother-in-law was the chief nurse and mother to all.

After one week of bed rest, and walking only once in the hospital, I was discharged. Lillian was in charge of getting me back on my feet. I remember watching her brilliant, gentle hands carefully change the skin draft dressing that covered most of my right buttock.

During my illness, I watched Lillian repair my husband's suits, crochet a tablecloth, and make me a nightshirt. Even though she was good at these tasks, her nursing skills far exceeded her homemaking skills. She had me stand when eating so I would digest my food better. After preparing my family's meals, she set my plate at the freestanding dishwasher in the kitchen, so I could stand and eat close to my family. I slowly regained my appetite. She also helped me deal with potential death without ever having to say much. Just as she had begun her nursing career in 1929, Lillian worked quietly in my home providing nursing care every day into the night.

Today, people ask why I am so close to Lillian. I say because she has *"hands of gold."* What would my family or I have done without her *"hands of gold"* during that scary period in our lives?

Lillian, now age 94, resides in a nursing home near Elmhurst. I have made a contribution in her name to Sigma Theta Tau International for a commemorative brick in the Center for Nursing Scholarship in Indianapolis, Indiana, for the library. And now, I lovingly dedicate this story of her life.

HELLO, MY NAME IS BETTY

by Betty J. Noyes

ello, my name is Betty and I am a nurse." That was the way my mother taught me to introduce myself. As a child, it was, "Hello, my name is Betty and I want to be a nurse." This may sound like a stretch of a childhood memory, but I know it to be absolutely true. It was the way my mother introduced herself, "Hello, I am Elizabeth Firsching Grove and I am a nurse."

Nursing was the central personal identification for my mother. Nursing was the core of her life. She contributed to the lives of many patients and their families, but most of all to me.

The family held mother accountable for choosing the best hospitals and doctors. Her obstetrician was "the best" that Columbia Presbyterian Hospital in New York City had to offer in 1944. I was always told to boast about whom he was and where I was born. Those were important identifiers to the family. However, we also had 12 other nurses in our immediate family. Each time I was told a story about them it always began, "_____, the nurse, did _____."

Mother's trek to work everyday was a normal part of our lives. When I was three years old, she would take me to work, and I would stay in the hospital lobby with my dolls. My role was to line up the wheelchairs of discharged patients in the lobby. She would periodically come down to see me, give me a hug, and tell me that she had to get back to her patients who were ill. I was to greet every visitor, including the doctors, who would relay messages. Almost every morning, stories would include tales of patients, doctors, "good nurses," and hospital life.

Mother worked most of her career as a staff nurse. She was first a licensed practical nurse and then received her registered nurse license after taking a challenging exam during WWII. Her pin, cap, and bandage scissors are still in my dresser drawer.

During the Depression, her father, my grandfather, developed tuberculosis and had to be admitted to a sanitarium for months. Mother single-handedly supported the family of four, a home mortgage, and even a car. She was familiar with the work ethic and mission of nursing so she provided food and shelter.

When mother became a private duty nurse, she sometimes cared for the rich and famous. She was assigned patients who were hospitalized in a small, elite hospital in Manhattan. She would stay with them for the entire course of their hospitalizations and frequently go home with them. I was told stories about when the doctor called and how the bed, bath, or walks around the estate for exercise went. My family would visit mother on weekends. We still have home movies of me as a toddler being carried around the grounds of beautiful estates on Long Island, Westchester County, and surrounding areas.

The patients would give me lovely gifts of clothes, toys, and pearls. I still have them. As you can see, these visits did have their rewards.

Mother would say she had to go to work because the patient needed her, the doctor had made a special request for her to care for his patient, or her patient had been readmitted and she had to be with them. Some of these relationships lasted for decades. Her commitment was always to the patient. I know that she offered tender loving care. I was left in the care of my grandmother. "Grossmama" supported the important role my mother was playing in the lives of so many others.

Mother became a department head for central supply when I was in high school and we were all proud. I was told this assignment was not a "promotion," just a different type of nursing. She was responsible for the sterility and distribution of patient-care equipment. When staff called in sick, we both went in and sharpened needles, wrapped instrument sets, checked autoclaves, and delivered carts to the OR and the nursing units.

When I was 3 years old, my mother gave me my first of many "nurse kits." She taught me the purpose of each "toy." I would play with them until parts were lost or a newer version became affordable. No game, other than "nurse" or "hospital," is in my memory. Mother dressed me in a curtain once to represent the cap of the WWI nurse. I was very happy. She always wore her cap proudly; it was her symbol of nursing.

Later in childhood, I was taught arithmetic and budgeting. Using her salary, I was challenged to calculate how many days mother would have to work to earn the amount of money to afford a desired purchase or vacation trip. That is when I learned nursing provided double rewards: professional satisfaction and a "good" salary.

I once considered teaching as a career. I vividly remember mother standing at the kitchen sink saying, "You can teach nursing." That ended my dilemma. The *Cherry Ames* book series about nurses was my childhood library. I read every book cover to cover.

During the summers of my childhood from ages 4 to 16 years old, mother was a camp nurse. Being an only child growing up in Brooklyn, New York, outdoors, nature, games, and sports were unknown. I once again learned her nursing career would "win" us a summer in the country. I was encouraged to be her assistant and would bring the "injured" to the infirmary.

From the age of 14, I worked as a junior volunteer in the same hospital as my mother. The pride of wearing a uniform was enormous. Although mine was not yet all white like my mother's, I could now wear white stockings and white shoes. I could make rounds, talk to patients, talk to nurses, and talk to doctors just like my mother did. I won many service chevrons and awards. Each ceremony was underscored with the pride of being a nurse, just like my mother. Short acceptance speeches included my commitment to the profession and my pride in providing patient-care services.

It was time to select my nursing school when I was a sophomore in high school. It seemed to me that the choices were St. Luke's Hospital, Lenox Hill Hospital, or Bellevue Hospital in New York City. The other 12 nurses in the family had attended big name diploma schools. Then came the shocker. My mother and I consulted the National League for Nursing in Manhattan. This was the "academic Mecca." I was extremely nervous meeting "those" people but was told they were "nurses," so it was going to be just fine. I vividly remember the office cubicle in which the meeting took place. My mother posed the question, "What kind of education should Betty pursue." The discussion lasted less than one hour and mother cried. The NLN staff recommended I should go to a high-caliber baccalaureate program.

The family conferences that followed were numerous. Every nurse in the family was polled and every opinion considered. Every conversation was repeated, every cost-benefit analysis discussed. In the end, the NLN authority was paramount. So the selection process began. I was to select a program that offered lots of clinical experience and was affiliated with only the best hospitals that had a school of medicine and other health professional schools on campus. The cost had to be budgeted. Mother would have to work extra days and shifts, as well as purchase insurance policies. I would have to work more hours in the hospital, with the understanding I needed to be included in as many patient procedures as possible to assure I had clinical exposure to supplement my academic education. All went according to plan. I borrowed textbooks from the hospital to begin studying various diagnoses, procedures, and drugs. I observed every patient procedure possible.

My name is Betty and I was going to be a good nurse, just like my mother. I worked every weekend and every holiday. Every nursing supervisor and even the director of nursing knew me by name. Most physicians greeted me and I was crushed when they didn't. I even knew the priest and the rabbi. Everyone knew my mother and she was sure I knew everyone.

My years in nursing school at the University of Buffalo were tense. I was always told grades were important but my clinical scores were paramount. The latter was always A+. The academic grades were satisfactory and came with hard work. I returned home every summer and worked at the hospital as a nurse aide. There was no time off. Every night, there was a joint debriefing on the drive home and reinforcement for positive encounters of the nursing kind. There was pride in nursing and in being a nurse, just like my mother.

Now, it is 57 years later, and I still say, "Hello, my name is Betty and I am a nurse and proud of it. I have nursing in my DNA and 13 nurses in my family. And I am proud to tell you my mother was an outstanding nurse!"

MARRIED TO A MALE NURSE, BRINGING CARING HOME: PHILLIP LEIGH MANDEL

by Deborah Mandel

You can't tell by looking at him what my husband, Phillip, does for a living. If guessing, his hobbies and interests would lead you down the wrong path. His hands are always rough from his construction projects, and his hair is usually unruly from his helmet. He loves to ride his motorcycle back and forth to work. He can be found around the house four days a week being Mr. Mom to our two sons, Matthew and Seth. He has the patience of a saint as well as a true gift for lecturing; we have offered to purchase a podium for him several times. His love for music is evident. There is not a shelf in the house that does not have a CD, tape, or album on it. He even plays the guitar when he thinks no one is within earshot.

Phil has a natural desire to fix things. He has a talent for construction and has created many household comforts, including an outside paradise. There is a project around every corner, with some left unfinished because he needs help. You see, Phillip is a nurse who carries this identity into all his other activities.

Phillip and I met almost 30 years ago in nursing school. We married two years later. Phil chose to put school on hold so that I could finish. He returned to nursing school after my graduation and received an Associate's Degree in Nursing from Kingsborough Community College. Phil always found emergency medicine exciting and rewarding. He worked in the emergency room at Kings County Hospital from 1979 to 1988. Phillip provided care for an inner-city patient population who experienced violence, poverty, neglect, and illness as part of their daily lives. Phil remained committed to caring for this population for years after he moved to New Jersey.

In 1988, after much cajoling, Phil finally left Kings County Hospital to become an emergency room assistant head nurse at Robert Wood Johnson University Hospital. After two years, Phil turned his expertise to advanced life support and found his niche in mobile intensive care nursing. Phillip has received numerous awards in his nursing career and has been honored several times for his life-saving efforts. This year alone, those he saved honored Phil five times at the Emergency Service Dinner for his life-saving contributions. It was an extremely emotional experience to see the people and their families my husband has so profoundly affected.

Phil's expertise has been an asset to his community, Spotswood. He donates countless volunteer hours to the Spotswood First Aid Squad. He also volunteers his knowledge of construction and tools to the Spotswood Community Playground Project. He was responsible for all the tools donated for a five-day playground construction project.

Phil is a good sport. He has been stuffed into Santa Claus and Easter Bunny suits for children's community events. He has served on every large community fund-raiser, working behind the scenes, picking up donations, setting up equipment, and providing any type of assistance.

Phil has provided CPR instruction to community members and fellow nurses. He tutors aspiring paramedics, nurses, and emergency medical technicians. He provides opportunities for them to ride along with a Mobile Intensive Care Unit. Phil is an extraordinary teacher and mentor. He has an ever-increasing number of requests to teach Advanced Cardiac Life Support, Pediatric Advanced Life Support, Cardiopulmonary Resuscitation, and Neonatal Resuscitation programs.

Phil's activities at work, at home, and at play include a caring element. Phil loves to ride his motorcycle, and even in this activity he has a commitment to help and care for people. He is an active member of the Knights of Life Motorcycle Club, a group comprised of men and women working in all areas of medical and nursing fields who come together from several states. This motorcycle club provides first aid and/or motorcycle escort for community and charity events throughout the year. Phil is extremely fortunate to combine his passion for motorcycles with his skill as an emergency care nurse.

I am truly lucky to have Phil as a friend, colleague, and husband. He understands the frustrations and the rewards of being a nurse and is able to empathize with me by providing perspective and support. It is unique to have a spouse who faces similar work challenges and who is there to share in the failures and successes of nursing. Writing about Phillip has been a labor of love. There can be no better way to describe Phil other than to say he is an ordinary, unassuming man who is proud to be a nurse and who has made an extraordinary difference in my life, as well as the lives of his family, patients, and those in the community.

There can be no better way to describe Phil other than to say he is an ordinary, unassuming man who is proud to be a nurse and who has made an extraordinary difference in my life, as well as the lives of his family, patients, and those in the community.

MARILYN DANNER IRISH:
DEVOTED TO FAMILY AND COUNTRY

by Peggy Miller

arilyn Danner was born March 23, 1927, in Iowa City, Iowa, to a close-knit family that included her parents Ruth and Earl, a brother Dave, and a dog named Louie. As a temperamental Pekinese, Louie was solely devoted to Ruth. The Depression was in full swing and times were particularly tough. Earl was disabled due to a cardiac condition and unable to work. Ruth supported the family by working as a secretary for a general practitioner. In retrospect, Marilyn doesn't remember a dramatic call to nursing. However, her father's illness and her mother's occupation were probably influences.

While at Iowa City High School, Marilyn knew she wanted to be a nurse, a decision strongly supported by her family. Marilyn graduated from high school in 1944, and to her great surprise she received a watch from her parents they barely could afford. The Girard-Perregaux watch with a sweep second hand was purchased at Hand's Jewelry Store in Iowa City. Marilyn wore the watch throughout her nursing career and eventually gave it to her daughter, Carolyn, when she became a registered nurse.

Marilyn enrolled in the bachelor's of nursing program at the University of Iowa. She doesn't recall how she obtained the $25 entrance fee, a great deal of money at that time. She joined classmates Jinx and Connie at the West Lawn dormitory, where the trio formed a close friendship that continues to this day. The students proudly wore school uniforms, white bib aprons, caps, and stockings. Long hours were spent in study and working on the hospital wards. Their training took place during World War II, when nurses were in short supply, so often it was the students who cared for the patients with little or no assistance.

Marilyn preferred working on the surgical ward, where nursing responsibilities included bathing patients, administering medications, taking vital signs, and assisting with exams. As a reference point for this period of nursing, Marilyn recalls giving injections of the recently discovered miracle drug, penicillin. Unlike today, many medications had to be crushed, heated in a spoon, and suctioned into a glass syringe. As another point of reference, cardiopulmonary resuscitation was not a nursing or medical intervention since it was not developed until the late 1960s. Typical of these times was the extreme deference of nurses to physicians. Marilyn remembers how nurses stood up when an attending physician entered the nursing station.

Marilyn looks back at nursing school as a wonderful time of high spirits, great camaraderie, and challenging classroom and clinical experiences, all of which provided a solid foundation for a nursing career. She still treasures the nursing pin she received at graduation.

Upon successful completion of the state board exam in Des Moines, Marilyn returned to work on the surgical ward at the University of Iowa. Uncertain about her next step, Marilyn applied to the VA Hospital in Biloxi, Mississippi, where she was accepted and assigned to a general ward. She loved it! While living in Mississippi, Marilyn was visited by her parents in June of 1950. Ruth, who had complained of headaches during the visit, subsequently had a severe, disabling stroke two months later.

Marilyn continued working at the VA Hospital since her parents' need for financial support was greater than ever before. At every opportunity, she returned to Iowa City to care for her mother. Ruth suffered a second stroke and died in December of 1950; her death was a devastating loss for Marilyn and her family. In order to be closer to her father, Marilyn transferred to the Hines VA Hospital in Chicago, Illinois, where she worked with young paraplegic veterans. She would work 11 nights in a row in return for four days off so she could return to Iowa City to be with her father.

Eventually, Marilyn returned to Iowa City and worked as a private duty nurse so she could be closer to her father. It was during this period that Marilyn's 18-month-old nephew, Mark, was admitted to the University of Iowa Hospital Intensive Care Unit after having aspirated a piece of carrot. Following a failed bronchoscopic attempt to remove the carrot, Mark's larynx swelled, necessitating an emergency tracheotomy. It was Marilyn, along with Mark's mother, who maintained a 24-hour vigil at his bedside. One night while Marilyn was on duty, Mark began coughing so violently that she feared he would die. To her great relief, the piece of carrot popped out on the baby's bib and Mark recovered promptly.

Having fulfilled family responsibilities during tough times, Marilyn decided to join the United States Air Force. However, she was unsuccessful in convincing Connie and Jinx to join with her. Nevertheless, Marilyn pursued her ambition and enlisted. In 1950, at the onset of the Korean War, she was assigned to Scott Air Force Base in Belleville, Illinois. Out of the entire nurse corps, Marilyn was one of only three nurses chosen by the chief nurse to attend flight school. For Marilyn, this opportunity offered greater challenge and excitement, as well as additional hazard pay.

Flight training was held at Eglin Air Force Base in Montgomery, Alabama. Marilyn remembers terrific nursing courses and flight training that included simulated parachute jumping. The nurses were required to wear parachutes during domestic transport of the injured soldiers. In the event of a mechanical failure, these valuable nurses and pilots were instructed to parachute to safety. Fortunately, Marilyn was never confronted with this situation and, to this day, is unsure whether she would have been able to leave her patients to follow that order.

Marilyn graduated from flight training and received her wings, which she still proudly owns. She returned to Scott Air Force Base, married an Air Force pilot, and worked at the base hospital. A favorite memory is the time she flew with 20 patients from Scott to Chanute Air Force Base in Rantoul, Illinois, so they could attend a University

of Iowa/University of Illinois football game. One patient's jaws were wired and she was concerned he might experience airsickness. To her relief, the wire clippers in her pocket were not needed. She does not remember who won the game!

Eventually, Marilyn was sent to Mountain Home Air Force Base in Idaho, where she worked in general nursing. Sometime later, she was transferred to the Strategic Air Command where she was required to be ready in 90 minutes for deployment anywhere in the world.

Marilyn and her husband were honorably discharged in 1953 when the war ended. They relocated to St. Louis where Marilyn went to work as a plant nurse for an automotive company. After the birth of her first child, Marilyn Lynette, she returned to the VA. She then decided to take advantage of the GI bill and, while working full time, began night school for her master's degree in nursing education and administration.

Marilyn became director of a school for licensed practical nurses after she graduated with her Master of Science in Nursing degree. There were welcomed interruptions in her nursing career for the births of daughters Carolyn and Cathi. Following a four-year hiatus for child care, Marilyn returned to the VA Hospital as a clinical nursing supervisor.

Following her divorce, Marilyn moved to Phoenix, Arizona, in 1972 and became a clinical nursing supervisor at the VA Hospital. Shortly after that, she became acutely ill with hepatitis she contracted from a patient. She received a disability and was never able to work again.

Marilyn's focus remains her children, as well as her adored menagerie of four lucky dogs, Bob, Gurley, Hillary, and Maus. Marilyn's career was challenged by adventure and increasing responsibility. Her dedication to her family and country is impressive and not without consequences to her own health. Her love of nursing and the Air Force influenced and inspired her daughter Carolyn, who is a master's-prepared nurse working in oncology at the VA Hospital in Amarillo, Texas. Carolyn and this writer became nurses because of Marilyn's influence and love of nursing.

NANA

by Anne E. Solak and Rhiannon E. Tennant

y grandmother's name was Annie Elizabeth Goodin. She was a nurse and my namesake. As I grew up, my grandmother was a constant part of my life. She had come from Australia to live with my mother and father shortly after their marriage in 1947. Some of my earliest memories are of listening to my grandmother's stories about her adventures as a young nurse during World War I.

My grandmother was born near the end of the 19th century, on July 22, 1883, in Ganstead, a small village in the north of England, some ten miles from Kingston upon Hull, a medium-sized city near the North Sea coast. She was the third of 12 children and the oldest daughter of a typical middle-class Yorkshire farming family. Because she was the oldest daughter, her formal schooling was cut short so she could help raise her brothers and sisters.

In the 1890s, many people in England, especially girls, did not travel far from where they were born. Yet, my grandmother, showing the adventurous spirit that would remain with her for her whole life, left home at 16 to begin her nurse's training at a hospital in York, far from her little village. In those days, students and nurses lived in residence at the hospital where they worked and trained.

We don't know exactly when my grandmother completed her training, but we do know she was working six days a week as a hospital nurse in 1906 when she met my grandfather, Harry Puckering. Harry and Annie saw each other once a week for two years on Annie's day off. One day, Harry suddenly left England for Australia. He told Annie he had nothing to offer her; he felt she would be better off without him. My grandmother was devastated. She missed Harry desperately and was on the verge of leaving for Australia to find him when World War I broke out in August of 1914. My grandmother hurried to join the war effort and enlisted in the British Army Nursing Service, known at the time as Queen Alexandra's Royal Army Nursing Corp.

Queen Alexandra's Royal Army Nursing Corp was a direct descendant of the group of 38 women, led by Florence Nightingale, who went to Scutari Hospital in Istanbul in 1854, during the Crimean War, to care for wounded British soldiers. By the end of World War I, some 100,000 nurses had served in France, Italy, Salonika, Egypt, Palestine, Mesopotamia, India, East Africa, and Russia. She served aboard the hospital ship HMHS Gloucester Castle, a converted mixed-service steamship. The Gloucester Castle was put into service as a 410-bed hospital ship on September 24, 1914. My grandmother joined the medical staff shortly before the ship left for the Mediterranean in November of 1914.

The Gloucester Castle medical staff provided service throughout the Mediterranean. The ship made a long stay at the Island of Malta. As a little girl, I remember my grandmother telling me how the smell of garlic permeated the island. She said, "To this day, I can't stand the smell of garlic. They used garlic in everything; they even put it under their pillows." She found out, however, the smell of garlic wasn't as bad as the smell of war.

My grandmother went from Malta to Greece and then, in April of 1915, to the beaches of Gallipoli in Turkey, where one of the most disastrous British campaigns of the war occurred. Annie was there for eight months between the invasion and evacuation. In January of 1916, over 200,000 British, Australian, and New Zealand soldiers became casualties. She and her fellow nurses lived in tents on the beach at Gallipoli, in constant danger, providing emergency treatment to soldiers before they were sent out to the hospital ships. The carnage on the beach was unimaginable and was one of the worst experiences of my grandmother's life.

After the Gallipoli evacuation, the Gloucester Castle returned to England. On March 30, 1917, the Gloucester Castle, although clearly marked as a hospital ship, was torpedoed by a German U-boat. Fortunately, it was close to the English shore and all but three of the 399 people on board were rescued as the ship was towed to port. My grandmother didn't recall being particularly afraid during the incident because she was so busy getting the sick and injured soldiers to safety. Little more than a year later, another hospital ship, the Llandovery Castle, was sunk in the Atlantic by a U-boat. The survivors in the lifeboats were killed by machine gun fire. All the nurses aboard the Llandovery Castle died. My grandmother always felt she was a lucky young woman.

After recovering from the attack on her ship, my grandmother was sent to Stavros, Greece. In early 1918, she contracted epidemic typhus, a louse-borne infectious disease with an approximately 50 percent fatality rate (this was before antibiotics). My grandmother always believed she contracted the disease while caring for refugees from the Bolshevik Revolution in Russia. Over 150,000 allied soldiers died from the disease during World War I. My grandmother was not expected to live; she was taken aboard a hospital ship using a cattle sling. She was sent to a large military hospital in Alexandria, Egypt. Her recovery was difficult; it took six months, and she lost all of her hair in the process.

In the fall of 1918, as the war was winding down to its end in November, my grandmother was sent to Marseilles, France. It was during this time the great Influenza Pandemic began, ultimately resulting in the death of 20 to 40 million people. My grandmother spent until the end of 1919 in the nursing service, caring for sick and injured soldiers. A small woman, my grandmother always believed her arthritic back was a result of her time in Marseilles, where she had to lift hundreds of sick soldiers. At some time during her time in the Mediterranean, my grandmother was infected with malaria and suffered two reoccurrences later in her life.

My grandmother Annie returned home from the war and lived with her mother until 1921 when Harry Puckering wrote her mother to find out whether Annie had survived the war and the influenza pandemic. Harry was doing well in Australia. My grandmother left her family again and, on December 21, 1921, married Harry Puckering in Mossman, Northern Queensland, Australia. They lived in a beautiful house on two acres, and Harry managed the local sugar mill. They had two daughters, my mother Alice and my aunt Beryl.

My grandmother never did any further formal nursing. The experiences of that most horrible war were enough for her. In Mossman, there was no doctor or hospital within 20 miles and only two cars in town, so for 10 years my grandmother became the local midwife. She never charged for a delivery and, in those days of large families, never lost a baby. She continued as the midwife and also provided emergency treatment for those in need until a hospital was built in Mossman in 1932.

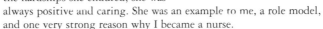

My grandmother experienced many more adventures, unrelated to nursing. She was a remarkable woman who remained busy and mentally active until her death in 1971. My grandmother will always be "Nana" to me. Nana was not only a nurse who helped people in need, she also risked her own life doing it. Despite the hardships she endured, she was always positive and caring. She was an example to me, a role model, and one very strong reason why I became a nurse.

NURSING HISTORY REVISITED:
A DAUGHTER'S REFLECTION

by Alma Joel Labunski

The year was 1917. The place was Manhattan, New York. The young, slim, vibrant, foreign woman (Ms. L.) exiting the large university door was feeling rejected, alone, and heavy-laden. She was an eager young woman who had recently immigrated to the United States. She had bright hope for achieving a successful medical education at the university. However, she was advised that, although her academic performance was exemplary, her command of the English language was poor and her resources were too minimal to progress through medical school as a self-supporting female student.

With continuing feelings of hopelessness, Ms. L. was perplexed about what she could do. She had traveled thousands of miles alone to Ellis Island to see the Statute of Liberty and to enroll in medical school for preparation as a physician. How could she ever face her family again? These thoughts were overwhelming. She reflected upon her previous envious position as a teacher of high school mathematics with a roof over her head and the ability to fluently speak seven languages in the "old country."

One month later, Ms. L. contacted a friend in Cleveland, Ohio. With her only bag in her possession, she boarded a train for the city. She was determined to find some field in which she could be of service as a newcomer in the United States.

With the nation involved in World War I and the escalated need for healthcare workers, Ms. L. entered the School of Nursing at St. Luke's Hospital, which had no required fee. In exchange for the "no fee required," she lived in the dormitory, worked 12 to 16 hours a day, seven days a week, and was allowed two hours on Sunday mornings to attend church. Two evenings each week were allocated for study. Even with their vigorous schedule, Ms. L. and her classmates became close friends. They worked, ate, slept, and played together and remained friends for a lifetime.

Immediately upon completion of the program, Ms. L. began public health nursing with the Visiting Nurses Association. Since little had been established for World War I veterans at that time, Ms. L. and two of her colleagues investigated the pioneering efforts of volunteers in New York City who had established the American Red Cross. Using guidelines from New York, Ms. L. and her co-workers initiated what was later to be called the Cleveland Chapter of the American

Red Cross. Those beginning organizational components paved the way for the creation of chapters throughout the United States.

The immediate post-World War I days required long hours and hard work with little remuneration. Nonetheless, satisfaction, pride, and completion were all their own reward, and Ms. L. and her colleagues eagerly reported "loving every minute" of it. They rubbed shoulders with currently acclaimed public health nurse leaders such as Lavinia Dock (a political community nurse activist), Carrie Hill (chief of the American Red Cross), and Lillian Wald (a public health nurse activist and founder of the Henry Street Settlement in New York).

Ms. L. moved to Chicago and learned the city had a St. Luke's Hospital. Sparked by her positive experiences at St. Luke's in Cleveland, she joined the public health nursing staff of St. Luke's Hospital. She sensed more comfort in Chicago where an immigrant, with no family in America and who very often was lonely, could find others with similar circumstances. It was in Chicago that Ms. L. unexpectedly promoted a friendship with Mr. J. who had also immigrated to the states from the same country. Their commonalities allowed them to openly interact. In 1925, their friendship blossomed into a courtship and marriage.

Although her single status changed, the newly married Mrs. J. continued to work as a public health nurse. Mrs. J. also became a mother of two daughters, Vivian and Alma. Mrs. J. worked as a nurse during the recession, the hardship of the Depression, and the loss of her husband's jobs and their home. She served as a staff nurse and supervisor in public health and in hospital agencies. She also served as an industrial nurse in occupational health, a school nurse, a physician's assistant in the operating room, an obstetrical nurse, and in the home as a private duty or home care nurse.

Mrs. J. functioned as the role model for hundreds of staff and patients (through close to 50 years of nursing service), including caring for national celebrities. However, she also insisted her daughters, especially the youngest who demonstrated great interest in healthcare, should never enter the field of nursing. Mrs. J. would say, "It is not the place or profession for a proper Middle-Eastern, ethnic woman."

As daughters Vivian and Alma were maturing, they were perceived and stigmatized as wayward (currently the term is "latch key") children and teens. Although unheard of in their community and in that era, the girls' mother was absent from the home; she was working. Their father prepared their breakfasts and lunch sacks and saw them off to school. Father also visited the schools after cleaning house regularly and preparing the dinner, all the while preparing the way for Mrs. J. to come home and take over.

During the girls' teen years, World War II activities kept Mrs. J. hard at work as a nurse. During those years, she worked long hours as the nursing shortage escalated. Always willing and enthusiastic, Mrs. J. never complained of fatigue even though illness, surgeries, and family deaths visibly drained her time and energy. In fact, absence from work was nearly nonexistent for Mrs. J. Although the family had no automobile, Mrs. J.'s work ethic demanded she walk every morning to meet the bus, in spite of subzero temperatures and snowdrifts up to her knees. Daughters Vivian and Alma watched from the bedroom window as their mom trudged in the quiet snow-packed streets of Chicago day after day, year after year, heading for work to provide nursing care for others.

In 1960, another nursing shortage impacted the nursing staff and the ability to provide adequate patient care. As an innovator and continuing "mover and shaker," Mrs. J. continued to create ways to improve healthcare for her patients. This time was no exception. She pioneered an intravenous therapy (IV) team of nurses to cover three shifts; they started IVs, monitored patients' IV sites, and changed the sites as needed throughout the hospital.

The IV Therapy Team idea "caught on," and Mrs. J. was soon sought by acute care setting personnel in Chicago and Midwest states to provide presentations. She was in such demand for presentations and IV care that fellow colleagues only wanted to be taught by "Tish," as she was affectionately known. Colleagues would say, "Tish is the only one who can teach us," and "Tish is the only one I know who can 'smell' a vein."

Mrs. J. was also an avid reader. She faithfully reviewed every professional journal from front to back. She believed the hallmark of a professional person was to continue learning throughout a lifetime. Mrs. J. continued to grow professionally, but continuing relapses of thrombophlebitis impaired her ambulation and pushed her into

retirement in 1963. Mrs. J. spent 48 years as a faithful nurse, providing comprehensive, quality-based service to improve the health and welfare of all people. Mrs. J. was an outstanding example of selflessness as she unconditionally gave her life, a life that spanned four wars: World War I, World War II, the Korean War, and the Vietnam War. Mrs. J. was the greatest force in changing lives, especially the life of one of her daughters.

Pressures for retirement grew increasingly as Mrs. J.'s selfless caring transferred to her husband who had suffered several strokes. She nursed him for six years before he died in 1969. Restlessness and feelings of loss prompted Mrs. J. to seek a southern retirement community where she would be assured of life care. She sought solace in her church, the community, and, of course, in the need to continue giving by assisting her neighbors, working on community projects, and volunteering healthcare in the skilled-care facility within the retirement community.

All the subscriptions to nursing professional journals continued to be reviewed and read by Mrs. J. in spite of short-term sensory failure. She insisted on being "well-prepared" for whatever might occur and to continue her dedication to lifelong learning.

Shortly thereafter, cancer did invade Mrs. J's body. The primary site of the cancer was the colon with metastasis to the liver and brain. Mrs. J. was placed in a nursing pavilion as a patient, but she continued to make desperate attempts to serve others by assisting the nurses. Mrs. J. was always a nurse; she was always nursing. Mrs. J. would make her own bed and joyfully, although painfully, serve other patients in the adjoining rooms. However, Mrs. J. finally succumbed to incredible fatigue, somnolence, coma, and death. Although hardly able to speak, Mrs. J., my mom, rejoiced, stating she was going "home" and would finally be reunited with those she loved, nursed, and lived for.

RUTH'S WALK AS A NURSE: RUTH I. ROBERTSON

by Kerry L. O'Brien

There was no specific event or person that triggered her interest in nursing. Ruth just wanted to be a nurse. She hoped to attend Bellevue Hospital School of Nursing, but her father refused. "If you go to that 'hospital,' you'll get the black bottle." (The black bottle referred to the Spanish Flu epidemic of the 1800s. Bellevue nurses became infamous for tying a dark blue bottle of medicine, a treatment for dysentery, around their waists and carrying spoons to treat the sick.) She decided to attend St. Catherine's Hospital School of Nursing.

Cousin Freddie dropped her off at St. Catherine's that first day in 1940. As she stepped out of the car, the key to her trunk slipped from her pocket and down into the drain. A long stick with chewing gum on the end helped her to successfully retrieve the key. This is how Ruth began her nursing journey.

Improvisation, critical thinking, the ability to adapt to both changing and unfavorable situations, a commitment to excellence, a calling to help others regardless of circumstance, and simple acts of caring: these phrases characterize both the personal and professional journey of Ruth I. Robertson.

One year after graduating from St. Catherine's, Ruth entered the Nursing Sisters of the Sick Poor. Working as a visiting nurse, Ruth and her fellow nuns were ahead of their time. They began to track outcomes of cancer patients, trending symptoms, and nursing care to determine the most effective symptom management interventions. Ruth pursued her BSN and MSN in nursing education at St. John's University. Through all of these activities, Ruth was facing an internal struggle. After 16 years, Ruth made the difficult decision to leave the convent.

After some soul-searching in the California sun, Ruth returned to the east coast. After running a chance errand for her sister in Connecticut, she stopped by to see an old friend at Bridgeport Hospital. This stop began the next phase of Ruth's life.

Ruth began as the assistant director of nursing. She functioned as an ombudsman, the "buffer" between administration and the staff, and was charged with improving physician, staff, and patient satisfaction. Through her meetings with patients, nurses, and physicians, she compiled information and formulated recommendations. While her recommendations were not always followed, she established herself in the Bridgeport Hospital community as a dedicated advocate for patients and the nursing profession.

Miss Margaret Madden assumed the role of director of nursing and taught Ruth her two most important lessons, "accountability" and "follow-through." Ruth pursued an MA in nursing services administration and moved into the role of associate director of nursing. Together with their team, Miss Madden and Ruth had the foresight to develop numerous specialty units, i.e., CCU, neurology, and orthopedics. They also facilitated the development of nursing practice specialties at Bridgeport.

Ruth spent 23 years at Bridgeport. When Miss Madden retired, Ruth was promoted to director of nursing. Innovation, creativity, and strong leadership, peppered with some personal disappointment, marked her tenure.

Ruth and her colleagues created the first upward mobility program for LPNs in the Connecticut area. This program was vital to elevating the educational preparation of practicing nurses. The team worked tirelessly with five local schools of nursing to revise the curriculum. Ruth presented the program and curriculum to the Connecticut State Board of Examiners. The program was accepted. Numerous LPNs from Bridgeport Hospital became RNs.

The success of the program and the commitment of Ruth and her team, especially Jean Pakacs, the education specialist responsible for clinical nursing education at Bridgeport Hospital, led Bridgeport Hospital administration into discussions with Sacred Heart University administration regarding a collaborative agreement. As a result of these discussions, Bridgeport Hospital became a BSN degree-granting institution. An incredible amount of time was spent with the Connecticut State Board of Examiners, Sacred Heart University nursing faculty, and Bridgeport Hospital's administration in developing this program. The project became Ruth's "pet project."

The board of trustees at Bridgeport Hospital made changes in hospital administration. Ruth, along with most of her senior colleagues, was terminated. The new administrator and his team did not have the commitment necessary to follow through with the project. Today, 17 years later, Ruth feels regret that she did not bring the program to fruition at Bridgeport. Ruth's idea of the program was ahead of her time in terms of value and innovation. The program was implemented years later between St. Vincent's Hospital and Sacred Heart University.

Upon leaving Bridgeport, Ruth decided to "take it easy" and work per diem as a nursing home supervisor one day each week. However, even in her more relaxed mode, her excellence and commitment were noticed, and within six months Ruth was asked to assume the role of director of nursing, a position she held for almost six years.

And there were many other activities Ruth initiated, such as connecting an impoverished pediatric burn patient with Shriner's Hospital for Children, enabling him to receive skin grafts and treatment for contractures; reducing a pregnant woman to tears of joy and disbelief when she offered her wet and dry paper towels to clean her hands after helping her with the bedpan; explaining the intricacies of using a stool sample card to a bewildered old man who called her "old timer" while on administrative rounds; teaching adults to read as part of a volunteer adult literacy program at Mercy Learning Center, even motivating one learner to do the crossword puzzles; advocating for her mentor and friend to receive proper and compassionate medical care and rehabilitation after her subdural hemorrhage; volunteering in the rectory office one day each week and counting collection money at St. Peter's Roman Catholic Church. These types of caring activities illuminate Ruth's walk as a nurse.

Ruth's life experiences as a nurse have made her a role model for the next generations: three family members and numerous former employees are nurses. Ruth was an excellent clinician and administrator. And Ruth's volunteering after retirement, her creativity and personal integrity, and her ability to initiate new and innovative programs place her in the forefront of nursing.

SHE STILL GIGGLES

by Heather R. Beebe

The patient, clutching a collection of Beanie Baby toys, greeted the new arrival with a proclamation, "Episcopalian nuns do not believe in gynecologists." She then turned on her heels and disappeared down the corridor. The arrival, a new graduate entering the unit for the first time on the first day of her first job, giggled and proceeded to the desk. Thus began my sister Alison L. Beebe's career as a psychiatric nurse.

Alison's interest in nursing began at a young age. In a fifth grade report on the human body, she described the intestines as "a bunch of worms." After consulting with our nurse grandmother, she realized there were many more clinically appropriate descriptions.

Alison followed a traditional path. She worked as a candy striper during high school as an introduction to nursing. During nursing school she made the less traditional choice of going into psychiatric nursing. During a medical surgical rotation, she sat down to chat with her assigned patient after having completed all the required tasks. The instructor entered the room and scolded her for "wasting time." At that moment, Alison decided a specialty that focused on talking with the patients was far more appropriate for her. She realized she had the empathy, interest, and sense of humor that enabled her to enjoy patients who had either lost touch with reality or endured it as a crushing burden. So she dove right in.

It was sink or swim when Alison started on the evening shift of a locked intensive care unit at a state psychiatric institute. The Beanie Baby toy collector and her fellow patients often outnumbered the beds. Mattresses would line the halls.

Police brought in the homeless as well as the criminally insane. Alison learned to delouse and to "fold" patients who needed restraint. She learned to clean up after patients who put their faces through meshed-glass windows. She dug out her maternal-child text when a psychotic postpartum patient joined the crowd. She also learned the burly assistants and metal detectors couldn't always protect her from assault.

Alison almost always came home with a bubbly disposition and giggled about some of the things that had happened that night. After all, laughter was often the best response to what she saw. Imagine a scene where a fresh-faced 20-year-old is approaching a man sitting

stark naked in a room full of visitors gratifying himself. In her most authoritative voice and keeping a straight face, she said, "Joe, this is inappropriate behavior, please put your clothes on." She received a marriage proposal from another unclothed patient as he jumped up and down on his bed, "Will you be my wife for life?" *Coitus Interruptus* took on a new meaning, given the frequency with which she disengaged patients in the midst of these behaviors. She used creativity and humor when she convinced a man to eat again by sneaking him M&Ms. Later she gave the same man a haircut, only to discover you can't cut an Afro with scissors!

Alison eventually moved from the ridiculous to the sublime. She relocated and found a position at a private psychiatric institute that was located on a beautiful campus with much greenery and conveniences, such as homemade cookies and a beauty parlor. The pace slowed, and her clinical approach shifted from "firefighting" to long-term psychoanalysis.

However, Alison's personal approach did not change. She remains lighthearted, empathetic, and nonjudgmental when dealing with patients. To this day, she likes to keep things simple and doesn't beat around the bush. She doesn't search for exactly the right words, believing her patients are people like herself, so she "tells it like she sees it." While this might be a bit radical in the world of psychiatry, patients appreciate these qualities and open up to Alison, which often expedites their treatment.

Alison's sense of humor often helps to diffuse very tense situations for both patients and staff. Her energy is contagious and co-workers find the work shift passes more quickly when she is around. She is still humbled by the idea she can help someone return to a meaningful life after struggling in the depths of suicidal depression. Every day Alison chooses to enter a world many would never choose. Alison is now 17 years into her career as a psychiatric nurse and she still giggles.

SUSAN, MY DAUGHTER: THROUGH THE YEARS

by Bernie Rimgale

It was 28 years ago when I was blessed with a beautiful baby girl. Through the years, she has brought much joy into my life for I knew she would do great things. From the time she was a little girl, she always expressed a desire to be a nurse. I worked at a very prestigious hospital, Loyola University Medical Center, in the Chicago suburbs. She was very curious, so from time to time I would take her to the medical center to look around. Her Aunt Trudy was a nurse who always told stories about her patients and their surgeries. My daughter could listen to these stories for hours.

During her teenage years, she volunteered as a candy striper, passing water and magazines to patients. She had a strong interest in reading about the Vietnam War and expressed a desire to volunteer at the Veterans Hospital, but I thought she was too young. She loved to hear war stories from her grandfather. After her junior year in college, she was accepted into the VALOR Program at the Nashville, Tennessee, Veterans Hospital. This was a summer externship offered to nursing students with very high grade point averages who went through a lengthy interview process. It was there that she cared for veterans who served her country; she just loved taking care of them and hearing their war stories. She would come home and tell me all about her day. She also learned many things from the doctors and nurses in the recovery room where she worked.

The years flew by and soon it was time for Susan to choose a school of nursing. Of course she sought advice from her Aunt Trudy, and Aunt Trudy had some advice for her. Susan worked very hard in her *undergraduate program* and graduated from the University of Tennessee with a Bachelor of Science Degree in Nursing, *summa cum laude.* I was a very proud mother.

Susan worked in Knoxville for 18 months before returning to Nashville and the Veterans Hospital. While there she took care of a woman veteran who had been in critical care in serious condition for several months. One night when the census was low, Susan had time to spend with this

woman. She told me how she had time to wash and style the woman's hair and helped another nurse shave the patient's legs. She said the woman was very grateful for making her feel so good.

I remember when Susan took care of a young woman who had cystic fibrosis. Not only did she provide the needed care for her condition, she also took the time to wash and French braid her hair. It gave the young woman such a lift. I also remember one night when she called me after work to tell me about losing her first patient. She was crying. I wished I could have been there to comfort her.

Susan also told me how she took care of a man with AIDS after "some sort" of surgery. He came back a couple of weeks after his release and gave her a big hug. He was very pleased with the care he was given by my daughter. I knew Susan provided much more than the needed physical care when it came to making patients feel better. She has a special way of caring for her patients.

I worked in the admissions office at Vanderbilt University School of Nursing, a graduate (MSN) program in nursing. I saw many nursing students come and go, and I, as a mother, dreamed of the time I might see my daughter attend the school. The years passed and Susan worked to gain experience after graduation from the University of Tennessee. After about 3 1/2 years, Susan applied to Vanderbilt's Graduate Nursing Program. She was accepted, and my dream was about to be realized.

Susan was always an excellent student. She attended a rigorous program while working part time as a nurse and graduated from Vanderbilt with a 4.0 GPA. One day, when I was getting off the elevator, I noted they were hanging the 2002 class photos on the wall. I looked up and saw her beautiful face staring back at me from the photograph. That was one very proud moment for me. I think I dragged everyone I worked with to see the picture.

I have worked with nurses for the last 28 years. The nurses I have worked with will always stand out in my mind and have a special place in my heart. I am very proud to have my daughter, Susan, join them. I am even more proud to say that my daughter, Susan, my niece, Michelle, and my cousin, Trudy (who is more like my sister than a cousin), are all nurses.

SUSAN, A DAUGHTER'S REFLECTION OF A MOTHER'S PRIDE

by Susan Rimgale

hinking back on it, I'm not really sure that I did want to be a nurse. I was more interested in the science of the human body and the "medical model" rather than the nursing model of care. I was afraid to go to medical school for fear of the time constraints it would put on my life. Someday I wanted to have a family and could not see doing that as a physician. Nursing was a way to be involved in the medical field without giving up "all my time."

Perhaps by some divine intervention, I had experiences where I realized I was being led through a journey of life. I had been a nurse for about a year, learning the "ins and outs" of a busy ICU nurse's routine. I don't think I had time to breathe, much less feel like I was spending quality time with my patients and families. I was just trying my best not to kill anyone! I was overworked and underpaid and wondered what I had got myself into.

Then I had the honor of caring for an elderly lady who was having an exacerbation of her congestive heart failure, complicated by renal failure, dialysis treatments, and sepsis. I got the chance to know her husband, who visited everyday. By the fifth day, the patient showed no signs of recovery; she continued to deteriorate. She was still cognizant and communicated with her husband and me about her wishes to be "let go." The cardiologist made rounds that evening and a big discussion ensued with the patient and her husband that focused on "her wishes."

A decision was made to extubate her, make her comfortable, and allow her to move on to what the next life holds. I stayed with her and her husband as she took her final breath. I can remember telling him that she was gone (maybe the second or third patient who I had watched die). With tears and a look I can remember like it was yesterday, he said words that I will remember for the rest of my life, "What am I going to do without her?" I wept. I knew of nothing else I could say. What had I experienced in my 22 years that could even begin to scratch the surface of the void in this man's life? I hugged him and wept. I cried for him and his wife, but also for myself and us all, knowing that one day we will all experience this type of loss, this type of heartache, this type of surrender.

That night I went home, drank a beer and toasted that man and his wife and their life together. I realized how very lucky I am. It was *me* who was there to share this experience with him, not the physician or anyone else. I realized then why I have been placed on this journey.

I'm sure that elderly man doesn't remember my name, and I'm quite sure he doesn't realize how much I needed him at that moment, probably a million times more than he needed me. The circle of life entwines us all as human beings, and what an honor and a privilege it is to be there when it begins or ends, as only a nurse can be!

I was inspired to write this after reading my mother's perception of me as a nurse. I couldn't be happier knowing how proud she is of me or how closely she listens to my stories, but I have to say that I am no hero for being a nurse. There are days when my patients get on my nerves and I don't think I can go back to work. But the most important lesson nursing has taught me is that I am a humanist. I want everyone to live the longest, healthiest, and most fulfilled life they possibly can. I want people to enjoy everything on this earth. Sure, the days I lose a patient are often really hard, but for me it makes the sun shine just a little brighter, the air in my lungs feel a little more invigorating, and my laughter a little louder because I now have an appreciation for just how short this journey is and how we must enjoy every second of it.

I'm now a nurse practitioner in critical care and don't have as much opportunity to share in these intimate experiences at the bedside. However, becoming a nurse practitioner has provided the perfect marriage between treating diseases and complications by the so-called "medical model" and still allowing me to care about patients from a humanistic nursing perspective.

THE STORY OF ANGELS: A FAMILY AND TWO SISTERS

by Debbie Downey Afasano

t was September 22, 1950, when my premature birth became big news in a small New England town. My mother always referred to it as "God's plan." My father spoke of how he was called back home from a fishing trip for this "special birth." The *Bridgeport Post* named me a "miracle baby." The delivering physician told the press that, "It was more than medical science that saved me." My mother, rest her soul, loved to tell the story of my birth as though it were a fairy tale.

Mom would explain, in a passionate voice, that shortly before I was born, Dr. Viola had lost his young son, Michael, to rubella. The doctor, a close friend of the family, was distraught and wondered about his value as a physician. During my birth, my mother insisted she had a vision of his son's face hovering above her. She described it as the face of an angel, the first angel to ever connect to my life.

Dr. Viola told my parents it was an intercession. My mother believed my premature birth renewed his confidence as a physician and his faith in God. It surely defined my life, for I am certain my purpose then, as it is now, was to be a nurse.

One of the first nurses to have an impact on my life was Lydia Hopkins. Nurse Lydia became my interim mother during my two and a half months in an incubator. She was considered a "high-tech" nurse as she regulated the oxygen flow and tended to me in my bassinet. I am told my living quarters were just a little bigger than a breadbox! Nurse Lydia was the soft voice and soft touch in the night. She was the vigilant angel of mercy who fed me, by eyedropper, until my sucking reflex developed. This nurse with the gentle adoring eyes influenced my life and my decision to become a nurse.

A yellowed newspaper article is on the wall in my office. It tells the story of a baby that survived, a baby so fragile local parish nuns prayed at her incubator. A divine plan was mobilized with my first breath. In actuality, it was over 20 minutes before the doctor evoked a cry using a hand-held resuscitator. When I was sent home, the local paper ran a picture of me on the front page. My parents, the physician, and Nurse Lydia surrounded me. Nurse Lydia is gazing down at me with the face of an angel.

Fifty-one years after my amazing birth, I am a nurse for a faith-based facility. How ironic is it that nuns prayed for my survival and today I work for the Sisters of Bon Secours. Today, I pray along with them for the strength and skills to support our mission to provide "Good Help to Those in Need." Today, as I look across the hallways of my facility and see the faces of angels, my purpose is crystal clear.

Angels have always surrounded my life. My Nana worked as a nurse until she retired in her eighties. She entered nursing school in her mid-sixties. She dressed in starched whites and polished shoes. She was the picture of professionalism with the face of an angel. Her white cap and white hair accented her rosy cheeks and sparkling eyes. Nursing made her vibrant, as though she came to life the day she became a nurse. I remember her confident gait and air of steady calm and reassurance. Her services were in demand and she earned a sterling reputation because of her attentiveness and willingness to make her patients comfortable.

She was a private duty nurse who blended the art of cooking into the art and science of nursing. If an apple a day keeps the doctor away, then certainly Ruth Butter's apple pie could cure whatever ailed you. My Nana talked about all the "old people" she cared for who were years younger than she! At her eulogy, I remembered the face of this white-haired and warm-hearted angel along with these words:

> *As I write I am feeling brighter, spirits lifting with the thought that part of you lives on in me; you've been my teacher, and I'm well taught. It is my hope that, in my lifetime, I can convey through thoughts and deeds the kind of love you gave so freely, you seemed to answer all our needs.*

My sister and I followed in my Nana's footsteps, both hoping to make a difference just as she did. My sister Pam is another angel. Pam is my mentor, best friend, and a nurse. I will never forget how she assumed the role of a compassionate nurse when we stood at the bedside of our dying mother. It was Pam, in the middle of her own grief, who reminded me, "Now is the time to make Mom proud. Now is the time to believe you are special and become all the things she knows you are." Pam helped me through the darkest time in my life.

Pam's confidence in me shaped my future and challenged me to look inside to identify my potential. She persuaded me to get my Associate's degree when I was an LPN and reminded me of my untapped potential when I questioned my ability to return for a BSN. Pam, along with several wonderful nurse mentors, helped me to realize my strengths and, in turn, bring the best of myself to the nursing profession.

Pam's ministry is in women's health. She travels abroad to impoverished countries to help them develop and improve women's healthcare services. She provides clinical, administrative, and leadership education. Using gestures, interpreters, pictures, and a working knowledge of key Russian terms, she has been able to introduce new models for healthcare in Russia, the Ukraine, and Belarus, where they have seen within her the **Лицо ангела**, which in Russian means the "face of an angel."

Pam's ministry is in women's health. She travels abroad to impoverished countries to help them develop and improve women's healthcare services. She provides clinical, administrative, and leadership education. Using gestures, interpreters, pictures, and a working knowledge of key Russian terms, she has been able to introduce new models for healthcare in Russia, the Ukraine, and Belarus.

by Ann Kobs

It was the turn of the century when two girls were born in Brown's Station, Iowa, near the Iowa/Illinois border. And it was in 1919 when both girls completed their studies to become professional nurses. Their Iowa nursing program was typical of the era. It was a two-year program that included "practical work in the wards, classes, and a complete course in cookery."

One of their textbooks even contained extensive handwritten recipes for various therapies, diets, and menus. For example, there was a recipe for how to make a mustard plaster. The recipe for mustard plaster for a baby called for one part of mustard, eight parts of flour, mixed with a white of an egg, vinegar, or lukewarm water. For a stout man, the mustard plaster recipe was six parts mustard and one part flour.

Another pearl of wisdom in the textbook was the care of someone who had ingested a "fine bone." The cure was to "suck on a lemon immediately after." The text also contained advice on how to use leeches for the relief of congestion. For purulent ophthalmia, the nurse was directed to "cleanse the patient's temple and, with a sterile needle, scratch the skin until the blood shows." Next, directly over the temple, the nurse was to place the mouth of the vial (containing the leech). The text contained a description of how the leech would bite almost instantly and drop off when it was gorged. "If the leech needs to be taken off before it is gorged, sprinkle a little salt on its head. Hemorrhage should not be checked unless profuse, in which case a piece of ice or alum applied to the spot will arrest the flow. If possible, the patient should be kept in ignorance of the application" (Beck, 1917).

The Iowa Code, prior to 1917, required nurses to be at least 23 years of age and of "good moral character." In 1917, a licensing exam was developed that contained 50 essay questions. The questions were divided into five sections, at least one of which had to be completed orally.

There were 10 questions on "diseases of men," to be taken only by male nurse candidates. The exam was required by law to include "elementary hygiene, anatomy, physiology, materia medica, and dietetics." The exam also included practical nursing questions about medical, surgical, and obstetrics problems, and the nursing care of children. The rules and regulations of the state board of health related to infectious diseases and quarantine were also in the exam. From time to time, other subjects required by the state board were included in the exam. The oldest examination on file was given in 1917 (Beck, 1917).

Both Helen and Elizabeth passed the licensure examination. As was the case in the 1920s, only the wealthy employed registered nurses, so Helen and Elizabeth were both employed by wealthy families. Both had chosen private duty as their career option.

Early family photo albums show Helen and Elizabeth with their patients. They were referred to patient assignments by physicians who had taught and worked with them during their schooling. Their patient assignments took the two of them throughout Iowa and Illinois

Helen and Elizabeth lived long healthy lives, outliving even their nieces and nephews. Helen's last private duty case was her beloved sister, Elizabeth. At age 94, Liz suffered a cerebral aneurysm. When Helen called her great-niece with the sad news, the niece asked whether Liz was in the hospital. Being a true caregiver and private duty nurse all of her life, Helen responded it wasn't necessary. Helen stated, "I will nurse her at home. She never wanted all of those machines." And so she did, for 10 days.

My mother and Helen's great-niece, Leora, remembers traveling in 1984 with the family from Clinton, Iowa. The purpose of the trip was to accompany Helen to the wake and funeral of her sister, Liz. Leora asked Helen, "What a wonderful red coat you have on today, where did you get it?" Helen, always a fashion plate, stated, "Penney's was having a sale last week, so I walked downtown to buy something nice for the funeral." My mother and aunt were horrified because Helen was supposed to be taking care of Liz at that time. To calm their reaction, Helen continued, "Well, Liz wasn't going anywhere."

Aunts Liz and Helen were my inspiration for a career in nursing. I have not yet met two more interesting women. They certainly didn't fit the mold of the day; they were career women. In all the years I knew them, Helen never started the day without face makeup and a stylish hairdo, even if it meant wearing a wig in later years. They had pride in their calling and pride in their work. They were truly women who made a difference by being real caregivers.

Beck, A.D. (1917). *A reference handbook for nurses* (3rd ed.). Philadelphia, PA: Saunders.

WHAT SHE TAUGHT ME IN LIFE, SHE TAUGHT ME IN DEATH

by Elly Burns-Prestage

The story I am about to share with you is a tribute to my daughter, Jamey Lynn Miller. Jamey died on August 15, 2001, nearly 10 months after being diagnosed with glioblastoma multiform (GBM).

vividly remember the call I received. It was a Saturday morning. The phone rang at about 7:00 a.m. I never thought it might be Jamey; she rarely called that early. What came next were words I never considered could be possible. "Mom, you need to come to Houston. I had an MRI yesterday and they have found what appears to be two tumors on my brain." Jamey and I, being nurses, knew the probability of survival. She was amazingly calm. Her husband was right at her side, and friends quickly responded by taking care of her children, Alexandra and Hank. When the test results became available, Jamey was admitted to the hospital. Without knowing this had taken place, I was met by a close friend at the Houston Airport and went directly to the hospital.

When I entered the room, I saw my daughter as beautiful as ever; one would never be able to tell something so serious was wrong with her. As usual, she expressed a greater concern for me than for herself, asking whether I was okay. At this point, pain flowed from deep inside my heart, "No, this was not okay. This could not be happening to my daughter." As I sat at the bedside and watched over her resting, I reflected on the extraordinary life of this 32-year-old woman.

Her caring, giving nature was evident at an early age. She was the protective big sister to her little brother, acting as his "ears" because he had lost almost all his hearing when he was barely six months old. At the age of 17, she announced she wanted to be a nurse. I was equally stunned and pleased. Jamey had started modeling. Her 5'11 stature made her a striking image, and she could have easily made a career of it. However, she wanted to be a nurse like her mom. We discussed where she would go to college and narrowed it down to the University of Pennsylvania, the University of Washington, and Villanova. After some discussion, we knew Villanova would be the choice.

Jamey's time at Villanova was filled with honors. She earned respect and adoration from her fellow students and teaching staff. Everybody who met Jamey shared the same view; it was never what she did as much as who she was. Jamie was truly the kindest person most people said they had ever known.

While at Villanova, Jamey met Rick, her husband-to-be. He graduated a year ahead of Jamey with a chemical engineering degree. His first position as a chemical engineer was in Houston, Texas. It was in Houston that Jamey started her career as a pediatric critical care nurse. She thrived in this role, rapidly gaining the love and respect of everyone with whom she worked. After working her shifts at Hermann Memorial Hospital, she would work a second job, caring for severely handicapped children. It was through her extensive work with children that she eventually became a research assistant to the head of the department of pediatric pulmonary medicine at Hermann Memorial Hospital. As with the rest of her career, she poured herself 100 percent into the role of the patient advocate. She also earned master's degrees in public health and administration.

Jamey once again demonstrated a level of compassion and caring unlike anything I had ever seen when she became a mother. I was so proud of her. I often thought how much better she was at mothering than I. Her grace and selflessness was beautiful. I would often simply just enjoy watching her and thank God for the privilege of being her mother.

When I hear her voice call my name, I know she has awakened and taken me from my reminiscent thoughts. It is now time for us to reach out, share our fears, our love, and the honesty she has always depended on me to provide. It is difficult to be nurses and know so much. You move immediately to knowing and understanding. You fast forward to the prognosis, which for Jamey came on her 32nd birthday; it was profoundly bleak. The neurosurgeon left us with little doubt that the tumors were indeed GBMs and that she would undergo surgery. The term debulking was used. This meant radiation therapy would follow. The survival rate is sickeningly small, yet Jamey projected no anger or self-pity. On the contrary, Jamey showed such grace and courage, putting everyone around her at ease.

During the 10 months of her illness, Jamey was never alone. Rick and the children cherished every moment they could spend with her. Her brother, Jason, came from Jacksonville, Florida, so many times I often wondered whether he would be able to keep his job. Her best friends, many of whom were nurses, took turns staying with her in the hospital. Her stepfather, Tony, quit his job and stayed in Houston to drive her to and from her treatments. Her mother-in-law and father-in-law were always there, taking turns with her care and also the trips to her treatments. Her father-in-law, Dick, and her stepfather, Tony, were touched by her determination to learn how to read once again, never giving up hope. My sister, Judi, spent nearly a month with her, at which time they spent hours talking about the things that meant the most to her in life. Peggy and Joanna, her sisters-in-law, dropped everything and came to be with her. Their close friends Janie, Hutch, and LeAnna provided support only they could give, because LeAnna had recovered from a brain tumor only a year earlier. They were all there, all the time.

Two days before Jamey died, she was moved to a hospice center where she was cradled with love and dignity. Great care was taken to provide us with the knowledge of what we could expect in the final hours of her life. We were all there, but it was me, her mother, who brought her into this world who would lay next to her in that bed and reassure her that it was time to leave my arms and let God wrap his loving arms around her and take her home.

It was near the time of Jamey's death that I found this Indian message entitled "Beloved Girl Child."

> *My beloved child, how I love you. Through all the years and tears we have shared, it is I who feels honored. To have loved you, taken care of you, then to release you and learn to let go. So I release you to the Great Spirit, setting us both free. Knowing in my heart it's time. You are my greatest love, but also my greatest pain.*
>
> *Signed-Blazing Sky*

Jamey achieved many honors in her short life. It was truly my privilege to be her mother. I want to close by expressing my gratitude and highest regard to all nurses. Please never underestimate the great gift of caring.

In memory of Jamey Lynn Miller, a scholarship fund has been established at Villanova University School of Nursing to provide another young person the chance to make a difference. More information about the SNAP (Student Nurse Association of Pennsylvania) honorary legislative award, established in Jamey's name, can be found at http://www.snap-online.org

WHEN I'M A NURSE, I WON'T LET BABIES CRY: GERRY'S STORY

by Susan A. Bisol

verybody went over," she said. "History was being made and I wanted to be part of it." Like many members of her generation, Gerry Bisol answered the call to serve her country without a second thought. It never occurred to her not to go. World War II was the largest and most violent armed conflict in the history of mankind. Today, more than a half century separates us from that conflict. Time has taken a toll on our collective knowledge of the stories and experiences of these distinguished WWII veterans. Gerry's life and her WWII story is part of nursing history.

Giaconda Isabella DiTommaso was born at home, the oldest of six children, to Italian immigrants in the "Patch" of Fitchburg, Massachusetts, in 1921. When she was old enough to begin school, her teacher changed her name to Geraldine, rationalizing it sounded somewhat the same and contained about the same number of letters. Today, Giaconda or Geraldine is called Gerry.

During her early years, Geraldine remembers the visiting nurses who provided care for her family. She especially remembers the nurses who cared for her mother during and after childbirth. The nurses' bags and their contents intrigued Gerry. She remembers the nurses letting her get necessary items from the bags. In 1932, when Gerry was 11 years old, her youngest brother Mario was born. The visiting nurse put Mario on his stomach, a position that he did not like. Mario protested loudly. Gerry told the nurse, "When I become a nurse, *I won't let babies cry.*"

Gerry's intention to pursue a nursing career became known to Dr. Mattia, the physician caring for immigrant families in the neighborhood. Dr. Mattia invited Gerry to assist him in some medical cases. Gerry still tells stories of assisting with tonsillectomies performed in the home.

Gerry entered Cambridge City Hospital School of Nursing in 1939. She was one of 23 to enter and one of 13 to graduate. She chose Cambridge City because it offered students $10 a month in payment. Gerry later learned payments for books and breakage were deducted from the $10. In school, "lima beans on toast" was the dinner menu every Thursday night. Fortunately for Gerry, Jacks Variety Store, across the street from the hospital, delivered toasted cheese, tomato, and wilted lettuce for 15 cents. "I still love toasted cheese with tomato," Gerry fondly states.

Training at Cambridge City was three years of work and study with only two weeks of vacation each year. Along with the rest of the students, Gerry worked seven days a week and only had one overnight pass per month. Geraldine recalls that if a student was late for breakfast, as she admits to being, the overnight privilege was lost. In 1941, war was declared. Gerry was a senior in nursing school. Many of the nurses working in the hospital left for war, leaving the senior students to staff the hospital. Gerry graduated in August of 1942. She stayed at Cambridge City as the head nurse on the obstetrical floor and delivery room. In 1943, Gerry and three of her nurse friends joined the Army.

Gerry has many experiences and memories as an Army nurse, all of which provide a rich history. Gerry's first assignment, as a newly commissioned second lieutenant, was at Camp Edwards. There she processed inductees. Gerry remembers a young man from Georgia undergoing a physical examination. Gerry gave him a cup and asked for a urine specimen. When she returned, he handed her an empty cup. When asked where the specimen was, he responded, "I drank it." The young man believed, based on where he came from, that drinking urine was a cure for many common illnesses.

In March of 1943, Gerry was transferred to Fort Devens in Ayer, Massachusetts. She opened the first female military ward. The Women's Army Auxiliary Corps (WAAC) was expanding and they needed medical care. The WAACs were the first women, other than nurses, to serve in the United States Army.

On June 4, 1943, Gerry boarded a train at 0200 hours and headed for Fort Kilmer, New Jersey. Kilmer was a port of departure where Gerry worked at the hospital base. In August of 1943, Gerry was sent to England on the HMHS Atlantis, a hospital ship. Gerry recalls that while crossing the Atlantic, the ship was hit by "friendly fire" from an Irish merchant ship. On September 4, Gerry disembarked at Greenoch, Scotland, and proceeded to the 120th Station Hospital in Tortworth, England.

On November 4, 1943, Gerry traveled from England back to Greenoch. She set sail November 5 on the Queen Mary. During this voyage, she nursed soldiers suffering from many different types of illnesses. Some of the illnesses included pneumonia, bronchitis, battle fatigue, and severe psychiatric conditions. "They were scared," she says. "They were just boys, some coped better than others." The ship arrived in New York on November 11, where Gerry received orders to return to Fort Kilmer.

Gerry recalls fun while back in the United States. Her face lights up when she relates a story about seeing Frank Sinatra on the Lucky Strike Hour. A drunken sailor in New York had given her Sinatra tickets. She and her friend, excited about the opportunity, hurried to the theater. To her amazement, they were the only Army personnel in the theater; all others were Naval personnel.

From Fort Kilmer, Gerry next traveled to Charleston, South Carolina. In South Carolina, the nurses were quartered above US Rangers. The Rangers, as she describes them were courteous but had "crazy haircuts." The Rangers were preparing to go to Italy. They had some of the most advanced equipment of their time. The Rangers said, "If we are successful, America will know; however, if we are not successful, the world will never hear about us."

In November 1943, Gerry boarded the USHS Arcadia. The ship broke down en route and was docked for repairs in Gibraltar for two weeks. Gerry arrived in North Africa on December 16, 1943. Here she lived in a tent and used

Midge Scotty Gerry.

open latrines. Her travels continued with a ride on the "40 & 8 Train" through the Atlas Mountains from Oran to Casablanca. The 40 & 8 was a French train that had previously been used to haul 40 men and 8 horses. The trip lasted *three nights* and *four days* and ended with her arrival at the 56th Station Hospital. Here Gerry waited to care for patients. In January of 1944, Gerry was transferred to the 50th Station Hospital to treat patients from the Angio-Casino battle in Italy. It was here that "the wounded began to arrive in vast numbers. They were 17- and 18-year-olds, crying for their mothers."

On March 17, 1944, Gerry, troops, and wounded soldiers boarded the General William Mana ship to return to the United States. On the ship, she cared for a Japanese-American soldier named Billy Moon. Billy lost his left arm and right leg during the fighting in Europe. Billy lay in his berth, listening to the other soldiers expressing their hatred for the "yellow bastards." Gerry still remembers the young man's face when she said, "They don't mean you." "I know, Lieutenant," he replied. Gerry cried with this young man, both for his loss and their sadness of the situation. The ship docked in Newport News, Virginia, on March 26, 1944. Gerry proceeded on to Camp Patrick Henry. As first lieutenant, Gerry worked in a venereal disease ward and administered one of the first injections of penicillin.

On May 7, 1945, Geraldine DiTommaso married Gene Bisol, a Marine whom she met through one of her brothers. On their first date, Gene and Geraldine went to church. Gene was literally her knight in shining armor. On one occasion, Gene rode up to her home on a white horse in full military uniform. Gene and Gerry were the talk of the neighborhood. They corresponded by telephone and letters throughout the war. Gerry and Gene had four sons. Their parenting philosophy was to teach the "boys" to be good and caring human beings.

Following the war and her discharge, Gerry worked as an industrial nurse and also in a urology practice. In 1951, Gerry became a civilian staff nurse in obstetrics at Fort Devens, Massachusetts. "I worked in OB for more than 23 years and celebrated "the first breath of the newborns all of those years."

In 2002, Gerry still works two days a week, taking blood pressures for the Council on Aging in Fitchburg, Massachusetts. She provides support and a listening ear to those who seek her counsel. In the past 15 years, she has nursed her mother and youngest brother, Mario, through terminal illnesses. Knowing she has helped someone each day, if only with a kind word, is what keeps her functioning and productive. Her own children have given her grandchildren, and she is awaiting the birth of her first great-grandchild. Gerry still believes "because she's a nurse, she doesn't let babies cry."

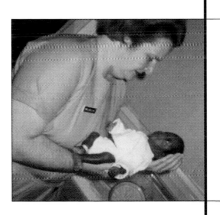

listening

PART III

FRIENDS LISTENING TO NURSES' STORIES

A NURSE SEEN THROUGH THE EYES OF A GOOD FRIEND: MY FRIEND, PEGGY JONES

by Sue Kamrad-Marrone

Peggy and I went to nursing school together, and I give her direct credit for getting me through school. With a disciplined study pal, I had no choice but to do as well as she did. We made it through the pressures and stresses of drug calculations, return demonstrations, and clinical experiences. We also built a lifelong friendship as we faced the challenges of school together. The challenges of nursing, as well as our friendship, continued long after we graduated from nursing school.

Peggy and I both accepted jobs in a coronary care unit (ICU) at a major teaching hospital in the Chicago area. We learned from each other and made fun of each other (a lot). We laughed and cried together from shift to shift. Peggy became known as the nurse who would do anything for her patients as well as the nurses.

As the years progressed, our friendship strengthened. Eventually we both burned out on intensive care nursing. The transformation was made from hospital ICU nursing to high-tech home care. Peggy was transformed as she took on a caseload of complex patients. Most of Peggy's patients had some type of intravenous access and therapy to manage. The territory was large, and sometimes the hours were long. Peggy never minded the challenges of providing home care.

Peggy went on vacation for two weeks. The other nurses and I had to cover her patients while she was gone. During those two weeks of Peggy's absence, not one of us on the team could fill Peggy's shoes. It was tough, if not impossible, to walk in her shoes while providing care to her patients. We all realized that Peggy had special relationships with her patients.

I was amazed by how much Peggy's patients actually cared about her. They all bragged about her! Two of Peggy's patients, whom I had taken care of during her vacation, stand out in my mind. They both kept me an extra 20 minutes just telling me how wonderful Peggy was to both them and their families.

One patient was actually seen more than Peggy was documenting. Peggy knew the needs of patient follow-up were greater than the number of approved visits. Peggy saw this patient on her own time because she needed and wanted to help the family.

The other patient never followed directions. He was always more noncompliant than compliant. The patient's wife was just as needy and wanted to be visited too. These patients were energy draining, and their family needs, as well as their medical needs, were of equally high demand.

All of the nurses, as well as Peggy's patients, were so happy when she returned from vacation. The nurses were just glad to give back her patient caseload. And I gave Peggy such a hard time, as only a friend could do, about being the "mother hen" of her caseload.

Peggy is and always will be one of those people who will go above and beyond; this is her philosophy and it is commonplace for her. I will never forget those two weeks that I provided nursing care for Peggy's caseload. I had to walk in her nursing shoes and realized that I just could not fill them.

The relationship I have with Peggy is like a sisterhood. The characteristics in our friendship are the same as those that Peggy has with her patients. She does not care who you are or where you come from. She only cares that she can make a difference for you.

Peggy is one of the most wonderful and caring nurses I have ever known. These same behaviors bleed right into her relationships outside of patient care to her family and to her friends. Peggy is a caring person who just happens to be a nurse. She makes an exponential difference in the lives of all those she touches. The needier the friend, family, or patient, the greater the challenge for Peggy. She wants to help. She wants everyone, patients and friends alike, to experience the best situation they possibly can. The best part is that Peggy is there to help all achieve this goal.

When we graduated in 1988, we did not know where our nursing careers would take us. But as the fabric of those years and careers was woven together, the sharing and counseling that occurred between us were outstanding. Our discussions centered on what our first new car should be, how we could get new boyfriends, what we should do with our old boyfriends, and when to leave our loser boyfriends. Nursing issues also were part of our talks, such as what stethoscope should we purchase, which clogs should we wear, what lab coat or warm-up jacket should we choose, and what continuing education programs would be most meaningful to attend. We also spent a lot of time discussing personal health issues, family health challenges, hard-to-deal-with death or loss events, and which geographic moves to take.

After 13 years, a few more career changes, and a couple more educational degrees between the two of us, Peggy is still the same. She continues to nurse nurses, friends, family, and patients. Peggy still has that same powerful effect on everyone who is fortunate enough to cross her path.

A STUDY IN VOLUNTEERISM
by Frances R. Vlasses

Y ou can find Julia Havey volunteering on Tuesday nights, running a class in the middle of a training ring with 20 dogs and their owners. You are struck by her ability to manage chaos, her offbeat sense of humor, her big smile, and the fact that, somewhere in the training center, her own dogs are obediently following her instruction. Although not immediately apparent, Julie is a nurse with 20 years of experience and an inclination toward critical care and high-tech challenges.

But this story is not about how she makes her living. The story I want to tell is about Julie's unpaid work with people and dogs. In this arena, her nursing skill shines through as she touches the lives of those she meets. Allow me to explain. Julie's definition of nursing is simply stated, "Seeing a need and doing something about it, without any expectations; that's what nursing is about." With this as her guiding principle, Julie finds herself, with leash in hand, on some interesting journeys that integrate nursing and animal assistance therapies. It was with this in mind that Julie got involved with the Yamoto* family.

Julie is a *volunteer* puppy raiser for Canine Companions for Independence (CCI), an organization that provides highly skilled assistance dogs for individuals with all kinds of disabilities except blindness. CCI puppy raisers make a 24/7 commitment to the care and preparation of a potential assistance dog for approximately 15 months. At work or play, Julie usually has one (sometimes two) assistance dog in training (ADIT) between the ages of 2 and 15 months at her side. She makes it look easy, but the telltale surveillance skills of an expert nurse come through in her talk of assessing, intervening, and evaluating activity that she plans to enhance the success of her pup.

One day, CCI Chicago received a call from a gentleman in New York whose father, Mr. Yamoto, was terminally ill with pancreatic cancer. He wondered whether anyone could bring a dog to visit his father at home. Although it was an unusual request for CCI, his home was convenient to Julie's work setting, and she agreed to visit with her current CCI pup in training, Linus. Her visit extended into a two-year relationship with this Japanese couple, during which time Julie

trained ADIT's Linus, Leann, and Jentry. She would sometimes bring along younger and older CCI dogs, and the Yamotos appreciated the whole working dog life cycle.

Julie often visits on her lunch hour. Her visits were "occasions" for this formal couple, sometimes including friends and lunch. Their son would call to talk with his parents during her visit. Julie stayed in the background, creating an environment for the dogs to do their magic. The Yamotos were interested in the dogs' progress in training. Julie brought a camera and photos and made an album for Mr. Yamoto to document their time together and to keep track of the dogs as they matured and left Julie's care for advanced training. She photographed Mr. Yamoto with the dogs, sitting on the floor, sometimes falling asleep with one of them by him. When he was

hospitalized, this album went with him. Julie and her ADIT attended Mr. Yamoto's funeral and continue to visit Mrs. Yamoto with her current ADIT, Conti. Although she can't explain why or how, she knows that her visits were an important part of this period in the Yamoto's family life. And although Julie insists that she stayed in the background, one can only admire the art and skill that went into the formation and maintenance of a long-term relationship with a family from an unfamiliar culture during a painful and sad event.

Sundays are hospital visit days for Julie. Her dog, Linus, participates in a selective animal-assisted therapy program at a local hospital, and Julie *volunteers* to drive him. In addition, Julie *volunteers* in animal rescue work, has cared for breeders and newborn pups, performs demonstrations on assistance dog work raising consciousness about the needs of those with disabilities, and participates in fund raising for CCI. She estimates that 120 dogs have come through her home since 1987. An astute observer of both human and canine behavior, she can be counted on to "think outside the box" in creating solutions for pet owners and assistance dog trainees that may only superficially relate to their dogs. While others benefit from her expertise, her perspective is always about how much she learns from each experience. She talks about how she stretches and grows from them and encourages you to do the same.

Julie believes that animals provide for an opportunity to improve the quality of life for many. She has seen how the powerful human-canine bond can enhance and empower the lives of those with physical challenges, and she is committed to this work. Julie makes this association to her nursing identity, "You can make a difference in someone's health status because you support this connection."

Julie's actions are open and deliberate. She cites the nursing process as the method easily applied to many situations to help her problem solve a disability challenge, a technology problem at work, or a problem in the canine-human bond. Her work with CCI exemplifies her nursing philosophy. Raising a pup for 15 months and then giving him up so another can have an improved quality of life, starting over with a new pup, seeing a need, responding with no expectations are qualities to be admired. It takes two years to fully train an assistance dog, and the waiting list is sometimes just as long. Julie knows that someone is waiting. She is currently raising her eighth CCI dog. Her *volunteer* schedule in combination with her work commitments would keep two people running. But Julie walks slowly, deliberately, with a dog at her side. More importantly, she takes her time because it takes time to develop the relationships along the way. She has committed to serve, and she is in this for the long haul.

*Name changed to provide privacy

A WALK ON THE BEACH

by Cheryl Vajdik and Carolyn Hope Smeltzer

I t was while Patty and her husband, Kary, were walking on the beach that Patty decided to be a nurse. She and her husband had talked frequently about entering the Peace Corps after their children graduated from college, but because Kary had a law practice he was devoted to that focused on children who need special schooling because of their disabilities, the Peace Corps was not an option. She thought about enrolling in the local LPN program, but Kary said, "If you are going to put that much effort into it, go into the RN program." And so she did.

Patty had no idea it would be so difficult to go back to school at 45 years of age. Even though she had a BA in English, she had to take numerous science courses to fulfill the prerequisites for nursing school. But she was determined to complete the degree because nursing would provide her with a way to work with people in need. She realized nursing would enable her to fulfill her life's goals. She was confident the hard work and challenges of being an "older student" would eventually pay off.

Patty graduated the same year her youngest daughter graduated from college. She could not help but notice the differences in their starting salaries and their "sign-on" bonuses. She was also amazed at how her daughter was recruited and how her daughter's choice of a job was based on her ability to move quickly "up the organizational ladder." Clinical advancement was never discussed when Patty was interviewed for her first nursing job. She was also astonished that, although she had so much more life experience than her daughter, hospital employers did not consider it a valuable asset. In fact, Patty took a job for less pay, with less opportunity for advancement, and with less desirable working hours than her daughter.

Patty decided she wanted to continue to learn and make the most of her capabilities, so she left her Lake Michigan home to work in the city of Chicago at a large teaching hospital. She was interviewed on an oncology unit and quickly discovered the oncology nurses really needed her. Patty also realized that she had much to offer oncology patients, such as wisdom, wit, humor, and of course, life experiences.

Soon after she started working with cancer patients, she began to question some of the treatment practices. She wondered why so many patients were dying in the hospital instead of in the comfort of their own homes or in a hospice environment. She also questioned the use of aggressive chemotherapy and radiation with their severe side effects that caused loss of appetite, vomiting, diarrhea, burns, fatigue, and an inability to perform the simplest self-care tasks. She wondered if the aggressive treatments caused more harm than good.

Patty soon learned the nurse is a patient advocate, as well as a caregiver, even though she had been a nurse for less than one year. Frequently, and appropriately, she questioned physicians about treatment plans, pain management, and hospice care. She discussed the prescribed treatment with physicians when it caused undo physical and mental suffering and it was clear the medical prognosis would not change. She was also concerned about the cost of care and that the family not lose all of its assets due to treatment that would no longer benefit the patient's quality of life. Even today, Patty continues to focus on ways to improve patients' quality of life and on how to help patients' families meet their needs.

A nursing faculty member once told Patty, "You think and act out of the box." She also believed Patty would have a hard time fitting into the hospital setting. Patty does think out of the box, and perhaps this is why she helps and cares for so many patients who are dying or receiving treatment for cancer. She brings care as well as humor into their lives. She makes both her patients and their families smile, even if they are in a crisis. Although she thinks "out of the box," she is extremely well organized when it comes to the care of her patients. And while she might be considered a non-fit in a hospital setting, she has been able to alter the way the hospital system functions, at least on her unit.

Patty feels the need to be organized because on her unit it is: *Go, go, go. If you are not organized, you can get caught up in the technical aspects of the treatments. If you are not organized, you have no time for the important and necessary acts of caring, listening, and providing healing and energy for the patients and their families.*

After listening to a patient recently and making him laugh for the first time in a long time, Patty received a $20 bill from him. Patty knew she could not keep it, and she also knew he did not have the energy to argue with her about taking it back. Patty did some quick brainstorming and finally decided to put it in the "nurse appreciation fund." When she told the patient her plan, he simply said, "Sounds like a win/win. I only hope all the nurses find time to listen to their patients like you do."

When asked how she became interested in nursing, Patty said, "I have always been interested in helping people in need." For many years before she started nursing school, Patty organized a group of Christmas carolers who went to the homes of the elderly living alone. The carolers did more than entertain those they visited. They brought food and blankets to them. A local Catholic church provided the food, and the other provisions were purchased with money collected from the carolers. Clearly, Patty has continued her care of others as she plays out her role as a nurse caring for those in great need.

Nursing has filled a need in Patty's life, but Patty has filled a void in the lives of those she cares for. Her approach and caring have made a difference in the lives of those who suffer from cancer. And while other nurses may do something similar with their patients, Patty's approach, caring, and devotion to the patients make her an extraordinary caregiver and one who obviously made the "right decision" that day on the beach when she decided to enter nursing.

A WEEKEND IN THE WILDERNESS

by Susan O'Neill

s they made their way to their annual camping trip in the woods of northern Pennsylvania, the rain began to fall. It was a torrential downpour! The twisting and bending roads made it necessary to slow down and search for the landmark to make the next turn. Three cars followed one another. Each one was filled with nurses who were all good friends.

This trek into the wilderness was a ritual. It was a time for a group of nurses who worked together, either presently or at one time, to be together to sustain important relationships. It was a time for renewal. It was a time for support; it was a time to be with good friends!

Tammy was in charge, as this whole affair was her creation five years ago, and she was already at the campsite waiting for the rest to show. She had moved to Idaho the previous winter to take a position as a nurse researcher. Everyone was especially excited, for this year was special because it included a much-missed friend and comrade. The majority of the nurses were critical care practitioners. Two of the newcomers worked in intensive care units.

"Here we are," said Judy as they got out of the jeep and started to unpack their gear. The rain had ceased, but there remained a muddy path. It took two trips to bring the supplies, so needed for the weekend, down the little hill to the site that would be home for them in the remarkable and beautiful world of nature. They were covered in mud and that made it even more fun. Everyone was happy and laughing and grateful. Even the sun peered through the clouds, as if to view the nurses' campsite, drying their space of land. They set up camp, pitched the tents, and started a fire.

It was amazing how the time together transformed them. It was amazing how they could free their minds to assemble for a great time. They had packed all the essentials needed to sustain life as well as many instruments of leisure. A CD player to provide music would be plugged into the only electrical outlet. They would cook over the campfire and make the water and bags of ice last for three days. The meals would be fabulous! They would hike, play, sing,

dance, eat and drink, and enjoy the kaleidoscope of life with vigor and joy pulsing through their veins. And they would do this because they were together, old friends and a support for each other. As nurses who worked hard and under very stressful circumstances, they had learned how to rest and redeem themselves by having fun with each other.

Of course, one of the high points of the three days was the "sweat." Every year they continued an old custom of creating a natural "steam room" with round rocks that had been baking in a fire all day. On Saturday night, everyone would get into their bikinis and crawl into a little hut they had constructed. They would dig a hole in the middle, place the red-hot rocks into the hole, and pour tea water—soaked in cinnamon, rosemary and thyme—over the stones. What a sensation and aroma! As the sweat dripped down their faces, they felt cleansed and invigorated. They knew this was heaven on earth.

As they celebrated life, each of them would drift off to a memory of someone they had cared for or someone they had worked hard to save but had lost. One thought was common: they were a crew, a platoon, all of the same mind with the same skills and tools providing care for others as nurses. The lingering memories of these joyful and happy days in the woods would one day help balance the stress and anguish of the difficult job of nursing.

When it was time to depart, it was hard to say good-bye, for this time together served as a time for gaining new energy for the future. As they hugged, kissed, and packed up and started off to home, they realized they had something special, something that all nurses needed—a way to gain strength, renewed direction, and purpose— and it was because they had each other. Was this an example of extraordinary behavior? You bet it was, for without this time together to relax, to touch base with those who understand the work of nursing and devotion to others, nurses often "burn out" or worse become distant and shielded from reality. All nurses should try to find a way to renew and support each other as this group of nurses has. It is truly a way to retain, sustain, and reward nurses for what they do for others!

BONNIE: NURSE, MOTHER, EDUCATOR

by Carolyn Hope Smeltzer

Bonnie always wanted to be a nurse, and her dream was finally realized when she entered nursing school. "Daddy's little girl" made her father very proud; he was so proud he presented her with a beautiful caduceus (medical insignia), which she wore every day.

Then the day came when her dreams were shattered. She left school to care for her ailing mother. Bonnie immediately, and forcefully, removed the caduceus from her neck and placed it in a bank vault. The caduceus and her dreams of being a nurse were locked up.

Bonnie had many successful years doing business in the "Big Apple." However, when Bonnie's youngest son, Lance, entered first grade, she saw an opportunity to reconnect with her dream of being a nurse. Bonnie, along with her son, entered school full time. Bonnie was in the University of Vermont's nursing program. She completed the program just as her oldest son, Scott, entered the university.

After Bonnie passed the nursing exams, she had one important mission to fulfill. Bonnie went straight to the vault and put on her caduceus. As she sat in the bank vault, she said to herself, "Dad, I did it!" Her dad was with her only in spirit that day. His engraving of special words on the caduceus was close to her heart as it lay against her neck. It had been 10 years since her father had passed away and 20 years since she had had the caduceus on her neck.

Bonnie is and always has been a true dog lover. When she was a young girl, her St. Bernard bit her in the throat. This event caused her to wrestle with her fear of dogs. She faced the situation with understanding and compassion. To express her feelings, she wrote a story about the incident. It was written from the dog's viewpoint, telling his side of the dog bite story.

This story allowed Bonnie to continue her limitless love of animals. This story also allowed her to forgive and not place fault on one misunderstood pet. Today, part of Bonnie's family includes two black, giant Schnauzers, Gus and Dillon. Both were rescued from uncaring homes.

Bonnie continues to write to express feelings and to help others cope with their own situations and challenges. *Sabrina* is a poem written after the passing of one of her pets. This poem has helped others who have lost a pet and touches the hearts of most pet lovers.

Sabrina

I loved you more than life itself
Your pictures all across the shelf
Your parents waiting from afar
Heaven is now where they are

You will know them when you meet
No longer blind, what a treat
Healthy now from head to toe
Running everywhere you go

Please come to me in my dreams
Life here is not what it seems
I can hug and kiss you there
Loving you without a care

I will always love you so
Wherever I may chance to go
I promise never to forget
Our last moments at the vet

My full life is what you gave
Knowing only how to behave
You loved until the day you died
Hugging you I sat and cried.

During her son's open school night, Bonnie sat back, staring at the left corner of the blackboard, which was filled with students' names. Bonnie questioned why the names were listed. "These children," she was told, "had either spoken out of turn or had not turned in an assignment." She was then told that the names would remain on the board for all to see until the children corrected their situations. All Bonnie could think about was how this activity could destroy the children's self-esteem. Children were supposed to focus on learning, growing, and developing a positive ego, not on how to avoid destruction of their self-esteem.

That night she realized the public school system focused on the competent, capable, and compliant. It left the other children to falter, especially with class sizes up to 40 students. Bonnie began to understand that her son, as well as other children, would have to struggle to get an appropriate education.

One morning, Bonnie received a telephone call from her son's teacher. The teacher informed Bonnie that Lance was eating bagels and Coke in a morning class. Bonnie said, "Great, he did not have a chance to eat breakfast, and now he will be better prepared to learn, not being hungry." The teacher said she did not care whether Lance was hungry, hung up the phone, and threw out the bagel and Coke. Bonnie and her husband, Stephen, knew that there had to be a better way to educate their son. They enrolled Lance in private school.

As time passed, Bonnie and Stephen became very interested in the beliefs and concepts of the private school, concepts that created positive energy. Students ate when they wanted and never went hungry. The food not only filled their tummies, but fueled their starving minds. Individual attention was the norm. The school was student-focused and friendly and also fostered self-esteem. The environment created mutual respect between teacher and student.

A no-homework policy, which improved each student's home life, was in full force. The philosophy behind the policy was to have the students do their homework at school, where the resources and teachers were available for support and tutoring.

The proms and social events were for all and were not dominated by economic means. The type of prom clothes did not dictate whether a student could afford to go to the prom. Students were welcome to come to the prom in a gown or tux or casual dress.

Bonnie, a mother and a nurse, wanted her son and the other children to have a learning environment where they could be educated, grow, and socialize with the respect and dignity they deserved. Bonnie and her husband currently own not one, but two schools. They have a business partner, Nina Kaufman. The schools have become a family affair. Bonnie focuses on the curriculum and the learning environment, her husband is the superintendent, and her son is one of the many students.

Years ago, Bonnie had major surgery. Like her earlier dog bite, she used this experience to better understand the issues facing the nursing profession from the patient's point of view. She gained a deeper understanding of the nurses on the front line. Bonnie's experience as a patient reinforced what her grandmother had told her in childhood, "You give with a full heart and a full hand." Bonnie saw the nurses treating patients based on her grandmother's philosophy; they were loving, caring, and competent.

One of the ways she now contributes back to the nursing profession is through her poetry. Here are two of her gifts to nursing.

A Day of Love

Valentine's Day will soon arrive,
A day of fun since we were five.
Hearts of red and pink are sent;
Words on cards we hope are meant.

Sounds of love flow through the air,
Hearts afire everywhere.
Romantic nights are the plan
For every woman and her man.

Shelves of candy are all we see
For men to give on bended knee.
Candles lit are all aglow,
Shining white like glistening snow.

As the day comes to an end,
We hope no hearts will need to mend.
You close your eyes and start to dream
Of next year by a running stream.

Quiet days and moonlit nights
Fill with stars like sparkling lights.
Valentine's Day will come again,
Love will blossom now and then.

Nurse's Day 2003

For years we struggle side by side
Evoking feelings we must hide
Today we hold our heads so high
Now all the world will know why

On Nurse's Day, glowing with pride
Respect will never be denied
Each day a nurse must show true heart
When no one else will play this part

Many a day may end in tears
Remembering them throughout the years
But when that patient smiles at you
Only warmth comes shining through

The only true profession to choose
With nothing you can really lose
Rewards in ways you cannot believe
Knowing why you can never leave

Working in teams all over the town
No shortage will ever get us down
So tired that we cannot feel our feet
But we will never admit defeat

Patient advocates are what we are
Our skills and caring will take us far
Admiration and praise we deserve
With legs of steel and an iron nerve

All of nursing celebrates this day
With kindness, more than you say
So treat yourself to something dear
For those with thanks you cannot hear

CALLED ON

by Chris Harris Vlasses

When walking into Dr. Ralph Shannon's operating room, 20 minutes before surgery, the first noticeable sound you hear is the most infectious giggle. The laughter of several other nurses follows Felicienne Muragijimana's deep belly laugh. As the surgeries draw closer, the mood changes, and Felicienne begins to lead nurses through morning preparations. Bouncing between the languages of Kinyarwanda, English, and French, she dances from room to room, playing the role of educator, nurse, anesthesiologist, translator, and patient facilitator. All of this is happening at the Kabgayi Mission Hospital in the Gitarama Province of Rwanda.

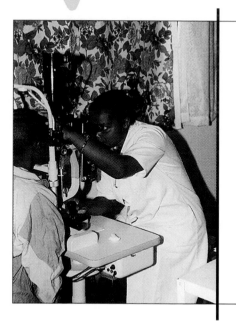

The work ethic of the spirited Gitarama native with warm brown eyes and a wide smile is amazing. While Dr. Shannon is the one performing the surgery, he is fond of saying that Felicienne is the *real power* behind the small eye unit. She is the first to arrive and the last to leave. She assists with the budget for the practice and is the obvious leader of the nursing staff. Like a good leader, however, she is steeped in humility and pride in her team. "It's not a matter of leadership," she says, "it is just a matter of feeling responsible. We are a team."

In addition to her leadership, nursing, and administrative responsibilities, Felicienne plays the valuable role of liaison between the eye practice and the Rwandan culture. For example, she is acutely aware that patients often travel for days to reach the clinic, and they almost always come without appointments. But if the team is too busy to attend to them right away, the patients may not have the resources to wait and will return home empty-handed. Felicienne knows that word-of-mouth stories, both positive and negative, have great influence in rural Rwanda. The stories inspire the staff to work weekends and holidays, serving patients, especially when workloads are high. And workloads are often astronomical.

Felicienne's team is one of only two ophthalmic teams serving Rwanda's 8 million people. The team fights an uphill battle against 16,000 cases of cataracts every year, often performing more than 10 cataract surgeries a day. Often, a fully anesthetized patient is waiting by the table as the previous surgery finishes. Their tiny autoclave chugs nonstop to meet the demand for sterilized equipment.

The team sees a total of 50 patients each day. When the team does community outreach at "more" rural hospitals, it is not uncommon for them to attend to more than 100 patients a day. However, despite the pace, Felicienne is remarkably sensitive to the needs of patients. Many patients are over 70 years of age and are in an operating room for the first time in their lives. They are often frozen with fear. Dr. Shannon's translator, Felicienne, soothes patients' anxieties. Her compassion is translated through her body language and by her motherly touch to those twice her age and, of course, by her rolling laughter.

As fate would have it, Felicienne was called into nursing when she had a swollen eye as a young girl. She saw the work of ophthalmic nurses firsthand and knew that she wanted to be a nurse. Although she does not like to talk about it, her nursing training was interrupted by the war and genocide that ravaged Rwanda in 1994. She remained away from home, at nursing school, during the first part of the massacre. When people were killed en masse on school grounds, she and many others were forced to flee to the forest. Thankfully, the atrocities of that time did not extinguish her desire to reach out and help others. Felicienne graduated from St. Elizabeth's School in Kabgayi in 1996.

In a country so stricken with tragedy and divided by hatred, it is all the more impressive and imperative that nurses like Felicienne are extending their hands to all people, crossing tribal and class lines. With the powers of profession and faith, Felicienne is part of a team that is healing both physical and emotional wounds by restoring sight to Rwandans and by opening their eyes to the power of a generous and loving spirit.

According to Felicienne, there are many "best parts" of her job, but she has a particular affinity for the cataract operations. "When you operate," she says, "you *give* something to the patient that you can't give with medicine." In truth, words can't describe the way people are changed by the cataract operations. Clinging to a relative, a patient arrives for a preoperative appointment. His eyes stare blankly, yet his grimacing face shows the frustration and humiliation of not being able to locate a chair in which to sit down without help. Three days later that same person will smile broadly and open the door for a grandson never seen before with head held high and shoulders back, as if a great weight had been lifted.

Partially because of the shortage of doctors to perform such surgeries, Felicienne is pushing herself to take her own skills even further and has already spent several months in Cameroon and the Congo in training. Felicienne wants to go to the Congo, where she will learn to perform cataract surgeries herself. As is frequently the case, however, political turmoil and tribal violence in the Congo have made the trip impossible.

While speaking about nursing, Felicienne radiates joy and excitement as she pauses several times for giggles and knee-slapping. In a quieter moment, she earnestly offers, "To be a nurse is not work, *it is a calling*. It requires patience and acceptance. You must adapt yourself to every individual person's needs, even above your own comfort. If you are not called, you will lose your patience, and you cannot be a good nurse." I smile and ask her if she has ever thought about being anything besides a nurse. "This cannot be," she says firmly, but then snickers at her own morose tone. "Once a nurse, always a nurse. Even if you change your occupation, you are still a nurse at heart. I don't think I could ever leave."

CREATING AN ENVIRONMENT OF HEALTH AND HEALING THROUGH PRESENCE

by P. Ann Solari-Twadell

"I feel so safe when you are here," says a patient at Westmoreland Nursing Center as Norene O'Brien enters the room. "It is always so nice to walk into work when you are here," a fellow nurse states as she greets Norene when she is coming to work for the evening shift. Each of these statements seems simple. However, it is only upon reflection that one can recognize a deeper message is conveyed about Norene. Norene's presence creates a special environment when she cares for the aged and terminally ill. There is something different when Norene is on duty. Through her attitude of acceptance, respect, kindness, caring, dedication, and regard for the whole person-body, mind, and spirit-something special is created.

In describing herself as "accepting, more of a listener, a mom by nature, flexible, and faithful," Norene creates this sense of wholeness. She speaks warmly of her Irish Catholic family of seven children. Norene was child number three. She developed into who she is as a result of loving parental and sibling relationships. Her older sister, Annamae, was a significant reason Norene became a nurse. Annamae, who was studying to be a nurse herself, would come home and enthusiastically share stories about being a student nurse. Norene listened to her sister's stories but did not instantly respond to her "call" to be a nurse. She first went to Dayton University to study business with the idea of working in her father's moving business. However, the study of business did not stimulate Norene's soul, for she kept remembering Annamae's excitement about caring for others. Norene transferred to Loyola University to study nursing. There she met her faith-filled companion of 34 years, her husband, Gene.

Today, Norene is the mother of five children and grandmother of three. Her daughter, Maggie's, description of her mother is consistent with Norene's perspective of herself. "I think my mom must have decided at a very young age that she was happy and satisfied to be the person she is and that she likes herself the way she is. This is the only way I have been able to figure out how my mom can be so accepting of other people, flaws and all. Due to her strong sense of self, my mom has always had the ability to immediately make people feel comfortable in any situation."

Norene's approach with both elderly patients and their families is most appreciated when she is there for the patient who is dying and for the family who must "let go and accept the patient's passage." Norene tells a story of one patient whom she came to know intimately over a 10-year time period. While providing medications and treatments, feeding, being with, listening to, establishing trust, promoting safety, and reducing fear, Norene came to know and minister to the patient as well as the family. When the patient died, the family requested she speak at the memorial service. Norene believed this was a "little thing" she could do for her patient and the family. Yet this "little thing" was so very important to all who loved this woman. As Norene spoke at the memorial service, family members came to understand not only how well their loved one had been cared for in her time at the nursing home, but also how much she and the family were loved and respected. Norene's presence and participation at the service illustrated her continued care for the family, reflecting her concern for the patient, and acknowledging her gratitude for this patient in her life. At the same time, it allowed the family to remember, grieve, and be helped by someone who was present for their loved one, as well as for them, through the years.

About two or three years after Noreen became a nurse, she faced several situations that validated she had selected the right profession. A woman in her early 40s had a cardiac arrest. Norene called the

Norene's patients have also taught her many lessons about living. She recalls caring for a woman who had no short term memory. Throughout the day, Norene fed her, kept her clean, and helped her in and out of bed. The patient continually asked Norene her name. Finally Norene said to the patient, "You know, I have told you my name at least 25 times." The patient replied, "Honey, would you mind making it 26!" This response reminded Noreen that patience is needed when caring for elderly patients, and if you can't be patient—don't be there. Another thing Norene learned is that "you cannot take life too seriously in a nursing home. It is important sometimes to be silly, to joke, and to laugh."

Life has presented many unforgettable events for Norene. With fondness, she tells of the time she heard her daughter announce the arrival of her first grandchild with the words, "Say hi to Grandma." It was a most memorable experience and one that reflects the values she holds about family and the importance of little things. "Being grandma," she says, is the reward for raising children that are good and responsible. She also loves being with the grandchildren, for as she says, "It is not like raising your own children where you must be responsible all of the time. I can be with, enjoy, share, and teach them and when I am tired, I can go home."

The author thanks Norene O'Brien for her years of friendship and Maggie Wren, daughter of Norene O'Brien, and Karen Forchett, RN, nursing supervisor at Westmoreland Nursing Center, for their contributions to this article.

"code" and participated in a vigorous and successful resuscitation. After discharge, the woman came back to the hospital to see Norene. With humor, the patient showed her appreciation by reminding Norene that, in her earnestness to save her life, Norene had broken her ribs. On another occasion, Norene cared for a man who had had a cardiac arrest. He shared his intimate experience of almost dying and seeing what he described as the "white light." He told Norene, "I want you to know that when I do die, I will be peaceful, because I was able to discuss this with you." And die peacefully he did. Aware of the relationship that Noreen had with this patient, the staff called her at home when the patient died. These experiences help confirm the appropriateness of Norene's selection to be a nurse.

FROM LESSONS LEARNED TO LOVE RETURNED

by Lori L. Fischer

Karen Prelog admits her childhood was not normal or easy. Her tale is an uplifting one about a girl who had a tough childhood, but whose life was miraculously transformed by hard knocks, faith, love, and the support of her children. From childhood hardships to adult support, Karen has become a caring, loving person and a compassionate nurse.

Karen's hardships began early in her life. Her mother was judged mentally ill and unable to care for Karen and her four brothers. Karen's father could not meet the challenges of raising his five children. Karen's paternal grandparents became the guardians of this ready-made family. Karen's grandparents lived with their newformed family in a small, three-bedroom home in the remote woods of the Upper peninsula of Michigan.

Karen's grandparents were hardworking. Karen's grandfather swept floors in a factory for $0.50 per hour. Her grandmother cooked, cleaned, canned, and baked. One of Karen's happiest memories is having "baked chicken" on Sundays. The chicken was usually killed on Saturday and shared with many other relatives the following day. Karen's family had a roof over their heads, food on the table, and a warm fire in the stove, but the home did not have running water, electricity, or indoor plumbing.

At the beginning of each school year, the "welfare lady" brought new clothes so Karen and her brothers would have a "fresh start" for the school year. This was always an anticipated time for Karen because she would get "girl" clothes and could put away some of her brothers' hand-me-downs. One time, she recalls getting an "old lady's" pair of gray shoes. She was so thankful, because she wouldn't have to go barefoot.

When Karen was 13, her grandmother died, and her brothers were "farmed out" to the neighbors. Karen felt unloved, unwanted, and very alone. At age 15, the courts decided Karen would live with her father and stepmother, so she left Michigan and moved to California. This was an exciting and tumultuous time for Karen. She wanted to start her life anew, enjoy new experiences, and be more in control of her destiny.

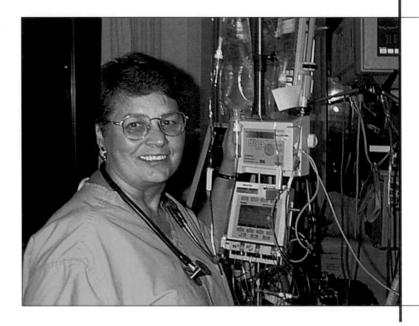

As Karen was leaving for California, a nurse, Irene, stopped by to say good-bye and to wish her good luck. When the bus was ready to leave, Irene generously offered Karen the sunglasses off her head. This simple act of kindness overwhelmed Karen. She had always felt worthless, alone, and unimportant. Karen believed Irene had given of "herself" when she handed her the sunglasses. To Karen, this kind, simple act was symbolic of unconditional love.

Living with her father and stepmother was not at all what Karen had anticipated. She discovered that her "new" parents were alcoholics who had little time or concern for Karen and her two half-sisters. Karen's memories of living with her grandfather suddenly looked desirable, so she moved back to Michigan.

Karen's new life in Michigan gave her hope, enjoyment, and an introduction to religion. Karen was gaining confidence yet realized her first 17 years of life would leave lifelong scars. She took secretarial courses because she had been told she "was not smart enough" to go to college. Karen did so well in the high school secretarial course that the principal hired her. While working, Karen attended Bible College where she met her husband, and they started a family. After 23 years, the marriage ended. Karen became the custodial parent of her four teenage boys.

Karen worked as a school bus driver, but the salary was not enough to sustain her family of five. Karen knew she needed a career. Karen discovered, through a career placement test, her strengths were in nursing, military, and police work. Nursing was Karen's choice. Her boys were supportive and encouraged Karen to pursue her career choice and schooling. Pursuing nursing was a three-and-a-half-year family project. Her boys tutored Karen, cooked, and performed many of the household duties. Karen frequently worked four different jobs during the week to meet their financial obligations. The encouragement and support of her friends, family, and community, and the incredible dedication of her children helped Karen succeed in becoming a nurse.

Karen's first nursing job was in an Arizona county hospital. Most of the patients in the hospital were indigent, poor, lost, lonely, or "down and out." Karen felt she could relate to and help the people whose lives mirrored her childhood. Throughout her nursing career, Karen has continued to care for people from all socioeconomic walks of life, including minor criminals and murderers. Regardless of the patient's background, Karen's commitment is to care for and demonstrate love to her patients. Karen is aware she may be the only person in the patient's life treating them with respect, dignity, kindness, and compassion.

In the past, Karen desperately tried to understand and make sense out of her childhood. She now believes her *past* has prepared her to be a compassionate nurse. When Karen walks into a patient's room, a little voice inside her says, "My patients will have a better day because I am *caring for* them and I *care about* them." Karen always draws from her past experiences and makes every patient feel loved, wanted, and respected. Patients' families are also comforted by Karen's nursing care. A family member said, "I am so glad that you are taking care of my father tonight. Now I can go home and sleep better, knowing that he is in your care."

Today, Karen is a burn nurse "in practice" and "at heart." A "big heart" is what it takes, Karen says, to care for some of the burn patients. One patient/family experience illustrates Karen's philosophy. Karen used both her heart and her nursing care practice to provide burn treatment to three children whose mother tricked them into playing a deadly game. The mother blindfolded her children, locked them in the shed, poured gasoline over the shed and herself, and then lit a match. The oldest boy, 14, escaped and rescued his 12-year-old brother and 8-year-old sister. Unfortunately, the little girl died at the scene. The mother and younger son sustained burns on 70 to 80 percent of their bodies. The 14-year-old boy received minor burns. The community and nursing staff were outraged that such a heinous crime had occurred. Karen, however, looked at the situation with a different perspective. She understood this situation could very well have happened to her and her siblings had her mother not been committed to a mental institution. As she cared for this mother over the four-month hospitalization, Karen learned the impact of untreated mental illness, depression, and desperation. While caring for the mother, Karen gave her a pair of symbolic sunglasses, characterizing the unconditional love she was given earlier in life by Nurse Irene. Through nursing, Karen has been able to give this mother love based on her own *lessons learned* through life.

HOME ON THE RANCH: PHYLLIS ETHRIDGE

by Carol Ann Cavouras

A ranch in rural Arizona may seem an unlikely place for a national nurse leader, but Phyllis Ethridge has created a great deal of change from this location. Spending her entire career working for one hospital, Phyllis has influenced nursing practice throughout the world.

Phyllis is a woman of great ingenuity and creativity. She has been able to foster creativity by developing programs that meet the needs of patients. Her peers describe her as continually envisioning a future far beyond what most people see. Phyllis has translated her visions into practical applications that have affected patient care everywhere.

Phyllis was born and raised in Boston, Massachusetts. While she was a teenager, her mother fell and then died from a subdural hematoma. This experience, coupled with her own experience during an appendectomy, created her interest in nursing.

Phyllis' dream was thwarted when she learned that, in Boston, graduates of schools of nursing could not take the state board examination until they were at least 21 years old. Phyllis had an older sister in Tucson, Arizona, who encouraged her to move to Tucson and enter the diploma program at St. Mary's School of Nursing. Phyllis did move to Arizona but was still too young when she graduated from St. Mary's School of Nursing to take the board examination.

But once she passed the state board exam, Phyllis became a nursing force that would not stop. She remained in the Tucson area, working at St. Mary's Hospital throughout her career, eventually becoming vice president of patient care services. Although acting in a leadership role, Phyllis could always be found at a patient's bedside.

Phyllis has always been a unique nurse and leader. Her soft blue eyes penetrate; her distinctive voice and laugh are unforgettable. She emerged as a strong advocate for the professional status of nurses. But more than that, she empowered nurses to fulfill their professional role and care for patients.

St. Mary's Hospital was on the cutting edge of nursing practice in the 1980s. Innovative programs, such as the credentialing of nurse competencies, salaried status, and self-scheduling practices, set the hospital apart from others as one of the original magnet hospital facilities.

Phyllis was also instrumental in the development of nursing case management in nurse clinics and home healthcare. In the 1990s, she used a $12 million grant to develop a community-focused professional nurse case manager group practice, a network of community health centers, and the world's first nursing health maintenance organization (HMO).

This HMO evolved into a system where professional registered nurses manage nonphysician, noninstitutional services provided for Medicare members. Never one to stray far from patient care, as she was developing these programs, Phyllis became the case manager for six people in her own neighborhood, a rural community 20 miles away from Tucson. She also routinely "took calls" for the case management team.

Phyllis tells about a 45-year-old homeless man who needed heart surgery. As an expert regarding community resources, Phyllis found him a place to live and food from the food bank, and assisted him in applying for social security. She followed this gentleman throughout his recovery period until he left Arizona to return to his home state.

Lest you think that Phyllis was all work and no play, while enacting these changes in the workplace, Phyllis raised six children who still live nearby. Phyllis also recognized the power of networking long before it was a buzzword. She has been active on a number of national committees and has always had a vision of creating a forum for nurses to interact and have fun together.

Recognizing that relationships develop while having fun, Phyllis decided to not only foster a better balance between work and play for each individual, but to help them contribute to the creative advancement of nursing practice. She hosted a retreat at her ranch with the idea of nurses spending social time together. The power of the event was awe-inspiring. Phyllis recognized that the burden of playing host diminished her ability to enjoy and participate, so she arranged for others to help her create an event that has developed into an invitational of nearly 100 nurses from around the world who meet in La Paz, Mexico, for a week. It still continues each spring.

Never one to slow down, retirement for Phyllis has not diminished her level of involvement. She remains active on six national committees in nursing and serves as a reviewer for the Magnet Nursing Service Program. Keeping a healthy balance, her nursing work is limited to Mondays and Thursdays, because the rest of the week is scheduled for fun. Phyllis is the coach, catcher, and relief first baseman for a Women's Senior Olympic team that practices twice a week at 7:00 a.m. These early morning practices have paid off. The team has traveled and has won recognition in national tournaments. Phyllis' athletic endeavors also include participating in two local golf leagues. In 1995, Phyllis was inducted into the Tucson Sports Hall of Fame.

Even with this busy schedule, family has remained important to Phyllis. She frequently enjoys her children and 13 grandchildren, assisting them with 4-H projects. And Phyllis' leadership has not diminished, either. She continues to urge her nursing colleagues to be bold and to think creatively.

MIRACLE WORKER

by Barb Ward

"The number of kids and parents who need help is just astounding. It can be overwhelming. So, I step back and think if I can make a difference in one child's life, then I've made a difference, and that's what I do." To hear Susanne Bjork talk about her day-to-day life, you'd think there's nothing that is extraordinary about it. However, as she nonchalantly tells about her family and her calling to be a nurse, she reveals that her life is indeed filled with a series of little miracles, both at work and at home.

Starting from the beginning, Susanne will tell you that she always knew she wanted to be a nurse. When she was in kindergarten, one of her class assignments was to make a paper doll representing what she wanted to be when she grew up. She made a nurse. In addition to her passion for helping others, she also had a special affinity for babies. She was always the first one to step forward to hold a newborn, so her step into neonatal nursing was natural.

During her first year out of nursing school, she knew nursing was the right choice. A baby was born with holes in its lungs and was having difficulty breathing. The parents were beside themselves with worry. She can still remember the look in that mom's eyes as she asked, "Is my baby going to be okay?" Susanne unfalteringly told her that the baby would be just fine. And that baby not only survived, but also thrived. That was the moment she thought, "This is it, newborn nursing is what I want to do." After moving to Greeley, she took a 6-year detour from the nursery and worked in an adult intensive care unit and a cardiac catheterization laboratory. Susanne eventually found her way back to the nursery and has remained there for the past 13 years.

Not every situation in her nursing career has had a happy outcome. One baby that she had helped deliver was born with no lungs and subsequently died. She grieved with the baby's mom. This was difficult for Susanne because she had just returned from maternity leave after her second child was born. "My greatest satisfaction as a nurse comes when I feel that I've made a difficult situation easier for a family." She was fortunate to be there the next year when the same woman delivered a healthy baby boy.

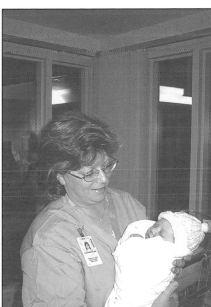

Over the years, her care and compassion have helped numerous families, and her generosity easily spills over into her home life. At work, she helps women as they bring the miracle of life into the world. At home, she and Larry, her husband of 16 years, raise two miracles of their own, 11-year-old son Seth and 14-year-old daughter Leah, as well as care for three foster children, 3-year-old Gloria, 20-month-old Beverly, and 10-month-old Georgia.

The circumstances that brought foster children into her life, not surprisingly, are an overlap from her work life to her home life. A baby girl was born at home and survived only by a miracle. Her mother was not so fortunate. The mother died when the baby girl was just a few days old. It quickly became apparent that the baby girl would need to be adopted, and as social services struggled to find a family for this little girl, Susanne and Larry searched their hearts. In doing so, they realized that they could give little children like this one a home. Although this little girl became a foster child of one of Susanne's friends, Susanne began to ask more questions about foster care families. Susanne was drawn (Larry would say possessed!) to stories of people taking care of foster children or children in need.

She heard of large, loving foster families and, somewhere down deep, she knew that she wanted to be one of those families. Medical complications a few years after the birth of her second child led to a hysterectomy. But now, with the miracle of her foster children, she explains, "I have all the children I always thought I would have." "I am lucky to have a wonderfully supportive husband and family," says Susanne. "It has made me want to be a better parent, wife, and nurse. Being a nurse and a mommy has taken me places I never dreamed of."

Susanne's generous spirit has not gone unnoticed by her colleagues. In the spring of 2002, she was honored with a Florence Nightingale Award Nomination. Although honored, Susanne admits the decision to compete for the Nightingale Award was difficult. She says, "I feel I simply have been doing my job, using the talents God gave me."

Susanne's colleagues speak of her talents with words such as caring, compassionate, highly competent, calm, and knowledgeable. Kari Waterman, RN, BSN, a perinatal educator for the Banner Health System, Colorado Region, wrote this when recommending Susanne for the award, "Unfortunately, in neonatal nursing, a nurse not only sees great happiness, but also sees great sorrow. Nurses care for babies and their families in amazing births as well as tragic deaths. Susanne gracefully captures the essence of nursing when she provides care to all families and babies."

Susanne will undoubtedly continue creating more little miracles in her life. Susanne will continue to grow and expand her knowledge as a neonatal nurse. She and Larry are planning to continue providing homes for other foster children when their three foster children move on. Susanne is truly a godsend to so many families in Weld County. She truly has many crossovers between her family and nursing life.

NURSE EXCELLENCE SEEN THROUGH THE EYES OF A PHYSICIAN

by Terry R. Light

ary Norene Jamieson grew up in a close-knit Irish immigrant family in Chicago. Because she was born with congenital hip and foot abnormalities, she underwent orthopaedic treatment and was in repeated casts. Today, Norene, as she prefers to be called, vividly recalls her own experiences, so when surgery is necessary for children, she is committed to minimizing both physical and mental discomfort for the children and their families. Her quick smile and open approach allow her to quickly establish rapport with kids.

Norene's mother believed it was important that Norene have a vocation. She proposed either nursing or teaching but decided Norene did not have the temperament for teaching. Norene agreed and chose nursing. Ironically, she now often serves as a role model for nurses and nursing students throughout the world; in a sense she is a teacher. With her family's support, she attended and graduated from St. Anne's Hospital School of Nursing, the place of her birth, on the west side of Chicago. She worked as both an operating room and emergency room nurse at St. Anne's from 1969 until, sadly, the hospital closed in 1988.

Norene's part-time work at the Shriners Hospital for Children in Chicago grew into full-time employment with the closing of St. Anne's. Her professional capabilities were recognized in 1994 when she assumed the position of nurse manager of operating rooms. In this leadership position, she provides direction for staff as well as hands-on patient care. Norene continues "to scrub" on complex spine and limb lengthening procedures to assure that the flow of the procedure is smooth. She is often seen comforting children prior to surgery and is constantly teaching her staff and encouraging all in the department to upgrade their skills.

Norene's most unique contributions take place outside the Shriners Hospital. Over the last 11 years, this dynamic and dedicated woman has organized and participated in 29 overseas medical missions. She has organized 17 trips to Colombia, 10 trips to Lithuania, and two trips to Jordan. Each of these trips represents a *vacation* dedicated to the service of children.

To support overseas medical care, in 1994, Norene and two physicians, Edward Millar and Peter Smith, established the Silver Service Children's Foundation. The foundation raises funds to support the overseas missions, providing dollars for airline tickets and transportation of supplies. An annual auction raises funds. Norene has enticed a local pub to provide the food and beer that puts bidders in a festive *bidding* mood. Throughout the year, Norene solicits auction items from professional sports teams, friends, local restaurants, museums, and businesses. Each year, the auction raises approximately $15,000 in support of Silver Service trips.

Boxes and medical supplies dominate Norene's basement storage area. She acquires materials as well as packs the supplies for each trip. Implant vendors, other hospitals, and Chicago corporations such as Mars Candy and Ty, the manufacturer of Beanie Babies, have responded to Norene's requests for donations. She organizes and inventories 30 to 35 large boxes of operating room supplies, candy treats, and stuffed animal gifts for each trip. Only one box of loaned instruments will return to Chicago. Unused disposable items are left with the host hospital.

The Chicago-based Lithuanian Children's Hope Foundation sponsors the annual trips to Lithuania. Norene, again, organizes supplies, recruits nursing personnel, and coordinates surgeon staffing with Shriners chief surgeon, Dr. John Lubicky. Surgeries take place at the Vilnius Children's Hospital. Once she arrives in Lithuania, Norene leads a team of nurses who unpack their surgical supplies, candies, and stuffed animals for the young patients. She is sensitive to local operating room customs but is adamant that American standards of sterility and technique be observed in the host operating room. The local nursing staff is integrated into the complex procedures undertaken by the visiting American surgeons. Norene is often the last to leave the hospital, making certain that all is ready for the next day's surgeries. Her day is not done. She prowls the stalls and stores of Vilnius merchants, searching for unique painted Russian lacquered boxes to give as gifts or to add to her collection.

Norene travels to Colombia with an orthopaedic team every April and October to an area plagued with guerilla activity and drug trafficking. Over the last decade, the team has cancelled only two trips because of political turmoil. Team members fly to Cali, Colombia, where armed guards meet them and accompany them to their quarters in Buga.

Two full days of clinics are followed by four very busy surgical days. The final day of the visit is devoted to education of local physicians and nursing staff. Dr. Julio Palacio, a Colombian orthopaedic surgeon, provides care for the children after the team returns to the U.S. Over the last decade, more than 5,000 Colombian children have been evaluated and 500 surgeries performed by the American team of volunteers.

Norene's extraordinary dedication was recognized in 2002 with a number of noteworthy awards. In early 2002, she was presented a certificate of appreciation from Valdas Adamkus, the president of the Republic of Lithuania. She was awarded the *National Association of Orthopaedic Nurses' (NAON) 2002 Outstanding Nurse Practice Award* in May. This award recognizes "the NAON member who has provided high-quality healthcare to the orthopaedic patient and has made outstanding contributions over his/her career to the field of orthopaedic nursing." Norene was also named the Nursing Spectrum *2002 Regional Nurse of the Year* for the Chicago and Tri-State Area. Connie Payton, the widow of Chicago Bears great Walter Payton, presented this honor to Norene.

Peter Smith, M.D., an attending surgeon at the Shriners' Hospital has commented, "Norene is truly an outstanding individual. She serves as a role model to all nurses by her work ethic, her patient-focused attitude, and her volunteerism." Hugh G. Watts, M.D., clinical professor of surgery at UCLA, commented, "I can easily say that I have never known or worked with anyone who is as competent. The striking thing is that Norene is able to create a wonderful surgical environment in a disadvantaged foreign hospital without getting frazzled or upset. She is a shining role model for anyone for her willingness to contribute to others less fortunate than she."

Although Norene was more than proud of her graduation from St. Anne's hospital-based nursing school, she wanted a university bachelor's degree. By taking courses in her "spare time," she achieved this goal in 1994 when she received a Bachelor of Science in Nursing degree from St. Francis University in Joliet, Illinois. Although it is hard to imagine that she has the additional time and energy, Norene volunteers each Sunday morning at the Chicago Field Museum of Natural History as an anthropology docent. In addition to leading tours through permanent Egyptian exhibits, she provides guidance to visitors to exhibits as diverse as the Dead Sea Scrolls, Baseball Hall of Fame artifacts, and a Cleopatra exhibit. Norene is now working towards a Master of Egyptology degree from the University of Chicago. Throughout her personal and professional nursing life, Norene Jamieson has served others with exemplary enthusiasm and professionalism.

PEOPLE AND PETS: A FULL LIFE OF ONCOLOGY CARE — LINDA BRETHAUER

by Carol J. Swenson

Few people search specifically for a home and land that can be reached only by a gravel road, but that is exactly what Linda Brethauer and her husband, Dave, did. They wanted to be rural, and they needed to have space for their large family of pets: six horses, seven cats, and three dogs. Their home is in southwestern Wisconsin, and besides their pets they have lived with several teenagers over the past five years.

Linda and Dave's horses serve a central role as they provide leadership to the local Spring Valley 4-H Club's horse project. This 4-H Club has the largest horse project in Rock County, with 12 to 20 children participating annually. Linda and Dave share their time and resources to teach the kids to groom and show the horses.

Giving and sharing of herself to pets and other people's children is consistent with Linda's giving and compassionate nature in the field of oncology. When asked to submit thoughts about Linda for this nursing story, again and again the words kind, compassionate, and concerned came to mind as they relate to patients, their families, significant others, and staff Linda cares for and works with. Linda always seems to sense when others need a listening ear.

Linda meets with patients and families to clarify cancer diagnoses or treatment plans that they may misunderstand or be confused about. An oncology social worker once stated, "Linda has a very compassionate way of conveying information that helps patients gain knowledge about what they may expect in the days and weeks ahead. She also lets them know that she will be with them when they need her."

Linda is an advocate for patients whether they are in need of more physician information, a wig to cover the results of chemotherapy or radiation treatment, a portable computer for a businessman so he can surf the Internet during an extended stay, or games for the long-stay adolescent patients. Linda is there to make the phone calls and has even resorted to begging to fulfill a patient's needs or desires.

Linda's career path has been one of lifelong learning, developing, and driving. She began as a nurse aide in a hospital while working on her BSN at the University of Wisconsin, Milwaukee. In Iowa, she worked for nine years as a nurse in acute care and public health. Linda obtained a master's degree, with a focus on oncology, from the University of Missouri. For this she commuted three hours each way between her home and the university.

Linda and Dave moved to their rural Wisconsin home in 1993. As an oncology clinical nurse specialist at Swedish American Hospital in Rockford, Illinois, Linda fulfilled her role as a practitioner and as a role model. Her daily commute was about one hour each way. After several years as a clinical nurse specialist, Linda decided she truly wanted to be an oncology nurse practitioner, so she earned a second master's degree from the University of Wisconsin, Madison. She drove one hour north of her home to attend these classes. It was never easy to complete her educational or career goals because Linda always had to travel great distances. But that never stopped her, for she is now a nurse practitioner in the radiation oncology department.

Linda currently travels 50 miles from her quiet, serene, rural site to the bustling site of her clinical practice and has never once complained about the time or distance being a hassle. She intentionally picks the back roads to enjoy the pastoral setting and adjusts her mind and emotions to the day ahead or the day just completed. No, Linda and Dave did not find a "farmette" on a gravel road, but their narrow paved road has frequent Amish buggies.

Her gift of giving is always there, even when her schedule is full and she has no more time to give. During a nine-month period of time while busy with her practice, Linda found time to be available for two friends whose husbands were terminally ill. She applied her vast oncology skills and knowledge to care for the patients and to support her friends. I was one of those friends who observed firsthand Linda's gentle, tender, loving care and professional approach during those difficult last days. She was there to support, comfort, and listen to me—what a gift of caring!

Linda was always a people person, and it could never be said that Linda put paperwork ahead of meeting with patients, families, or staff. She is an asset to the oncology program and the entire health system, but even more important is that she is a trusted colleague and friend.

There are not many people with six horses, seven cats, and three dogs, and even fewer who have loved, nurtured, and named those 16 pets. Their very human names are Clark, Sid, Love, Delhi, Logala, and Ebby (the horses); Emma, Sophie, and Bill (the cats who live in the house); Mac, Hazel, Sally, and Carrie (the cats who live outdoors); and the dogs, Desi, Fergus, and Eunice.

Linda's oncology nursing career has been a highlight of her professional life for people and even for her pets. One of her horses, Logala, was treated for cancer. Linda's life is truly full of people and pets as well as caring for those with cancer.

PRIVILEGED TO SERVE

by Ida M. Androwich

When Adele "Corky" Miller first transferred to Dominican High School in Milwaukee in the early 1960s, many wondered whether she would be stuck-up or unapproachable. As a daughter of one of the major Milwaukee brewing families, she had had many opportunities that other classmates did not or would not ever have. We soon found out that in Corky's family, privileges were tightly associated with social responsibilities. She was one of the crowd, yet a leader in scholarship and community service, and definitely a leader in seeking fun!

After high school, Adele finished her baccalaureate at Santa Clara and her master's in education at Stanford. Before starting her family, she spent a year in Tanzania, East Africa, working with her sister, Robin, at the Salvatorian Secondary School. This was to be the beginning of a number of Adele's international volunteer service trips. Loret Miller Ruppe, another of Adele's sisters, was the director in the Peace Corps. Adele had the opportunity to assist Loret in planning and participating in the Peace Corps' 25th Anniversary in Tanzania.

Adele started "multitasking" long before we knew what the word meant. As she was raising her three children in Maine, she began to manage the Highland Acres Dairy Farm, one of the few dairy farms in the area. Adele described herself as the "herdswoman" for over 100 head of cattle. She supervised four employees and coordinated the hay harvest for the 500-acre farm.

In addition to the work on the farm, Adele remained heavily involved in the community. She taught at St. John's School, coordinated students in community outreach programs, and initiated a government self-sufficiency policy related to agriculture studies. About 15 years ago, in the late 1980s, Adele realized that, while she gained great satisfaction from these community service activities, she wanted to be more directly involved in improving the quality of life for those who needed healthcare. This led her to seek a career in nursing. She graduated *summa cum laude* from the University of Southern Maine in 1991.

Since becoming a nurse, Adele has found great satisfaction in a variety of practice roles. She continued to maintain her activities on the farm but also became involved in a wide range of somewhat unique roles. She also was now able to use her nursing knowledge to create a new niche for her involvement in community activities. Whether it was staffing a first-aid station during a walkathon, coordinating community events, or advocating for clients within the medical community, Adele found a way to make a difference.

The holistic perspective she brought to her own life had now become a part of her nursing practice. Over the last decade, she has worked and continues to work at a home care agency, providing private duty nursing care for patients with a variety of chronic illnesses. Some of her patients are quadriplegics or have terminal cancer, diabetes, epilepsy, and/or cardiac illnesses that require care that is intermittent. Adele's care enables them and supports their ability to remain at home. Since 1994, she has also been a nurse at L.L. Bean, conducting thousands of employment health assessments. She serves as the substitute nurse for the Town of Brunswick School System and is also a volunteer teaching assistant in the school's special education program.

In 1993, Adele traveled to Belize in Central America to work in the Presbyterian Medical Center in a clinic in the small town of Patchakan. She and another nurse provided healthcare and ran the clinic for a month while the usual staff members were on vacation. During a typical week, it was not unusual to assess and treat over 100 patients as well as provide outreach care and education to the surrounding villages.

However, Adele's international heart is in Tanzania. This year, she was able to return again for several months to volunteer in the community. Armed with a nursing background, she was able to teach English and agriculture as well as nursing. One of her creative ways of teaching is to engage the nursing students in developing plays for fun while learning nursing and healthcare concepts at the same time.

Several notes from an earlier journal about Tanzania capture Adele's views. "On a beautiful early dawn it is wonderful to watch the women returning from a well with their buckets of water on their heads and their bodies wrapped in bright, colorful prints. They often have a baby on their backs and a huge smile covering their faces. Behind the school are several mountains. My favorite entertainment is to climb one and watch the sunrise. To climb, exerting every muscle, and then be rewarded by an overwhelming view for miles around is wonderful." Adele's views of Tanzania also capture how she approaches life and nursing, creatively and always combining all her skills to bring richness to others.

In 1993, Adele traveled to Belize in Central America to work in the Presbyterian Medical Center in a clinic in the small town of Patchakan. She and another nurse provided healthcare and ran the clinic for a month while the usual staff members were on vacation. During a typical week, it was not unusual to assess and treat over 100 patients as well as provide outreach care and education to the surrounding villages.

RUTH

by Carolyn Hope Smeltzer

R uth has been a nurse for more than 60 years. Never missing one year of service, Ruth admits nursing or being a nurse is just her. Ruth is a nurse who was never meant to be a nurse. Ruth was following in the footsteps of her ancestors to become an educator when fate took an unexpected turn. During her senior year of high school, one of Ruth's friends asked her to walk with her to City Hospital so she could fill out an application for the school at the hospital. Miss Kathryn Cullen, the director of nursing, greeted both girls and insisted that Ruth also complete an application. A friend of the family, who just happened to be on the hospital board of City Hospital, learned about Ruth meeting Miss Cullen. He insisted that the profession of nursing needed girls like Ruth. Ruth listened but had no desire to be a nurse. She did not know any nurses; she had only been in one hospital in her life, and her heart was set on being a teacher. She had already been accepted into the educational program at Colby College in Waterville, Maine. As Ruth puts it, "In those days there were three choices for women: teaching, nursing, or clerking at the local five and dime." Ruth wanted teaching to be her career.

Ruth's patents were surprised, skeptical, but supportive of their daughter, who was considered a "spoiled brat who had never done any labor" when she did enter nursing school. The family was convinced that Ruth would never finish nursing school and would return to her first dream of teaching. They found it amusing when Ruth actually had fun cleaning 75 bedpans each morning or looking for lost surgical sponges until the wee hours of the morning. Ruth had fun doing these and other tasks because she was with her friends, the other nursing students. Ruth says that she found nursing exciting from day one. Ruth stuck with nursing for two reasons: she liked nursing and she was a "hard-headed Irishwoman" who was not going to succumb to the family's predictions of her future.

Ruth tells many stories of having to "toe the line" or risk being thrown out of nursing school. Everywhere she turned there were more rules, rules from administration and the upper classmen. The rules included being on time for breakfast (6:30 to 6:40 a.m.), opening doors for upper classmates, having all required equipment in the "deep pockets" of the bib apron uniform, being in your dormitory room by 9:45 p.m., and remaining a single woman. Students were expelled for being late more than three times for breakfast or for not having their scissors, bandages, nail files, or pens in their pockets when they reported for ward duty. It was also clear to Ruth that you did not have "rights" until you were capped or an upperclasswoman. Despite the rules and not being capped, Ruth had a great time due in part to her best friend, RoseMarie. RoseMarie was sweet and had a brother who had just graduated from his residency program. These two factors allowed RoseMarie to break a few rules without repercussions, and Ruth tagged along for the ride. Ruth describes this experience as taking advantage of politics. Ruth and RoseMarie remain friends to this day.

Ruth's first patient has never been erased from her mind. When she was asked to feed a dying patient, she was scared and shaking but did not walk away from the task. The patient died the following day from cancer. This experience caused Ruth to avoid dealing with the dead. She would give care to any person who had a speck of life but when that was gone so was she. She credits herself for using her "baby blue eyes" to get male orderlies or male nurses to take the dead patients to the morgue. Ruth has never been to a morgue nor has she any desire to visit one. In reflection, she believes nursing is for the living and when a patient dies there is a failure. She also acknowledges that she has to face her own mortality every time a patient dies.

During Ruth's 60 years as a nurse, she has never applied for a job. They always found her. After graduating from nursing school, she became a nurse on a male medical ward. She recalls the pay being $75 a month with a payback of $10 for her room, board, and laundry. Her next position was in an isolation hospital that treated mostly children. It was during this time period that she met and married Edward Dooley. They had four children. She valued spending time with her children and family and needed work flexibility, so she took on part-time nursing jobs, all of which equaled more time than full-time employment. She was an ambulance nurse and an "on call" nurse as well as a private duty nurse. When her kids questioned where their mother was, the oldest child, Paula, would say, "Ma has had enough of us kids and she went to work." The truth was that Ruth loved her family and she loved working as a nurse. Ruth was very happy and successful in balancing her home life and her nursing life.

One summer, Ruth decided to work as a nurse in a juvenile detention center. Her children remember this job extremely well because their mother came home from work with the following two rules. "In life, choose the right things to do," and "Not knowing is no excuse for doing the wrong thing." To this day, you can hear her adult children saying, "I did it because it was the right thing to do, and not knowing is no excuse." These two rules have now been passed down to her nine grandchildren.

When Ruth's youngest child, Gregory, entered kindergarten, Ruth became a school nurse. Ruth was working part time in her husband's dry cleaning business when a client approached her to become one of the two nurses in the school district. Ruth accepted the position for only one year but retired from school nursing 25 years later. She used both her nursing skills and "raising kids" skills in this role. The duties ranged from caring for numerous broken bones, cuts, or stomachaches to counseling children on the importance of education, learning, hygiene, and health.

Ruth used a lot of hugs and kisses when counseling and treating children. Because she had dealt with a lot of the "tricks" of her own children, Ruth soon recognized that about 75 percent of all the children asking to go home sick were coming from the math class. So Ruth developed a school rule. If the student was still sick after math class they could go home, but the student was not allowed to go home sick before or during math class. She could count on one hand the number of children who returned to the nursing office after

math class. When Ruth started as a school nurse, there were two nurses in the district for 3,500 students. When she retired, there were six nurses for 2,400 children. When Ruth started as a school nurse, less than one percent of mothers worked. When she retired, this number rose to 74 percent.

During the last 15 years, Ruth has volunteered in a nursing home, bringing caring and compassion to a few women who were not as fortunate as she in terms of mobility. Seven years ago, Ruth's pastor, Father Trainer, asked her to get involved in the newly formed parish nurse program. She became a board member and attended numerous educational sessions so that she could learn and provide valuable leadership to the program. In addition to these two responsibilities, she provides weekly nursing care in a free clinic for under-insured or noninsured patients. Ruth is also a nurse for a spiritual camp. She was asked several years ago to be a nurse for one day in the summer. The one-day camp nurse promise quickly became a week of service, and, needless to say, she is still keeping that obligation. Because of her commitment to serving the community, she was asked to be a member of a board that provides human services to inter-faith relationships and families.

Ruth combined her loving mother qualities and nursing skills to provide home care to her daughter Paula, who was suffering from cancer. Ruth used all her talents, love, wisdom, and common sense to allow her daughter to die with love and dignity at home in her mother's house. Because of Ruth's relationships in the community, friends, family, physicians, and priests made house calls to Paula. All home calls ended up in the dining room. The table was filled with food and the room filled with hospitality.

When asked her age, she simply replies, "Can you keep a secret?" If you answer yes, she replies, "So can I." She does not share her age because she fears she will be stereotyped as old and not able to contribute to the community. Ruth continues to have a thirst for knowledge and learning. She also continues to be active with both of her loves, nursing and family.

SEEING IS BELIEVING

by Chris Harris Vlasses

omewhere between Florence Nightingale and Evil Knievel, you will find Ingrid Cox, a driven, adventurous caregiver and educator. She traveled to Africa almost 15 years ago with a two-year air ticket and still has not used the return ticket. She is still serving others in Africa. Ingrid's perception of her London education in nursing is in sharp contrast to "what and how" she considers nursing today. "It was so controlled," Ingrid says of nursing in London, "with starched uniforms and caps and learning how to do flower arrangements and 'things.'"

Within a few short months, while stationed on London's rough East End, Ingrid fell in love with both nursing and care of the underprivileged. "Wearing this pristine uniform everyday, you eventually feel quite proud of yourself," she says, smiling, "but suddenly you come to the other end of life. You are no longer being sheltered. There is no nurse tutor behind you, saying, 'C'mon, Nurse Cox, do this.' You have to do something else all by yourself, and I think that's why I started to enjoy nursing. The fact that it was a challenge was energizing. It wasn't just something that was as regimented as I thought it was going to be; you got praised for using that initiative and that was fun."

Ingrid's experiences in London also reflect her adventurous spirit. She spent a year "squatting" in an abandoned apartment and also became extremely interested in mountain climbing. At the conclusion of her education, the combination of her desire to help others and to live life to the fullest brought Ingrid to Africa. She and a physician friend found healthcare jobs in Zambia. The two women decided to celebrate with an ice-climbing trip, and while on top of an ice-covered mountain they received word from Ingrid's father that their jobs had fallen through. The two friends still had plane tickets to Nairobi, Kenya. They both decided to not let their setback ruin their plans, so they flew to Kenya with no jobs. They set up camp in a youth hostel.

Over the next few months they traveled the Kenyan countryside, interviewing for positions and climbing every mountain they could find. When all was said and done, Ingrid had climbed almost every major range in East Africa and found herself hired by the Kikuyu mission hospital, only 27 kilometers from Nairobi. While powdering gloves in the operating theater, her curiosity led her to become quite interested in the work of Dr. Mark Wood, who was on the ophthalmology team at Kikuyu. Before long, Dr. Wood asked Ingrid to return to Moorfields Eye Hospital in England to train to be an ophthalmic nurse. The training would help Ingrid manage Kikuyu's new 75-bed eye hospital.

Blindness, particularly preventable blindness caused by cataracts, is an enormous problem in East Africa, where 20,000 out of every one million people lose their sight each year. There are 55 million blind people in the world; 45 million of these are in Africa and Asia. Cataract blindness is the major cause of blindness in developing countries affecting over 35 million people and it is curable. The problem is compounded by the fact that there is only one ophthalmologist for every one million people in many parts of Africa, compared to the European standard of one for every 150,000 people. It is estimated that the population of curable blind people will rise from 45 million to 75 million by the year 2020. If the disease is not controlled and treated, this population will be unable to work. They will become dependent on care and financial support from others, therefore having the potential to cripple the fragile African and Asian economies.

With this in mind, Ingrid eagerly accepted her role as "head ophthalmic nurse" when she returned. She began by hiring and training an entire staff. "It was good to be at the start of something and to establish the standards and quality control," she recalls. The fact that two-thirds of Kikuyu's current staff consists of the original team Ingrid hired and trained 12 years ago is a testament to the value and quality of her work.

In fact, many of the staff stayed much longer than Ingrid. When unmarried Nurse Cox announced that she was pregnant, she was promptly fired by the mission hospital. At 37 weeks pregnant, Ingrid was reading the classified ads and noticed her old job. She spoke to the administration, interviewed, and was hired again only to be fired for a second time a week later. She then left to deliver her first child at Kikuyu.

Feeling that it was time to move on, Ingrid spent the next two years working as a Theater Nurse Tutor at Nairobi Hospital, a private institution serving wealthier patients. Fate once again intervened and two years later Ingrid came across a classified ad for her old position at Kikuyu. While many might scoff, Ingrid interviewed AGAIN! Why? "I loved working with the patients there," she says. "The thrill of removing a bandage each morning and seeing somebody's sight restored makes you, even now, go soft in the knees and get a bit teary. It's just magnificent and that to me is the reason I was in Africa. It wasn't looking after rich patients in Nairobi hospital just because they could afford the surgery. I was there to work with the *wananchi,* the people who couldn't afford anything else. I just wanted to give them the best that was around."

For the third time, Ingrid was hired by Kikuyu, now affiliated with the German Non-Governmental Development Organization (NGDO) Christian Blind Mission International (CBMI). She set up a course in ophthalmic theater technique and without training assumed administrative and financial responsibilities so that clinicians were free to perform surgeries. "But that is part of what you do as a nurse in Africa," she says, "you just take things on." Her job expanded to fund raising, managing the overseas nursing exchange program, visiting physicians and students, and the acquisition of new equipment.

While at Kikuyu, Ingrid helped with the first audit of a cataract unit in Africa. During the study, Smith Kline Beecham contributed money for a free week of surgery. In that week, Ingrid's staff saw 700 patients a day with 400 surgeries performed. Almost 68 percent of the patients had come from a five-kilometer radius of the hospital. Although the hospital had been performing subsidized surgeries for 23 years, money had been an obstacle for these patients. Always ingenuous, Ingrid obtained sponsorship from a Kenyan business to support a team and a bus for free community-based service.

In her 12 years at Kikuyu, Ingrid states that she "worked herself out of a job." At least this time she left on her own terms. Passing responsibility completely over to her Kenyan staff was "a real thrill" and exemplified Ingrid's firm belief that the role of the mission healthcare worker is to do great things as well as to play a larger role by training others. The job is far too big to do alone.

Ingrid has worked in Nigeria, Rwanda, Sudan, Kenya, Tanzania, Uganda, Somaliland, Cambodia, and Somalia, where she and the team's plane were shot at while attempting to land one New Year's Day. Ingrid teaches and supervises many operating room teams all over eastern Africa as part of an affiliation with a worldwide program called Vision 2020 that aims to eliminate preventable blindness in the world by the year 2020.

Ingrid remains most excited by her work performing community-based surgeries in the field. "The locations are amazing," she says. "You operate even in the most remote places. In a turkwel, a mud hut, you dig holes in the dirt floor to stabilize an ordinary bed. You take off the headboard and that becomes your operating table. Your sterilizing area is a little bit of twine and bamboo outside. People walk for days, sometimes weeks, when they hear that the eye unit is coming. They have nothing at all and they are so grateful. You start at 6:00 a.m. and work until 9:00 or 10:00 p.m. constantly boiling your own drapes and sterilizing over hot coals. It's just amazing."

So how does being a nurse in Africa compare to working in Europe? "Being a nurse in Africa is much better," she laughs. "In Africa you can push your skills, extend your skills, use your initiative, and give more than is dictated by the rules and regulations. 'The Right for Sight' (Vision 2020s motto) is why I'm here, and I think I can do more here to further that mission than I could in the UK. Sure the UK has pleasurable things, such as my grandparents, television, and everything else, but I have mountains out here . . . big ones."

SHE NEVER TURNS AWAY

by Judith (Judi) A. Jennrich

"I was always the nurse, even when we played house or dress-up as kids," Nurse Margaret (Maggie) Terry proudly states. Her sisters and brothers would take turns playing mom and dad. Her sisters would wear fancy party dresses and fight over who would play the queen. But Maggie was always the nurse, no matter what types of games they played. "That was my role, and I would never give it up. Even when we were little, the kids would come to me when they fell down, because 'I was the nurse.'"

Maggie remembers being close to her grandfather, especially when he was ill with skin cancer. She wanted to take care of him. He lived with her family, and toward the end of his life her mother would give him injections. At that time, they had glass syringes that needed to be handled with care. Maggie would take the syringe when no one was watching and practice, pretending that she was giving shots. After breaking only one, she became very proficient in her "pretend" injections, dreaming of the day that she would become a nurse and make her family and everyone else feel better.

In Belize, at age 14, primary school is completed and graduates are eligible to take a national exam to continue high school. Those with the best scores are offered jobs to teach in primary school during the day and attend high school in the evenings. Maggie passed the exam with high marks and was asked to teach at Libertad Methodist, the village school. She was able to teach in most of the grades, and while she considered herself to be a good teacher, her dream was to attend nursing school. She graduated early from secondary school but still had to turn 18 to enter the Belize City Hospital School of Nursing. The school is in the largest city in Belize, about 100 miles from her village of Libertad, one of the northernmost villages in the country. In Belize, going to "the city" was likened to leaving the country, far from your village, family, friends, culture, and way of life. But Maggie gladly accepted this sacrifice to follow her calling.

All reports from former teachers, fellow students, and family describe her as an outstanding student nurse. They remember her as very serious about her studies, dedicated, dependable, caring toward her patients, and enthusiastic about all rotations and assignments. In fact, she loved all of it.

Maggie became better known as Nurse Terry, a formality practiced in Belize. Her first nursing assignments after graduation were in the medical wards of the Belize City Hospital where she worked for three years repaying her school debt. She was then transferred back home to her village's District Hospital in Corozal Town where she worked for another three years. Her patients always thought that they were her only patients, because she always made time for them until problems were solved. She was always willing to go that extra mile for her patients and their families.

While she loved her work in the District Hospital, she longed to work as a rural health nurse back in her village, with family and friends. Nurse Terry hoped to work on the prevention of health problems and be a consistent provider of healthcare for people of all ages with all kinds of problems.

For the next two years, Nurse Terry returned to Belize City to dedicate herself to a rural health nursing post-graduate course, which included midwifery, community health, and clinical courses that would prepare her to assume the role of rural health nurse, hopefully in her village. She fondly recalls the first day of class. The supervisor of public health nurses came to address her class, describing the role of the rural health nurse and the possible locations to which she and her classmates could be assigned after graduation. The place that stuck in her mind was in the most southern district of the country referred to as "backa bush," a Creole expression for an extremely rural location. The supervisor acknowledged the challenges, hardships, and of course, the great need for a rural health nurse to make a one-year commitment to the Toledo District, 200 miles from Belize City. She went on to describe the area as one that was extremely large with rugged terrain. The population of the rural village of Crique Sarco and the many surrounding smaller villages totaled less than 1,000. The Ketchi and Mopan Mayans, Amish (speaking neither English nor Spanish in some cases), and transient Guatemalan cultures were unfamiliar to Nurse Terry. The nurse who took that assignment would have to rely on her two feet, a horse, and a canoe to reach her patients. Not only was the area isolated and rural, but also it averaged over 200 inches of rain annually, which did not facilitate ease of any sort of transportation. The supervisor then asked for a show of hands from the 26 students. How many of them were excited by this challenge? Most of them eagerly raised their hands, including Nurse Terry.

Two years later, when the student nurses' rural health course was completed, this same supervisor returned to discuss the various posts that were available for the graduates and reminded them that most of them had raised their hands for Crique Sarco Village in the Toledo District. She asked whether anyone was ready to leave the next day for that post, mentioning that it was a "hardship" post in dire need of a trained rural health nurse. In spite of the incentives, only one hand was raised. Nurse Terry said, "I will go where I am most needed" and prepared to leave the following day for her long,

lonely bus ride to the nearest town, Punta Gorda, "backa bush," Crique Sarco Village.

The town's public health nurse met her in Punta Gorda. She insisted that Nurse Terry get a pair of boots, warm clothing, a lantern, and a hammock. She was given a ham radio, a bag of medicines, and some food and water. She was told to "try out" the post. Others in the position had lasted less than a week. She was also advised that a "volunteer nurse whose care was questionable" from one of the churches in the area was currently manning the post and reluctant to have a trained rural health nurse come into her area. Nurse Terry left early the following day and after a bus, a skiff, a canoe, and much walking, arrived 12 hours later in the village of Crique Sarco to find no one waiting or expecting her at the clinic.

She slept soundly upon arriving at the room adjacent to the clinic. When she awoke, she was met by the "volunteer nurse" who said that she was surprised that Nurse Terry had come at all and that it was time to go on a home visit. Through the cold and rain, the two nurses carried their supplies on a 12-mile trek. They walked, wading through streams with their boots on, to reach the very small village of San Benito Point on the Guatemala border. It took all day to get there and another day to return. As they saw their patients, it became clear to Nurse Terry that should an urgent need arise for a physician or extensive care, it would be nearly impossible to transport the patient. She attempted to discuss this with the nurse but was met with resentment and the retort, "It just can't be done because of such obstacles" as weather and distance. They walked back to their clinic in mud so deep that Nurse Terry lost one of her boots. She described this trip as "torture" for her because of the physical aspect of the trip, as well as the tension created by the lack of communication between she and the other nurse.

This first jaunt was a three-day trip and she hadn't even been there a week! The nurse then asked her, "So, do you still want to stay here after all of that?" It was as if she had been given her biggest test with the nurse hoping that she would be like the others who returned to the towns or villages from which they came. Nurse Terry replied that she would, indeed, be staying, and that there was "nothing that she could do to keep her away." The other nurse left the following day, taking much of the equipment and supplies from the clinic with her.

Nurse Terry worked hard at her job. She learned about the way in which the different groups cared for each other, dealt with pregnancies, deliveries, injuries, and medical conditions. As she became more involved with the general health of the community and the schools, she became a "fixture" in the various small villages. She assisted local community health workers in upgrading their skills in such areas as treatment of diarrheal diseases, teaching them how to administer oral rehydration solutions, start IVs, manage complicated deliveries, perform infant resuscitation, and postpartum care.

One day a young boy fell from a tree and a farmer had to run to Nurse Terry for help. It was apparent from the physical exam that the boy had life-threatening injuries and needed to be treated immediately. No chopper or boat would be available for days. Nurse Terry, undaunted, carried him many miles to the river where a group of fishermen took her and the boy to Punta Gorda in a small dory. They paddled for 12 arduous hours until they reached the town where the boy was treated. He survived!

This incident was the catalyst for the village people to look for a boat to travel to Punta Gorda for help when it was needed. It became her mission to obtain a skiff that would be available for the clinic at any time for any emergencies. She held village meetings and met with church members to convince them that they should not have to be dependent on outsiders should an emergency arise. As a result of her efforts, Kiratimo International, an affiliate of Rotary International, contributed to village donations to provide a motorboat for the health team. This water ambulance was instrumental in saving numerous lives for the villages "backa bush."

These efforts were the turning point in convincing the villagers that Nurse Terry did care about them and would go the extra mile. She became a leader in the community and was called upon to solve problems and to assist families with difficult issues. She cared for all of her "family." For example, when a patient died, she would help prepare the body and assist with the funeral, the cooking, the baking, and just about everything.

Nurse Terry is a nurse, a social worker, and a caregiver. She cares, shares, and does what needs to be done with so little fanfare. No

one realizes how things get done, except that when she is involved "big things happen." There was now a decent clinic, improved health standards and care for the area, more educated community healthcare workers, and easier transportation for those who needed medical attention. Nurse Terry left her southern rural health post after 18 months to return to her home, the village of Libertad. And although Libertad is the opposite end of the country, and in some ways the world, she left a legacy. The rural health nurses who followed her always return with gifts and greetings from her former patients and friends who remembered that when they called "Nurse, help me" she did.

Nurse Terry is currently fulfilling her goal of rural health nurse in her own village of Libertad, which has an active and well-functioning health center. She plans and carries out educational programs, distributing invitations for healthy living programs to the people on foot or on her bicycle. When nursing students spend time with Nurse Terry in her clinic, they comment that she "does and sees everything and cares for all types of patients and situations," most of it outside of regular clinic hours. Her days are filled with home visits to check on newborns that she brought into the world the night before and to check on wounds she sutured the day before. Her day usually ends with a stop to visit the frail elderly who she has known and respected her entire life. Watching her, one is imbued with the love that she has for her work as a nurse in her village. The students are most touched when they hear that she has quietly stayed the night and held the hand of a terminally ill cancer patient as he takes a last breath or had an unexpected caller in active labor during the night that she delivered on her living room floor! Thus, it isn't unusual to find Nurse Terry attending a mandatory rural health nurses' meeting in town looking a bit tired. Yet she is clearly present to learn how to implement new government health initiatives on such things as mother-to-baby transmission of AIDS. She is constantly improving the health of her village people whether they are family or her friends who are her patients, or whether there is a need to seek help locally or out of the country. Nurse Terry has never turned anyone away. She remembers all of her patients and has never once stopped caring. In her modest way, she brings great honor to the title of nurse.

SOMETHING TO SING ABOUT
by Irene Stemler

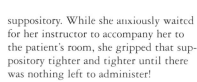

"**I** knew with all my heart I wanted to sing to nurse audiences but I was afraid. I didn't have much to sing about. I'm really not that special," Deb Gauldin confessed to one of her mentors. Kristin Lems replied, "Deb, *all* women have a story to tell, you just happen to tell yours through song."

Kristin validated just how important it is for women to share their stories with one another. Deb gained confidence in her ability to entertain and motivate nurse audiences. This confidence, along with talent and motivation, helped propel her career as a professional speaker, specializing in healthcare morale. Deb needed someone to believe in her, and now Deb offers the same message and wisdom to her audiences.

"I feel extra tender about singing to nurse audiences," explains Deb, "because they are a subset of women, mostly, who are particularly overworked and under-appreciated. They seem to need the message about being gentler with themselves more than most."

First and foremost, as Deb will tell you, she is a wife, mother, sister, and daughter. She has always been a champion for women's causes. She was turned down by the U.S. Peace Corps after applying at age 10 and tried to join the NAACP at age 13! Deb moved through the ranks of healthcare one step and one *conviction* at a time. She started as a "sunshine" geriatric volunteer. Then she advanced from the Junior Red Cross to a hospital candy striper to a nurse aide to a licensed practical nurse to a registered nurse. And most of those experiences somehow managed to wind up in a funny story or touching song.

As nursing students, we've all experienced that terrifying moment when our instructors actually expected us to *administer something therapeutic* to our patients. In Deb's case, it happened to be a Dulcolax suppository. While she anxiously waited for her instructor to accompany her to the patient's room, she gripped that suppository tighter and tighter until there was nothing left to administer!

Deb established her own professional speaking and entertaining business in 1993 and has been "on the road" across the country ever since. Her glamorous, high-profile travels have taken her from Whatcheer, Iowa, to Wahpeton, North Dakota, to Waukesha, Wisconsin. She has also been to Marshalltown, Mellon, and Muncie. Of course, there are also a few hospitals in Dallas, Philadelphia, Kansas City, and Chicago that have heard of her as well. And what does she find when she enters those hospitals?

"I see people absolutely *craving* to be appreciated and valued as human beings and as nurses. These are especially difficult times—the workload is greater, and the staffing is tighter. I'd like nurses to realize that they are the heart and soul of healthcare. Nurses are constantly giving—but they have great difficulty receiving. I like to ask my audiences what they need from me during the program. They usually say that they'd like something light and funny. Rarely do nurses ever get the chance to be thanked publicly for their hard work and long hours.

"My mission is to *nurse the nurses*. I help them remember why they chose the profession in the first place. That's why I like to sing *I Always Wanted to be a Nurse.*"

Music: to the tune of Somewhere Over the Rainbow©

Somewhere back in my childhood,
I longed to be a nurse.
I'd cure all of my patients,
No one would die or grow worse.
I wanted to be Florence Nightingale, Clara Barton, too.
Everything that Annie Sullivan did for Helen Keller,
Why, that's just what I would have done, too.
In nursing school, we wrote care plans and used our hearts
    and used our hands.
Remind me.
We saw each patient as a whole, we nurtured body, mind,
    and soul.
At the bedside is where you'd find me.
There've been many changes through the years, some for
    the better, some seem worse.
But if you want to see true conviction, look into the eyes
    of a nurse.
If patients handle all they see with courage and dignity,
Why, oh why, can't we?

Music and humor transcend age, gender, and geography. Deb's CDs are being used in educational settings around the world, including Israel and Japan. There are some universal truths about nursing that we just can't ignore, and just have to laugh at it. "Nursing is like the Mafia," laughs Deb. "You're in it for life—you know too much!"

Something about nurses, they never rest.
When you see one coming toward you,
You're being head to toe assessed.
It may seem as if they are passing by
Inside they've made a note:
Skin turgor, scleral color,
And that's just above your throat!
from Nurses Never Rest™ ©2000

Deb doesn't seem to rest, either. She's busy recording a sixth CD, and she also writes and illustrates a humor column for *The Journal of Perinatal Education*. She has contributed to a recently published, award-winning patient teaching guide by Mosby and has been featured on the National Public Radio Program, The Infinite Mind.

When you ask her today if she feels any more special motivating and singing to nurses, Deb laughs and says, "I don't know about 'special,' but I do know that every one of us has something to sing about! I just try hard to live the message I'm sharing."

THE BRIDGE GROUP

by Frances R. Vlasses

They placed something sacred into my hands. "You have to realize that what you heard here has never been said out loud." But even outsiders knew that this bridge group had special qualities. I had watched the group develop over the years, laughed over their escapades, and admired their commitment. The bridge group was an integral part of each of their lives.

Carol and Jane met in 1969. The youngest members of nursing service administration at Thomas Jefferson University Hospital, they had to stick together. The bridge group was formed soon after and was joined by Maureen, Marie, and Ginny. It started with no expectations in an atmosphere of total acceptance. It grew to include group travel to Portugal and the Caribbean, visits to Maureen when circumstances relocated her to Germany for six years, spa days, and the annual Blues Festival in the Poconos. On and off over the years, they even played bridge (they tell me there was a deck of cards on those Germany trips). Last year, they started keeping score. And so it continues now, a group sparkling with laughter and the rich history of stories and traditions.

They describe themselves as: Maureen, the natural caregiver; Ginny, the organizer and homebody; Jane, a peacemaker; Marie, who brings balance and perspective; and Carol, everyone's role model for how to be a good friend. Since the Jefferson days, they have never worked together. Their bond goes well beyond their jobs. They meet every six weeks, ostensibly to play bridge, if there's time, that is, after catching up on the news and someone remembers the cards. So what makes these fair-weather bridge players stay together? They just clicked, Maureen says, because of a similar philosophy of nursing and a shared, perhaps crazy, 60s notion that each could make a difference. Marie speaks of a deeper connection that exists as well. Although there is no easy way to go through life, in her experience, nurses benefit from watching patients deal with trials. They learn to disregard superficialities and form steadfast relationships. To this, the bridge group adds a sense of humor and intellectual curiosity.

Their professional lives span an impressive list of specialties, titles, and accomplishments as they provide leadership in major healthcare delivery systems and education; provide care and vitality to a retired senior community; teach and mentor young nurses, physicians, and nurse practitioners; nurse in primary care, critical care, and occupational health; and serve a diverse inner city population. Together they represent two diploma schools, four bachelor's degrees, four master's degrees, and one PhD. In the group there are five certifications as family nurse practitioner, adult nurse practitioner, and gerontologic nurse practitioner. Their combined years, as practicing nurses, span 152 years. Yes, they have influenced many lives and surely made a difference.

During the 33 years they have been together, they have seen the development of a friendship that even they themselves have difficulty verbalizing. They have seen each other through marriages, births, job changes, illnesses, empty nesting, and aging. Behind the veil of this every six-week bridge game, they have stood by and watched these transitions for and with each other, but not just as casual observers. The truth is that they have served witness to and supported each other through them all. They have been the ears that listened, the brains that problem-solved, and the hands that cared for each other. Jane says, "We are a support group for our joys and "unjoys." Yes, that is mostly what I hear in their conversation, laughter, peace, and much joy in having had each other to weather it all.

They only remember two minor disagreements over the years. Actually, I can't figure out whether they even agree to play bridge. However, this they do agree on, in Ginny's words, "These are the people I call on without reservation and sometimes before family."

They do not judge; acceptance is unconditional. They will be there, sharing an uncommon wisdom that comes from living their own lives so deeply intertwined with the mixed blessing of suffering and healing. This is a rare piece, this lifetime friendship, and they treat it with a reverence that is felt more than spoken. Marie says, "I get so much from this group and none of it has to do with bridge."

Is friendship among nurses different than other friendships? Qualities such as unconditional acceptance and timing, and the ability to be present for others and to care for each other if sick are clearly cherished in their friendship. And, as many nurses know, these same qualities mark excellence in practice. "Nursing is the bedrock of the group," says Jane. "You know that we do it for each other."

THE POWER OF PRAYER AND FRIENDSHIP: CARLA'S STORY

by Sheila Kelly Ames

This is a story of a nurse's faith and friendship in a small, rural community. It is also the story of the binding power of prayer. Carla Witzleb Hill was born on February 1, 1953, in Dixon, Illinois. In 1969, at the age of 16, she began working as a nurse aide at the KSB Hospital in Dixon. It was this experience that led Carla to seek a career in nursing.

Carla graduated from the University of Iowa Nursing Program in 1975, married her high school love, Roger, and found herself back in Dixon at the local and only hospital. The first 15 months were spent as a staff nurse in the newly formed Home Care Department. After the birth of her first daughter, she joined the Obstetrics Department.

While working in the maternity unit, she taught prenatal clinics for 10 years. In this role, she prepared numerous couples for one of the most important events of their lives, the births of their children. Carla was truly having an effect on the community.

During this time, Carla and Roger experienced two miscarriages. Carla, due to her strong faith, had always believed that each experience is given to us in order to learn and grow. While praying and healing from these losses, she became active in the local SHARE group. She became a hospital resource for parents suffering miscarriage, stillbirth, and early infant death. In this capacity, Carla reached out to numerous couples over the years. The compassion she showed to others in similar situations of grief and loss has been mentioned often, and community members value Carla's impact on their lives.

Carla and seven friends, in 1996, formed a weekly prayer group to say the Holy Rosary at St. Anne Catholic Church. Their prayers were for a dear friend who was terribly ill. Carla, a magnetic, amazing mother of six, encouraged us to pray to Mary, the Blessed Virgin. She forged us into a bond that has lasted six prayer-filled years.

We lost our wonderful friend, Ann, but realized prayers for others were a tremendous mainstay in our lives. We became even closer as friends, sharing good times and bad, celebrations and sympathies. The goodness of friends was never more evident, whether laughing or crying. Our spiritual lives grew and this growth was amazingly evident to each one of us. The rosary group was cemented in faith and friendship.

The rosary group also had an effect on Carla's spirituality. In 1997, she made a decision to become a parish nurse for St. Anne Church. She now assists with monthly blood-pressure readings after Masses, makes home visits, takes communion to the sick, assists with blood drives, and facilitates school health presentations.

In all of the post-rosary conversations over endless cups of coffee, we came to realize that Carla had taken care of every one of us after each of our babies were born, which is a total of 23. She had known us as long as our children had, touching our lives with her fine expertise and skill. In effect, she was part of all of our families. It is even more amazing that we did not realize her impact with the delivery of *all of our children* until almost 30 years later.

Carla does everything to perfection, whether it is decorating her beautiful Victorian home, caring for her family, or giving meds and advice. She also shares and spreads her spirituality. She combines all of her passions, nursing, faith, family, friendship, and community. She is the consummate nurse.

October 26, 2001, was a deciding day for Carla. At the age of 48, Carla underwent open-heart surgery. This was amazing to all of us, because she was a strong, dynamic woman who simply never stopped moving. It seemed that she was to be temporarily slowed.

Carla's mother, Betty; her husband; and her three children all pitched in when Carla arrived home from the hospital. The rosary group decided it was now time to take care of Carla. We wanted to return the many favors she had given us over the years. We gathered weekly to pray in her home, around the bed that had been moved into the living room. We fluffed pillows, brought tempting goodies, and prayed. We stopped in daily to bring meals and even became Carla's chauffeur until she was given permission to drive.

One rosary group husband, a retired judge, even did the yard clean up for Carla and Roger. But it wasn't just the rosary group that helped, it was all the people over the years that Carla had nursed and assisted in her kind way. Carla and her family were overwhelmed with the outpouring of generosity from the community. We recently celebrated her six-month recovery by praying the rosary. Prayers work wonders, and so do good friends. The community, Carla, her family, and friends all wanted her back nursing the community.

Carla is now back working in the recovery room at KSB, the same local hospital where, as a teenager, she was a nurse aide. Carla has completed her own cardiac rehabilitation and now offers her help in the Cardiac Rehab Department. As a nurse and a former rehab patient, Carla began to offer firsthand assistance to other recovering cardiac patients. Her personal experience is being used to help those in a similar situation, just as she had done before when she lost her premature babies. As a nurse, she's the best. As a prayer group member, she is a blessing. Carla blends her own life experiences and lessons into her nursing practice so she can improve care for others.

THE PRESENCE OF MICHAEL WORKING MAGIC

by Fran McGibbon

It was the fall of 1999 when I first met Michael Mullan at Hunter-Bellevue Nursing School in New York City. He was a nurse with an associate degree, returning to nursing school to pursue a baccalaureate degree. Little did we know how fortunate we were to meet and work with such an extraordinary young man. He was a young man whose simple, courageous decisions on September 11, 2001, would leave us reflecting and missing his presence for many years to come.

Michael had a wonderful presence at Hunter-Bellevue Nursing School. He challenged the faculty, embraced his student colleagues, and worked hard to achieve his goals. More vividly, I remember this rambunctious, fun-loving, mischievous guy who quite easily made our classes fun. By the way, as many firemen are, he was tall, dark, Irish, and very handsome.

Michael Mullen was not just a nurse returning to school. He was also a firefighter and a Captain in the United States Army Reserves, Nurse Corps. Michael was a member of Ladder Company 12 of the New York City Fire Department. Ladder Company 12's firehouse is located on the west side of the city, in an area known as Chelsea, which is very close to Ground Zero. On September 11, Michael had switched his day off and was working for a fellow firefighter. His company was one of the first to respond to the early reports of the World Trade Center disaster.

Michael's Ladder Company 12 was assigned to the Marriott Hotel. There brave firefighters were working as fast as they could to evacuate the building. While helping some of the hotel guests down the stairs, Michael heard a "Mayday" call on his radio. I've been told that he was on the fifth floor when he turned around and went back up to help a fellow fireman. So many times I have thought about just how close Michael was to making it out of the building alive. But we all know that it was "his" decision to go back. He was never ordered to do so, he just wanted to do what was right, to help another firefighter.

In the early hours after the fall of the Twin Towers, Michael was reported missing. I remember watching TV and seeing his mother on the news. Mrs. Mullan was recalling the story of her son's disappearance on September 11 and asking anyone with information to contact the fire department. I was shocked. This couldn't be the same Michael Mullan that I knew. It couldn't be the Hunter-Bellevue nursing student I knew. It couldn't be Michael, my friend.

The following day, while I was at work at Beth Israel Medical Center, I received a phone call from the director of Hunter-Bellevue Nursing School confirming my fears. Our fun-loving nursing student/firefighter was listed as one of many New York City firemen lost in the rubble of the collapse of the Twin Towers. Our hearts were broken, our spirits crushed. The healing and recovery from the loss of Michael has been slow. In my mind, I still see Michael rushing to class, waving in the hallway, or telling a joke. He was always ready with a joke or prank that would keep us laughing and make learning fun.

One of Michael's fellow firefighters told us the story of the time that Ladder Company 12 had responded to an automobile accident in Manhattan. A Federal Express truck had injured a pedestrian as he crossed the street. The pedestrian was not injured too badly but did require medical assistance. When the pedestrian questioned Michael about how long he would be in the emergency room, Michael responded, "Remember, it was a Federal Express truck. I guarantee it will take overnight!" This is how the guys in the firehouse remember him. He never let anything get him down. He had a special gift of finding humor even in the most difficult situations.

He was compassionate. After his death, his family received countless letters from previous patients and families he had helped. The themes of caring and kindness were evident in many of the different scenarios, from taking care of an elderly patient to calming down a scared toddler, to making an awkward adolescent feel important. This was Michael's approach to nursing. He had a healing quality and saw the need to address the emotional side of each patient.

Michael was a captain in the U.S. Army Reserves, Nurse Corps, and I was present at a memorial service they held for him in Fort Totem, New York. During the program, one of the more mature reservists, having been moved with emotion, shared with the group how Michael had made her elderly mother smile. She candidly voiced, "No one could make my mother smile. Michael made my mother smile." Her honesty and heartfelt emotion moved me as well as many others to tears. This was just another example of Michael's simple way of making others feel happy.

My personal memories of Michael are very similar to those who knew him. I teach a physical assessment class at Hunter-Bellevue Nursing School. Michael was one of my students. Or I should say Michael was one of my teachers. I have some uneasiness saying this; however, in retrospect, I think I learned much more from Michael than he learned from me. He made the class so enjoyable. He worked hard at developing his skills and was proud when he could perform with some degree of expertise. Once he had mastered a skill, he was quick to help his fellow classmates understand the concept as well. Had his fate been different, my guess is that teaching may have been an area he would have chosen and one in which he would have excelled.

I think of Michael often, but one thought continues to haunt me. When Michael was in my class, during the winter months, the nights were cold and dark when we would leave school. He would watch me from a distance walk safely to my car. Even when I objected and told him to go his own way, he would stay to make sure that I was safe. As fate would have it, I had the pleasure of speaking at Michael's funeral, and I thought it so ironic that God gave me the final opportunity to see him, my friend, HOME that day.

Michael's classmates, fellow firefighters, reservists, and teachers all loved him. He made a difference in our lives, and his presence is sadly missed. However, his memories and fun-loving, kind spirit will always live in our hearts.

Although Michael is no longer with us, his presence certainly is. When I met Michael's parents at one of his memorial services, we realized that they and my parents were from the same neighborhood in Belfast, Ireland My father was one of the chief draftsmen who assisted in designing the World Trade Center, and the original drawings are still in my mother's home. What a coincidence that Michael's fate brought him to the tragic events of the World Trade Center. One of Michael's cousins, who visited Michael's funeral, assisted my mother with tasks such as painting our home. Michael is still working magic to keep our lives connected.

THE SMILE IS IN HER EYES

by Sheila McNally

I t's Monday morning. Pretend you are checking into the ambulatory surgery unit at Rush-Presbyterian St. Luke Medical Center. It was your decision to have breast reconstruction after your mastectomy. Your husband and children said, "We love you just the way you are." Quite frankly, everyone is glad you survived your surgery and chemotherapy. It was an inner voice that pushed you toward seeking breast reconstruction. You wanted to be made whole again. You are handed a gown so you change into it. You say good-bye to your family and hop on a gurney to be pushed into an operating room. It's a different world in here. Everyone is wearing blue clothes, has his/her hair covered, and is wearing a mask. You've been here before and the memory alone makes you anxious. You meet a nurse and she says, "Hello, my name is Carrie. I will be the nurse taking care of you today." You see the smile in her eyes and you know she will do just that, take care of you.

Carrie asks you simple but important questions. What is your name? Do you know who your surgeon is? What operation do you think you are going to have done today? She engages you fully while she is gently covering you with a warm blanket. She asks you to move over to the operating table and makes sure you are comfortable as she places a pillow under your knees and a safety strap across your legs. Her eyes, her warm touch, and her gentle voice put you at ease and you know you will be alright.

You have just met Caroline Kunz, RN, CPSN, nurse clinician of the Eyes Nose and Throat and Plastic Surgery Services at her best. She is doing what she loves to do. But there's more to know about Caroline, much more.

I met Carrie over 23 years ago. Even then she was working in the operating room at Rush and was involved in the care of plastic surgery patients. She calls herself the handmaiden of the plastic surgeons. I know that everything she does in the operating room is performed in the best interest of her patients. In my mind, she epitomizes patient advocacy. She believes that surgery is a team effort as she spends her day interacting with peers, nurse managers, surgeons, residents, medical students, anesthesia personnel, surgical techs, and housekeeping staff. She is a critical participant in the team effort that helps them succeed.

Often her work occurs quietly in the background. But I know it is Carrie's preparedness and actions that affect the outcome of the surgical care given to the patients. Carrie pays meticulous attention to every aspect of the surgical theater knowing that her actions will benefit her number one responsibility, the patient. I have witnessed her planning for equipment, prostheses, supplies, and staffing for surgeries. She quietly instructs the residents on information she knows they need in order for that particular surgery to run smoothly. I am always amazed at how much information she stores in her head, regarding all the special needs of the surgeons. Carrie makes each surgeon's particular case appear like it is the most important surgical event in the world.

I would characterize Carrie as a caretaker who is always thinking of others. She demonstrates this in her everyday work. Carrie goes above the call of duty to take her show on the road. She has completed five or six medical/surgical missions in the Philippines, mostly in Mabalacat and Davao. These missions were accomplished to provide plastic surgical procedures on children with cleft lip and facial anomalies. Most of Carrie's "medical mission" trips have been self-funded. Carrie is an important member of the surgical team as she is the one who assembles the supplies and equipment necessary for the care of these patients overseas. On the road, 12-hour-plus days are the norm. Carrie always returns from these missions with a smile on her face and in her eyes. She talks about the fulfillment of taking care of these children in need. Carrie's storytelling speaks to her inner passion for providing care to patients, regardless of whether she finds herself in a "state of the art" university medical center or in an improvised "mash unit" for children in a third-world country.

THE STORY OF KARIN

by Patricia Birck

I am one of four Americans and 16 Swedes on a luxury train, riding through Africa. My husband and I are with a couple from Colorado. It quickly becomes apparent the Swedes all know each other well but go out of their way to speak English when we are present. Eating together in the dining car and spending our free time in the club car, we all eventually become friends. The stories we tell as we travel help us learn about each other. As each story is told, the African landscape passing by gives us insight into the others' personal lives. Each story told helps us learn and gain respect for each other. One of the stories has always remained fresh in my mind. It is the story of Karin. It is Karin's story that I am about to share.

I hear a heartfelt, guttural laugh—a laugh so hardy that I want to feel and laugh that way too! The laugh comes from "Kar-in," though she tells me, "just call me Karen." She introduces her husband as "Göran," but says to just call him "George." I do not know it at the time, but it is Karin's job and life to make people more comfortable. Karin is a nurse.

George (Göran) is handsome and slim, soft-spoken and subdued, with silvering hair and pale blue, kind eyes. He is a doctor. Karin is of medium height and solidly built, with shiny brown hair that frames her face from below one ear, up and straight across her forehead, and straight down to below the other ear. She has lively blue eyes that seem to be aware of all that is happening in the room. She wears a flowered magenta blouse, full blue-checkered skirt, and patterned magenta knee socks. The socks have a different theme each day. Karin is friendly, fun, open, and appealing!

Göran seems to have led a privileged life. We learn, by listening to the others, that he is a superb equestrian and an avid hunter. He and Karin met at the hospital. They have two college-age children. At dinner one night, Göran explains why he now works in the emergency room. He is unhappy with the socialist system of medicine, and this works better for him. As the patients come in, he is there to provide short-term urgent care. He takes his six weeks of vacation, races his horses, and hunts. He also travels with Karin. "It is a good life," Göran says.

But it is with pride in his voice that he tells me about Karin, who works in the oncology unit at the hospital. Few of her patients are destined to be released to enjoy happy, productive lives. Their fate is probably sealed when they arrive on her floor and yet she fills each one with hope and confidence. It is Karin who helps her patients get through the next treatment. It is Karin who remains with her patients, holding their hands, telling them that it will be okay. Göran says, "It is heart-wrenching work; each time a patient dies, Karin is devastated, feeling another defeat. But it is her work and it is her choice." We later discover that the pride he takes in Karin's nursing expertise is grounded in personal experience as well.

I notice him quietly toasting her across the table one evening. "Skoll, Karin," he says as their eyes meet. They seem to both respect and enjoy each other. Holidays are abundant in Sweden, and Göran and Karin travel a good part of the year. They do things together at home, too. "Ya," says Karin, "I go with Göran when he hunts! We take the dog and walk the forest looking for a moose. It is a good life!"

In celebration of their 25th wedding anniversary, Göran and Karin decide what they would enjoy most is to go somewhere and spend a few days alone. They accept the offer of friends to use their vacant lodge in the remote Chilean countryside. Arriving late at night after flying into Santiago and then traveling over dirt roads for hours, they realize they are quite far into the wilderness, probably about 100 kilometers from the nearest little town.

At 2:30 a.m., Göran is awakened by sounds outside the house and sees a large red stag attacking their rental car. He shouts to the stag, who gallops away into the darkness. Göran steps down from the porch to inspect any damage done to the car, when he realizes the normally shy red stag did not run back into the forest. He had hidden in the shadows. The furious animal attacks Göran, knocking him to the ground. Again, again, and again, the deer's rack enters Göran's body and is withdrawn. He can feel the tines go in through his wrist and exit his upper arm. He is sure the skin of his arm is ripped off. His stomach is being gorged. His knowledge of medicine tells him internal injuries are inevitable. His knowledge of animals tells him that the deer is so aggressive because it is in the rut (mating season). He has no chance of getting up unless the deer is distracted from the attack. With the light of the moon silhouetting the deer's face, Göran draws forth his last bit of strength, makes a fist, and pokes the deer in the eye. The deer retreats. With his very life slipping away from him, Göran manages to crawl back into the house.

Karin is having a lovely dream. Göran is calling to her, he needs her. The dream becomes a nightmare when Karin wakes and sees Göran covered in blood and sand. Seeing her husband on the edge of death, Karin puts away her anguish-she acts. She acts as a nurse. Not even asking Göran what happened, she puts him on the bed, dresses, and rushes to the car. She can still hear the stag in the back of the house as she pulls away. About a kilometer away, she happens upon the house of some Indians. Large dogs come running down the driveway. As Karin approaches the driveway dogs bark, warning her to stay

away, but she ignores them and shouts, *"paster noster,"* the very few Spanish words she knows. Karin makes herself understood to the Indians. Though they have no phone, the Indians have a radio and make contact with the authorities. Then they follow her back to the lodge and back to Göran.

Karin gives Göran steroids and other medications that she has in her handbag but knows there was no possibility of stopping all the bleeding. Convinced he will die if he loses consciousness, she feeds him spoonfuls of water, talks to him, and keeps him awake for the next three hours. As dawn approaches, an ambulance arrives with a young doctor and a nurse. Though very, very weak, Göran tells the young doctor that he must insert a needle into his right lung to release the pressure in his chest so he can breathe.

After a two-hour ambulance ride, they arrive at a town with a small clinic. Two surgeons are waiting, and Karin watches as they open Göran's abdomen and lift out his intestines to start the repairs. Göran had two punctured lungs and over 28 perforations from the stag's antlers. In the afternoon, along with one of the doctors, they board a small airplane and are flown to a large hospital in Santiago, where Göran is admitted to the intensive care unit for three weeks. Göran does recover with the loving, nursing care of his wife Karin.

Should you ever pass over the Oresundsbro Bridge between Sweden and Denmark, it is possible that you will meet Karin. She works at the information desk and now helps travelers. No longer at the hospital, she is still caring for others in a different way, a trait that will always be with her because she is a *nurse* and she is *Karin*. Although her job has changed, her life has not changed. She is still making people feel comfortable.

TRAVEL NURSE ON A MISSION

by Lori L. Fischer

They say there are no atheists in hospitals. When people are dying, everyone believes in something. When all hope is lost, patients turn to a higher power for assistance. Sometimes they turn to a travel nurse like Robert Silvis.

Bob Silvis was born the youngest of four children in Pittsburgh, Pennsylvania. Even as a child, he enjoyed helping people. His parents were ordinary people. His mom was a housewife, his dad was a mechanic. He looked up to his older brother who became a doctor and to his sister who became a nurse. And it was his family, especially his brother and sister, who would influence his life in ways he could not imagine.

Bob was a medic in the U.S. Army Research Unit at Ft. Dietrich, Maryland. Bob tried to walk away from the medical profession when his assignment was complete. He was young and newly married, and had three children by the age of 21. Bob spent the next 10 years trying to find himself. He worked in factories and fast-food establishments. He focused on supporting his three children. Bob eventually became a single dad at age 29, surviving paycheck to paycheck.

Bob's career path was meaningless and unfulfilling. Nursing was calling him. When Bob was 32, his brother offered to fulfill his little brother's dream. He made it possible for Bob to attend nursing school. His brother paid Bob's rent and supported him and his children. Bob was finally ready to have a career that would involve him physically, mentally, spiritually, and socially. He was desperate to find himself, and nursing could define his character and give him a title with respect and honor. While in school, Bob was not always sure that nursing was his vocation. However, his family *did* know nursing was for Bob. After Bob graduated from nursing school, his family members said, "You have finally arrived in a career you can embrace, and you are a natural as a nurse."

Bob has been a nurse for seven years. He recognizes being a male nurse presents challenges and opportunities. He is also aware he often provides care to the more difficult patients.

Bob was recently assigned a terminally ill patient who was also a nurse. She was a difficult patient who conspired to get her nurse peers in trouble. She would repeatedly ring the buzzer, file complaints, and lash out at anyone who would cross her path. She was lost, angry, frightened, and taking it out on the world, especially her caretakers. Through caring and dialogue, Bob was able to understand her behavior and gain her trust. He restored peace in her life through his words of inspiration and comfort.

Bob aids in the healing process of all his patients. His mission is to confront difficult situations and embrace tragedy with a caring approach. Bob bonds patients with their families and friends when it is patients' time to leave this earth. His nursing work is based upon compassion, not a paycheck. He quickly gains the admiration of his patients, peers, and managers as they see this humanitarian at work.

Bob also does part-time nursing through an agency on the side while working as a traveling nurse. His agency position once sent him to a drug and alcohol rehab floor. Bob was scared to death because he had no prior experience in this nursing area. However, when Bob walked through the door, he was no longer afraid; he was sad with a heavy heart. The patients were docile, lost souls trying to get through the day. At that point, Bob realized that he could not have arrived at this point had he not turned his life around at age 32.

While at the rehab unit, Bob cared for a 28-year-old female patient who had become addicted to drugs while in nursing school. She tested positive for MRSA (methicillin-resistant staphylococcus aureus) and had sores all over her body. She did not have the money or insurance to visit an appropriate doctor for her condition so Bob called an infectious disease specialist. The doctor was more than willing to donate his time and expertise for a fellow clinician. This is an example of how Bob wants all of his patients to have the best care possible.

Bob's initial call to me was after the September 11 tragedy. I was the staffing coordinator for a traveling nurse agency at the time, and he was anxious to head to the northeast and help the burn victims, since burn patients were his specialty. I was able to get him as far as Maryland. Bob also responded to one of my e-mails regarding a nurse who had lost everything in a fire. The nurse, Barbara, lived in Atlanta, Georgia. Bob and his wife, Linda, graciously ordered "scrubs" for the nurse and mailed them to her. Barbara was overjoyed and very appreciative of their help. This kind of spontaneous help is an example of what Bob loves to do. He seeks opportunities to help others both inside and outside his job.

Bob has found harmony in nursing. He has found his calling and with his wife is currently on his way to Alaska to work his nursing magic. He continues to spread the word of God by "love thy neighbor," and "do unto others as you would have them do unto you." This is Bob's philosophy and mission in life, and it is certainly his philosophy of nursing.

Bob has found harmony in nursing. He has found his calling and with his wife is currently on his way to Alaska to work his nursing magic. He continues to spread the word of God by "love thy neighbor," and "do unto others as you would have them do unto you." This is Bob's philosophy and mission in life, and it is certainly his philosophy of nursing.

WENDY'S LEGACY

by Loretta Jean Aiken

Wendy Ellen Gross was my friend for three decades. We worked years of night shifts in ICU together. She was funny (and a lot of fun), a great nurse, and smart. She was the essence of *Entertainment Tonight* on the graveyard shift. Staff from many departments came to Wendy for a laugh, for a pat on the back, or to ask her opinion about china, crystal, or some far-off, exotic place. She was the unit "expert on everything" (EOE). She referred to herself as the "EOE in Residence."

Everyone loved Wendy. The staff, management, and patients loved her. On more than one occasion, Wendy was asked to speak at the funeral of a special patient. On especially hard nights, Wendy would ask me, "Who will be there to take care of me when I am old and sick?" I would laugh and make wild promises of good care when her time came.

Four months after Wendy's 50th birthday, she seemed healthy one minute and almost dead the next. She had a massive vaginal bleed. I knew in my heart, from the moment it happened, that something was terribly wrong. Her diagnosis of cancer was grim, her prognosis deadly, and her life expectancy very limited. But Wendy took on her cancer like everything else in her life.

Even though her daily living revolved around surgery after surgery, multiple bouts of chemotherapy, many blood transfusions, nausea, hair loss, and countless hours of agony, she always found something to laugh about. She held court on the oncology unit and carried on life in her usual manner. She gave love advice to young physicians, encouraged and mentored less experienced nurses who cared for her, and supported other patients and families. She entertained the staff with tales of travels and comic events from her 30-year nursing career. And through it all, she never asked, "Who will take care of me?" She didn't have to.

From the time of Wendy's diagnosis, the phone rang off the hook. Nurses she had worked with during those 30 years flocked to help her. Friends gathered on the unit and let Wendy entertain them about the trials and tribulations of "patient-hood" or anything else that suited her sense of humor. The nurses invited us to share and participate in her hospital experience. We cried together during set-backs and sagging spells, and celebrated the day she was able to walk again and the day her dog came to visit.

Nurses kept vigils at her bedside when she was weak and confused and pulled at her lines. Nurses bathed her, did her nails, fed her, and told her little tidbits of gossip to keep her entertained. They cooked, bought groceries, walked her dog, weeded her garden, and reminisced with her about old times. Other nurses wrote cards, brought flowers, sent teddy bears and stuffed animals, and bought outrageous Dolly Parton wigs for special visits from previous bosses, former boyfriends, and patients she had cared for.

It was nurses who helped Wendy through intravenous therapy, dressing changes, paramedic visits in the middle of the night, temperatures, sepsis, hemorrhages, and nasogastric feedings. But it was Wendy who helped the nurses around her deal with their feelings of frustration, helplessness, and hopelessness. Wendy believed that for everything in life there was a purpose and somehow she was exactly where she was supposed to be, doing what she was supposed to be doing. We all went to comfort Wendy. Instead, she comforted us.

Wendy fought cancer for a little over a year, but finally nothing could stop the disease. She lived until the springtime, when nature was renewing itself with flowers and beauty. She knew that we could make it without her.

And still, the nurses were there. Nurses planned her wake, catered at her funeral, talked about the many good deeds she had done over her nursing career, and sprinkled her ashes in the nature park she loved so well. Wendy's wealth was the number of people who were so faithful in caring for her. Her joy was life and the patients she cared for so dearly. There will never be another Wendy, and I will never laugh with anyone as much as I did with her.

Now, sometimes after long, weary shifts on the ICU, I'll ask myself, "Who will care for me when I'm frail and helpless?" But then I smile, because I already know the answer. There will be *nurses* who will do for me what I have done for others. It was *Wendy's* legacy, and I know it will be *mine,* too.

PART IV

NURSES DEFINING THEMSELVES THROUGH PATIENTS' STORIES

A NURSE'S PERSPECTIVE

by Katherine (Katie) Koehn

I've been an oncology nurse only a short time and have never met anyone like Scott. Many people found him to be difficult and demanding, yet somehow we formed a bond because of his aggressive disease and a failed bone marrow transplant. Scott had numerous admissions to our facility. Leukemia was consuming his short life, and during the last few weeks of his life, I was privileged to spend a lot of quality time with him.

At the age of 37, Scott had lived a varied and spicy life. His body had interesting and comical tattoos, such as ruby red lips on his upper right arm. We loved to kiss him there and he loved it as well. Somehow we knew that this was his way of allowing us to become closer to him. He reveled in the stories about his "wild" behavior that both his mother and brother shared with us during his long days of hospitalization.

One of our best days together occurred when the doctor instructed me to remove his central line because it became infected due to his severe neutropenic state. He was also continually bleeding due to his severe thrombocytopenia. After a thorough physical assessment, which revealed continued bleeding from numerous sites on his body and severely depleted blood counts, I began the task of his physical care. Another staff member and I spent most of the morning with him, trying to clean him up, turning his frail, wasted body side to side to remove sheets covered with his blood. Scott could hardly open his eyes, but his other senses were very intact, as he continually asked me to hold him, begging me not to let him go. "Please don't hurt me," he cried, "you know I'm trying not to be a baby." He knew how perilous his condition was and this was definitely a man not ready to leave his world.

The actual removal of the central line caused a projectile stream of blood to leap from his open wound. Both my nurse friend and I thought that this was Scott's moment to leave us. Scott kept asking

us, "What's wrong? Am I bleeding?" After a quick assessment of his vital signs, we applied constant direct pressure over the exit site. We constantly talked to Scott and told him exactly what we were doing and why we were doing it. Keeping him posted was very important and allowed us the opportunity to give him honest and realistic feedback. We never thought his clotting factors were sufficient to allow us to remove our pressure dressings (our hands) and the carefully placed sandbag but, as always, he surprised us.

As we finished his care and were getting ready to leave the room, he asked me to stay with him awhile. I sat at his bedside, holding his 37-year-old hand, and cried with him. He asked about my baby and since it was almost Halloween, I told him about my one-year-old daughter, Emily, being dressed up as a flower princess. He loved hearing stories about my "normal" life. A veteran nurse came in to provide moral support to both Scott and me. We asked Scott what his best memories were. He replied they were those memories involving music. Since Scott loved music and the music business, we decided that his heaven would be filled with wonderful music. He then proceeded to name singers neither one of us had ever heard of but for Scott those were his angels. This was the only time he ever allowed himself to speak of heaven and his death. As I finally left his room that day, eyes swollen and heart breaking, he thanked me for taking care of him. I was overcome with the incredible sense of grace this man possessed, taking time from his suffering to thank me for what I did.

Scott dealt with his disease not unlike I would. He had little time for anyone not willing to participate in his goal to reach Texas. Time after time, he would be admitted for sepsis or neutropenia, looking more and more wasted with blood counts dangerously low. Time after time, he talked about getting well enough to go. He badgered his physicians, and I spent many mornings standing at the nursing station discussing a strategy to divert his attention away from the inevitable question, "When can I go to Texas?" Using skills I did not know I had, I supported him by telling him the truth about his current status. "Your counts have to come up. You have to stop bleeding, and you have to be able to make the plane trip" were all things I told him in honesty. His primary physician's nurse practitioner became skilled in the techniques of evasion as well, as he pummeled her with questions on her daily rounds.

Sadly, that day never came for Scott. He never made it to Texas. But in the last two weeks of his life, he did get to sit by his pool, dangle his feet in the water, and play with his dogs. He got to meet my baby and my husband. I got to meet his beloved animals. His sense of humor was evident all around his house, especially as he showed me his stick dog that stood guard on his front porch.

As oncology nurses, we constantly wrestle with the issues of acceptance. Patients move through various stages during their treatments. Helping patients in their process through this painful path is always difficult, and in my short years as an oncology nurse, I continually feel challenged by how to do it best. Scott had great difficulty admitting that he was not winning the war against his disease. He never wanted to discuss dying and his every effort was focused on "what can I do next?" He constantly talked about going to Dr. Anderson for "a miracle." He sought reassurance from the staff caring for him and from me specifically about his next hope, his dream of a "miracle cure in Texas." What he wanted was a guarantee that there was something more out there, just another few months or weeks to live.

I learned a great deal from caring for Scott. I learned that sometimes patients never give up and are never ready to meet the inevitability of their deaths. As prepared for that certainty as oncology nurses are, our patients don't always share that vision. Helping patients on their own terms is a valuable lesson for us all. I know that in providing Scott with an honest assessment of his current status, I never robbed him of his hope. I learned that it was okay for me to help Scott focus on his goal. I learned that it's great to celebrate the little things in life. From dangling my feet in the water to kissing my baby, Scott taught me that seemingly small things enable all of us to go the distance. As a nurse and human being, I thank Scott for all the lessons he gave me that I can now share with other nurses and patients.

HEY DOT, THEY TOOK THE RESPIRATOR OUT OF THE ROOM!

by Donna Horrocks

"Hey Dot, they took the respirator out of the room!" Talking that way to Dottie was needed. Normalcy, or just a hint of it, would often be the only thing that would bring Dot back from wherever she went in her mind. Sometimes, just the presence of her family would make her alert again. But most of the time it was left to us, the nurses. When Dottie's family was unable to bring back her sense of humor, we became the ones who could. Perhaps if she were part of our own families, it might have been different.

Incapacitating, life-threatening, and debilitating—these were the words that explained Dottie. We knew the diagnosis and the results. Her family had only the most rudimentary knowledge of what was wrong with her. Before coming to the hospital, Dottie had lived at home "bed to chair" for years. She never had the chance to tell us herself. Her family said that she had enjoyed life with her loved ones, but that came to an end when one night she had respiratory failure and was "intubated in the emergency room on arrival."

After seven weeks in the intensive care unit, still on the ventilator, we were not able to know Dottie as her family did. What we did know of her was expressed not in words, but in actions and silent behavior. Every nurse who has dealt with a seriously ill patient knows of these subtle communications, the mannerisms, the gestures, and the sadness. What you see in their eyes is the fear of being alone.

Whether it is the apprehension of breathlessness on a patient's face, or the "needing one more thing look" before you leave the patient's room, you know it is all about fear. For me, it was easy to recognize. I lived with that look for years. One of my parents suffered with chronic lung disease. So with Dottie, it was easy.

Everyone was reluctant to remove the respirator from Dottie. We all made excuses. I hoped for a bit of the communication from Dottie. I learned later of the comfort Dottie felt with the cycling of the ventilator. She told me as long as she heard the cycling, she could sleep. Ironically, it was when we removed the respirator that she became afraid. I almost knew what she meant. At home, as long as the oxygen concentrator was humming, there was little fear for my mom or me.

The day we decided Dottie no longer needed life support was a tough day. Naturally, she had been doing well and she met "all of the criteria for removal." But there was more. Dottie had decided not to be placed back on the ventilator if her lungs failed again. For Dottie, it was an easy decision to make. With Dottie's words of "not another ventilator," I was reminded of my mom and how difficult the day was when she told me she was too tired to go on and wanted no pacemaker or respirator.

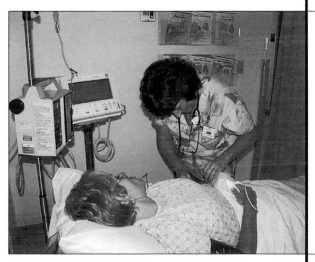

During the few days that we kept Dottie in ICU, we chatted as
much as Dottie wanted or could without feeling breathless. All the
nurses sensed there would be a loss on the day she would be transferred out of our unit.

Packing up Dottie was not easy; isolation equipment, oxygen stores,
and many, many supplies had been brought into her room and never
taken out. The equipment left first. That provided me with time to
be with my friend, Dottie. We laughed about the time she told her
husband that she was moving in with me when she got better.
Like so many nurses, I understood the look she gave me when she
had to leave.

Then it was serious. We both needed reassurance. Dottie and I, at
the same time, took each other's hand. I said it again, a little quieter
this time, "Hey Dot, they took the respirator out of the room."

*Like so many nurses, I understood
the look she gave me when
she had to leave.*

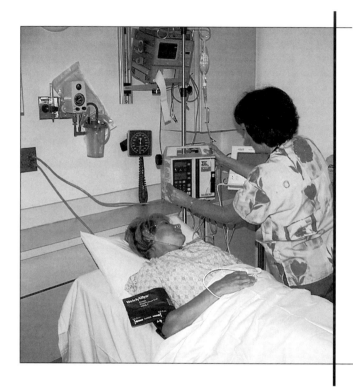

JULIA'S GIFT

by Carole Leomporra

t was the 1960s and I wanted to be a nurse. I wanted to be a nurse to help people. I had been a candy striper at ages 14 and 15 and a nurse aide at 16 and 17. Graduating from high school in 1966, I was off to the best nursing school in the country. Yes, I was off to be a nurse to help people. What I didn't know at age 18 was that I was going to be a nurse to help patients as well as a nurse who learned from patients.

After graduating from Los Angeles County-USC School of Nursing, my first two years as a registered nurse were spent in a huge county hospital in Los Angeles County-USC Medical Center. I worked on a neurosurgical unit and then the locked psychiatric unit.

I wasn't too sure that I was helping people though, especially on the locked psychiatric unit. I practiced nursing in a professional manner and was constantly amazed at what the brain could do to people. I wasn't quite sure that psychiatric nursing was my calling, and as it turned out, I worked on the unit for only a year.

My story about Julia begins while I was working at Sloan Kettering Hospital for Cancer and Allied Diseases. Yes, I moved from one coast to the other. We had an all-RN staff and I was oriented and reoriented to the philosophy of caring for surgical patients who were dying from cancer. I had never worked on an oncology unit and never nursed in a setting like Sloan Kettering. This was a hospital of hope, peacefulness, caring, loving, and being with patients. This is where I learned "to learn" from my patients.

I was a young registered nurse, living in Manhattan, working the evening shift, and engaged. I had it all! I loved my life and my job. I was excited about getting married and moving to Malaysia.

I came to work each day full of life, excited to be with my patients, thoughtful in my care, and interested in their stories and their families. I met many wonderful people. I cried with patients and hugged family members. Once again, I was seeing and feeling it all. There was something very different about working with cancer patients at Sloan Kettering. It was such a hopeful environment, a realistic hospital where honesty was prevalent, and patients were central to their care.

As a 23-year-old woman, I really connected with one of my patients. Her name was Julia. She was 25, a professional woman with a large, caring family. Her mother and many aunts came in every evening to be with her. They always laughed with Julia and, after getting to know me, included me in their bedside discussions. These were discussions about life, about their lives, about Julia's life, and about my life.

Coming to work and visiting with Julia were very special to me. We became friends and learned that we had much in common. You see, Julia was engaged to be married just eight months before I met her. She had a successful career, was in love, and had a future, just like me!

As it turned out,
this was to be Julia's
wedding night attire.

Well, not exactly like me. Julia was a patient at Sloan Kettering. She was dying because of a brain tumor. She wore brightly colored hair bandannas, pretty nail polish, and a wonderful smile on her face, with make-up specially applied by her aunts and sometimes by me. Julia would tell me about her former fiancé, the plans they made together, and the experience she had when he left her. Yes, he walked away from their love when Julia's brain tumor was inoperable and she did not have long to live.

My time at Sloan Kettering was soon coming to an end. The staff was starting to have parties for me, and I was packing to leave for Miami where I would get married. I would sit and share my evenings after work with Julia. She was so excited for my plans and me. We would laugh and cry together. She would talk about my future. She would help me decide which clothes to wear for my special occasions. She would give me tips for my hair and make-up. She would ask me how I spent my days off. Julia was interested and cared.

The date of our wedding was moved up due to my fiancé's work schedule. I barely had time to buy a wedding dress and certainly never thought about my wedding night bedroom attire. I had so much to do. I had no family around, just a couple of good friends, but still so much to do. During my last few days at work, Julia asked me about my nightgown for my wedding night. "Oh Julia, I've not even thought about it."

I was distributing the 6:00 p.m. medications to my patients. Julia was weak, very frail, and surrounded by her mother and two of her loving aunts. They called me over to Julia's bed, gave me a hug, and asked me to sit down by Julia's side. Julia was handed a box by one of her aunts. She took the box, wrapped with wedding paper, and handed it to me. "Take this, Carole. I want you to have it." I graciously opened the box and fumbled for the right words when I saw its contents. Julia was giving me a beautiful white silk nightgown with a matching robe for my wedding night. As it turned out, this was to be Julia's wedding night attire.

It is now 31 years later, and I am married to the same man and planning to reenter nursing, once again to learn from my patients. I am writing about Julia's gift to me. I sit looking at the beautiful nightgown and robe that Julia gave me. I share the story with our daughters, now 17 and 20. I share the goodness of people like Julia with them. As they ponder their future, wondering what life will be like for them, I remind them to always remember Julia.

MICHAEL FINDS A FAMILY: A FAMILY OF STAFF NURSES

by Rebecca Caldwell

The mission of Bon Secours Health System is to bring compassion to healthcare and to be good help to those in need, especially the poor and dying.

These are the words that decorate the walls of St. Francis Hospital in Greenville, South Carolina. Little did the eighth floor staff nurses realize the impact of these words until one Christmas season.

Michael was a 30-year-old patient on the eighth floor who had various end-stage diseases, including renal disease. He also had been diagnosed as HIV-positive and had a brain mass. From time to time, he had the mentality of a young child.

The staff's struggles started when there was no place for Michael to go when he was to be discharged. He was unable to stay alone and had been abandoned by his family. Because of his complex medical needs, it took more than four months to find a facility that would accommodate his needs. During the wait to find him a home, Michael became more than just a patient; he became part of the St. Francis family.

Michael participated in all the nursing unit's celebrations and holiday events. He attended the staff parties or decorated the unit during different holiday seasons, including the Christmas tree. Michael was so full of love and compassion that he stole the hearts of all who met him. Nurses throughout the hospital got to know him. They would visit him, bring him goodies, and take him to the hospital cafeteria to eat. The staff truly "adopted" Michael.

One day, a placement was found for Michael. He was elated to have a "new home." The first thing Michael did was go to the gift shop at the hospital where he found a rose to give to his social worker, Laura, as a thank you to her for finding his new home. Michael had a large going-away party that was filled with many gifts and tears. To help with his transition to his home, Heather, a staff nurse, bought him rugs, pictures, and plants. Heather felt that it was important for Michael to have a "homey" room.

Soon after Michael's departure from St. Francis, the eighth floor staff received a call from a local hospital. Michael was in the emergency department and was very upset. The emergency room staff didn't know Michael's history, so he kept asking them to call our unit. After they did, Heather went to the hospital to reassure and calm Michael. She was able to get Michael back to his "home" facility without another hospitalization.

At Christmas, the nursing staff decided to focus its annual project on Michael. The nurses and staff began buying gifts, clothes, plants, and other items for his new "home." Then, a week before Christmas, Michael was readmitted to St. Francis. Shortly thereafter, his family decided to stop his dialysis. The staff struggled with many emotions but decided to make Michael's last days not only the best for him, but also memorable for themselves.

Fearful of his limited time, the staff celebrated Christmas early for Michael. During this same time, Michael decided he wanted to rededicate his life to Christ So he was re-baptized in the chapel, and the staff made it a "day to remember." After Michael's Christmas celebration and baptism, he was transferred to another unit for terminal care. But he continued to visit our floor daily.

Michael died peacefully shortly after his transfer. The staff still share Michael's stories and memories. He touched so many lives; he touched so many of the nurses' lives. Looking back, staff realize, in the end, Michael was "at home" in St. Francis Hospital with the family of nurses who cared for him.

NOBODY

by Sarah Ann Johnson

"Not again," I said in exasperation, eyeing the bird's nest at my feet. It had once again fallen from its branch of the magnolia tree that hung over the walkway. My morning routine was such that anything requiring attention before driving to the hospital usually had to wait. But for me, this situation was an emergency. As a child, I was always told if a human touched a nest, a baby bird, or an unhatched egg, the mama bird would abandon it, never to return. I had never taken the time to find out whether this was true or simply a myth, but I wasn't taking any chances. After throwing my purse and lunch bag into the back seat of the car, I dragged an old ladder to the tree and went to the garage to grab the box of latex gloves. To complicate matters, I accidentally knocked down three cans of spray paint that rolled into the end of my rose garden where nothing ever grew. Ignoring the cans for the time being, I carefully put the gloves on without touching the outsides. "It's a good thing I got up early," I said to myself, gently scooping up the nest and placing it on the thickest part of the branch. I tossed the gloves in the trash bin, returned the ladder to the garage, and returned the paint cans to their original position. I backed out of the garage and headed toward the usual "hurry up and wait" traffic.

When I reached the hospital, I whipped into the first parking space I saw and ran inside. I punched the time clock with exactly one minute to spare. My relief at this accomplishment was only temporary. The chaos in the emergency room told me that there would be no shift change report and probably no lunch break.

While standing on the edge of a rolling stretcher and doing chest compressions on an elderly woman, the charge nurse yelled out, "All I can say is jump in and do the best you can." As I tossed my purse into the locker and my lunch into the refrigerator, I took a deep breath and said to myself out loud, "Here we go." Grabbing the next patient chart in the rack, I made my way to the first examination room.

I opened the door to find a nine-year-old boy sitting on the stretcher. He was holding a small, pitiful-looking potted plant, which was actually just a small sprig in an old plastic butter container. "Hello," he said cheerfully. "Well, hello. Whose child are you?" I asked, looking around for a parent. His cheerful smile faded just enough for me to notice. "They say I'm nobody, but you can keep me if ya want. Can I use that sink and put water on my plant?"

"Sure you can," I replied. "Where is your mother?" "I don't got none," he said. "That's kinda why I'm nobody, but you can be her if you wanna. Do ya already got kids? They say ya can keep me longer if ya don't got no kids already."

I had no words. Thankfully I was spared when the conversation was interrupted by a social worker who entered the room. She never did call him by name. "He was climbing a fence at his foster parents' house and fell," she said. "He has a cut on his side."

"Let me see," I said, raising his torn shirt to reveal an abdominal laceration. As I pulled the shirt over his head, small bead-like objects that had been in his shirt pocket flew in my face and hair, settling in the room like confetti. "What on earth is that stuff?" I asked.

"Them's seeds," he said. "Ain't ya never planted no seeds before?" "No," I said, eyeing his laceration. "I've never been too good at growing things. But the people I bought my house from left a rose garden."

His wound was too superficial to cause any permanent damage, yet definitely in need of stitches. I couldn't help but notice how badly the child smelled. His brown hair was matted and he looked as though he had not bathed in at least a month. Any part of him that touched the white sheet of the stretcher left a dirt mark. The child laughed delightfully and occasionally winced as I irrigated the wound with saline. "This must be how flowers feel when they get watered," I said as he continued to squeal.

I set up a suture tray next to the stretcher. He promised not to touch it and gritted his teeth as the physician numbed the wound. To distract the child, I asked about his plant. "That plant is my friend," he said. "I growed it from when it was little. I cut it off a bigger one. It's the only thing they let me take with me."

The physician gave me the "ER glance," that two-second, emotionless stare of support we give each other to cope with situations when we feel helpless. The stare is generally followed by stoic professionalism on the outside that masks the tears dripping down our insides.

After the suturing was complete, I dressed the wound and went to the donation closet to find a shirt. I returned to the room with a blue designer sports shirt that had never been worn. I left it in its package and let the child open it. It was like I had handed him a bucket of candy. He hugged me and his smell stayed on my scrubs for the remainder of the shift. I didn't try to bathe him because there were too many emergent cases that day but I remember wishing I

had. When the child left with the social worker, he was wearing the dirty shirt and was carrying the new one. Don't you like it?" I asked as he passed the nursing station. "Oh yes. It's the bestest one I ever got. I'm savin it for special times, like birthday parties," he replied, smiling, clutching his prize. "That's a really good idea," I said.

He left the emergency room with the social worker. When I went to clean the room, he had left a note written on a piece of paper towel, "Dear Nurse Shara, Thank you for my favorit shirt." He left me his plant. Like the rules in most hospitals, it was against policy to accept gifts from patients, but he looked so happy when he left. Tracking him down to return this pitiful sprig of a plant in an old butter tub simply wasn't what he needed. I took the plant home and planted it in the corner of the rose garden where nothing ever grew.

One week later, the lifeless body of the child was transported back to the emergency room. A car had struck him after he had climbed a fence and ran away from his new foster home. I bathed the child and folded his favorite shirt. I knew then my suppressed grief only scratched the surface of what a mother feels when she loses a child. It is not professional to become attached to a patient, but my humanity overrode my professionalism at that moment. In the silence of the morgue room, somebody grieved for nobody.

In the spring of that year, pink azaleas bloomed in the corner of my rose garden where nothing ever grew. They were so beautiful, so bright, and so much like their previous owner. They too smiled through the darkness, dodging rocks and thorns along the way. And like him, they climbed, running wildly as they grew with dirt-covered faces toward the sun, until they finally found their place among the roses.

THE MANY FACES OF COURAGE
by Diane Scheb

iane Scheb is the acute pain program coordinator and clinical nurse specialist at the Sarasota Memorial Hospital in Sarasota, Florida. She directs the clinical activities of the interdisciplinary Acute Pain Service at the hospital. She became interested and passionate about pain management because of the suffering encountered by her patients. She writes, "I feel so proud of what has been accomplished here and humbled by the human experience of unrelieved pain due to surgery, disease, or trauma. It is truly a privilege to do what I do. It feels like God's work."

Diane's three stories are the ultimate examples of nurses' daily walk with suffering. Diane's writing takes you into the myriad emotions nurses experience as they walk this walk. Their pain, frustration, compassion, strength, and courage are evident in these stories.

Death Be Not Proud

"Could I please go with you?" The freckle-faced, pigtailed 10-year-old little girl looked up pleadingly at me. "I don't want to stay here anymore." I couldn't say that I blamed her as my eyes slowly took in the now familiar sight. An almost lifeless body lay in the hospital bed. At 80 pounds, bald, cachectic, clutching her right chest, grimacing and groaning with every intake of breath, Jane looked like a concentration camp victim. Breathing had become a laborious, intense chore. The freckled face little girl was the daughter of this suffering woman. Clearly, both individuals had had enough. "Of course," I said, "come with me. I need to make pain rounds. You can be my assistant and help patients feel better." "Maybe," she said. "Could you be my mom just for today?" "Absolutely," I said. "You know that my mom is probably going to die today. She is very sick, and I'm sad that she hurts so much."

I was more than sad that she hurt so badly. I was frustrated and angry. Working in the Acute Pain Service, our job is to provide approved medical protocols to relieve hospitalized patients' pain. There had been so many positive pain outcomes with other patients. Yet with this 43-year-old terminal cancer patient, I felt that we had failed.

I met her in January. I had been told that the operating room was totally silent when her thoracotomy was performed. Never before had anyone seen such internal ravaging of functional tissue. The surgeon was subdued and stunned. The patient was so young and had such a young child. The pictures in the chart were the visual descriptors of what could not be described in words. There was extensive malignant disease around the lung and into the chest wall itself. The pain in her chest and difficulty with breathing was the external manifestation of what was inside her body.

In terms of advocacy and pain management, we had done everything that we knew to alleviate her pain and anguish. She had a huge intravenous narcotic infusion. She had an epidural with both narcotic and local anesthetics to block out the horrendous, torturous pressure in her chest. And at the end, she even had an Ativan drip to take away the anxiety of not being able to breathe. And yet, she still struggled and moaned almost to the very end.

So the question is, "Why?" Why did someone have to suffer so much and go through so much pain and agony? There is no answer to that question. It's like asking where was God at Auschwitz.

And yet, incredible good came from this tragedy. Consider the events of September 11 where, in the face of disaster, heroes arose from the clutter and debris to save lives and sustain souls. Think of the firefighters raising the flag. That was America at its best. So, too, this same phenomenon happened in that tiny hospital room. And this time, the heroes were caring nurses and doctors, determined individuals, who stepped up to the imaginary plate in the face of a hard ball, swung, made contact, and hit a home run.

Consider that:
- A pain management physician came in on his own time to place the epidural. He made himself available 24/7 for consultation and pain medication prescribing.
- A group of young post-surgical nurses, who had never cared for a terminally ill hospice patient, gave of themselves and offered care, support, concern, and effort to this patient and her family. Their dedication and compassion sustained a distraught family through a very difficult ordeal.
- A week where the acute pain beeper was eerily quiet. The other "problem patients" paled in comparison to what we were dealing with here. It almost seemed to be a spiritual sign that we were in the right place at the right time and doing the right thing.
- A family, formerly distant and not in touch with one another, showed that they could pull together and finally sat together in that hospital room showing that, in the end, family matters most and that courage and strength can be drawn from another's presence.
- Finally, the "reception" that Mandy and I received from hospital staff, physicians, and patients as we made rounds. Smiles, handshakes, and compliments about what a pretty little girl she was and how helpful she was as my pain assistant. No one asked any questions about what a 10-year-old child in shorts and a tee shirt was doing in the ICU. It was Mandy that pointed out the sign on the ICU door that clearly stated no one under 12 was allowed to enter. I said that, for today, it was okay. For that day, ANYTHING was okay.

"Can you just put my mom to sleep like we did our dog last summer?" "No," I said. "That is not what we do. But I promise that we will do everything we can to make your mom comfortable and her journey peaceful." And just as nature never extinguishes itself, so too, in the hours to come, she was transformed. Her body gave up and the horrendous breathing stopped. She finally looked peaceful and serene. All the heroes breathed their own sigh of relief. And they should marvel and be appropriately recognized for their contribution to this effort.

Special thanks to these heroes: Dr. Erb, Dr. Sarkis, Dr. Stephenson, Dr. Hoefer, Dr. Hautamaki, Tara Stolpe, Sara Anthony, RN, Stacy Walfe, RN, Holly Ernst, RN, Elizabeth Bornstein, ICM, Steve Appelbaum, Pharmacy, Dave Jungst, Pharmacy, and the Acute Pain Service nurses. Our heartfelt thanks also go out to Sue Shkrab, who cared for the caregivers—she is an unsung hero.

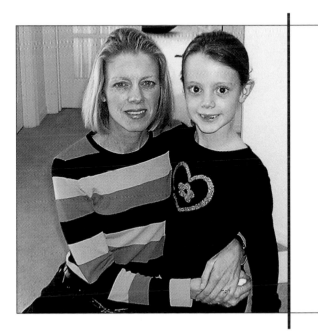

A Picture's Worth A Thousand Words

Her emergency room record listed symptoms of breathlessness and mild back pain. Her wallet held little money and the pictures of the joy of her life, her nine-year-old son. Batteries of tests, a respiratory arrest, a diagnosis of metastatic cancer, and, two weeks later, this 35-year-old woman would be dying in an ICU unit. In her hand would be the 3 × 5 school picture of her son. Unrelentless pain had taken over her body.

And that is when I met her. My eyes slowly took in the sight. Her form was almost lifeless except for intense difficult breathing. Her brow was diaphoretic; her face was pale and ashen. Her eyes were wide with fear. A large, obtrusive C-PAP mask was taped to her face to force air into her diseased lungs. Her body was rigid with pain. Her left hand, clenched tight, held the precious picture of her son. Her right hand held mine. This 35-year-old woman looked into my eyes and whispered, "Help me."

I looked into those terrified eyes and something inside of me ignited. I knew that this woman, dying of metastatic cancer, could be more comfortable. I also had the strongest feeling that this woman's hours were limited. Practically sprinting to the oncology unit, I collaborated with her oncologist. Tearfully, he explained that this situation had shocked everyone. She was so young with such a bad prognosis and with so little warning. We agreed on a pain management plan, and I called the orders over to the ICU.

Two hours later, I rechecked her. There was a marked change. Her respirations were 44/minute and she looked exhausted and with a higher pain intensity than previously. I asked her if the pain was any better. She shook her head and squeezed my hand and said, "I'll be okay." My fears were materializing. This woman was going to die today. I increased the narcotics and gave encouragement to her primary nurse, who was a true angel. Throughout this most difficult day, Nancy, her nurse, toiled to help the woman and then her family through the dying process. I was touched by her empathy and compassion.

A few hours later, her son arrived with a card for his mother. Bravely, he walked past us and into his mother's room. His dad was waiting there. Both man and child lay on the ICU bed, arms around the woman they both loved. It was one of the saddest sights I have ever seen.

And, afterwards, she smiled at me for the first time. The pain was gone. Her face was relaxed, the breathing easier. She was able to move her body in bed now. She still clutched the picture of her son. I knew that I had made a difference that day. . . .

And that's what it's all about. That is why nursing is a rewarding and challenging profession. We have the privilege of seeing humanity in its greatest hours of need. Through our care, concern, and knowledge, we can bring comfort to those in pain and hope to those who are desperate. There is no higher calling. It is nurses who hold the patients' well-being in the palm of their hands. What an extraordinary opportunity to do some good in a world where there is a lot of "not so good." It is a chance to "right" some of the "wrong." When nurses give of themselves in this way to patients, something intrinsically happens inside of them. The satisfaction and increase in professional self-esteem are unparalleled in any other profession. And, in turn, it comes back to the nurse—somehow, in some way. When you go home at night, you know you made a difference—what more could you want?

. . .The C-PAP mask had been removed. Anti-anxiety drugs had been given. She appeared comfortable and at peace. Her respiration slowly decreased as the hours went by. The picture now lay on the bed.

The Story That Had To Be Told

The story simply had to be told. Months later, I still could not enter that hospital room. The nurses who cared for him still had a haunted and tearful look in their eyes whenever his name was mentioned. And the look remained when he was not mentioned. Multiple counseling sessions, a patient care conference, and a post-mortem evaluation had not healed the wounds. Maybe it was because we could never heal his.

Looking back, it was amazing how little we knew about him. Considering all the time we spent with him, we could count the facts on one hand. He was a cowboy. He had lived with a wonderful lady named Martha for 2 1/2 years. He had planned to take a vacation to the Florida Keys after his first chemotherapy treatment. He had children up north. And probably most important of all, in the words of one quietly eloquent nurse, "He was the bravest man I have ever known."

Toxic epidermal necrolysis. Most of us had never heard of it, let alone cared for a patient with it. The formal definition of this dreadful disease was that it caused "widespread detachment of the epidermal layer of the skin, which results in exposed and exudative dermis." The translation-living hell!

Apparently it was caused by drug hypersensitivity, in this case allopurinol. Recently diagnosed with colon cancer, Frank had started on his chemotherapeutic regimen of which allopurinol was a part. Several days after the ingestion of the allopurinol, he developed an erythematous rash that quickly spread all over his body and face. The rash turned into blisters and vesicles. It was as if his entire body had developed third degree burns.

And then the peeling started. Left out of this somewhat theoretical description was the pain and agony that this man suffered in the care we rendered him. The skin on his back, buttocks, and back of his legs would literally stick to the bed and come off his body daily. His back became a bloody, torn mess. His care required the nurses to apply a cream to all of the wounds three times a day. And he insisted on standing during this torturous procedure. To roll side to side in bed was excruciating for this poor man. So, breaking every nursing rule in the world, we allowed him to stand as we slathered the cream to his denuded body. The only evidence of the pain we were inflicting was an involuntary wince as the cream touched the nerve endings on the skin. Sometimes, barely audible, swear words would come from his fissured lips.

And where was I in all of this? When I was approached about this patient's pain management, the nurse showed me the medication record for days past. It painted a sad picture. Oral narcotics, sedatives, anti-nausea drugs, even Benadryl had been given to try to alleviate the excruciating continuous pain. My contribution to his care was to escalate the narcotic dosing, make it intravenous, and add anti-anxiety medications. The results were much improved but not complete pain control.

The reality, however, was that not even high dose intravenous narcotics and anti-anxiety medications could take the entire edge off the pain. The "gift" that I gave him was to heavily sedate him and send his respiratory rate to 6-8 per minute. But at least, during those times, he was offered respite and peace.

Tongue in cheek, I said to the physician, and anybody else who would listen, that he ought to be intubated so that his body could be supported during this torturous time. Then we could take all the pain away without having to worry about him breathing. Little did I know.

Afterwards, I remember telling his oncologist that I had failed. He smiled a wise smile and said, "Diane, I fail every three days when one of my patients dies." Looking him straight in the eye, I said I was not used to the feeling.

My feelings of failure were the same as the angelic heroes who afterwards felt they had failed this patient. This story is as much about them as it is about this patient. Care, concern, anguish, and effort are mere words to describe the dedication and compassion portrayed by the staff nurses who cared for him. Together, we gave him continued courage and hope as we all worked to learn more about the disease and how together we all could better care for him.

Afterwards, we concluded that we could not do what nurses usually do for patients. We could not touch him (it hurt too much), We could not feed him (he could not swallow). We could not tell him that everything was going to be okay (we knew in our hearts that it would not).

So, why did this story have to be told? What good came out of it? The good is simply this. In this man's final hours of need, these nurses and I who were directing the pain management, trying to care for him, trying to keep him safe, valiantly trying to anticipating his pain, valiantly trying to treat his sepsis, ministering to his defeated spirit, we nurses were there showing him support, love, and emotion. At one point on that dreadful Sunday afternoon, every nurse on the unit and I were in that man's room. At the very least, this man knew, without a doubt, he was cared for. He knew we were fighting for his life, his dignity, and his soul. Therefore, we did not fail. We provided a lighthouse in a terrible storm. We continually gave hope when there was none. We gave of ourselves when our own spirits were empty and sad. We all cried tears of empathy and shared in his unabated suffering. And that is why this story simply had to be told. In that hospital room, human spirit met human spirit in the hour of greatest need.

The sounds of the helicopters said it all. Similar to the choppers on "M.A.S.H.," intuitively I knew what had happened. We were airlifting him out. He was going to die. The bravest man in the world was going to a better place. The story simply had to be told!

THE MARINE, A NURSE, AND THE WALL

by Jacqueline Rohaly-Davis

I was a new oncology/hematology clinical nurse at Edward J. Hines Jr. Veteran Administration Medical Center, Hines, Illinois, when I met Steve. Steve was a 47-year-old, strong, good-looking gentleman with a stoic expression. He was over six feet tall and well built. Steve's demeanor was frightening as he stood tall and proud in silence after just being told he had advanced lung cancer.

With an expressionless face staring at me, I nervously introduced myself, explained my role, and began to teach Steve about his chemotherapy treatments. I asked Steve if he understood or had any questions. Steve just stared intensely while holding the teaching booklet; he did not answer my questions. I reassured him that I would be with him for his first treatment and gave him my business card. Steve shook my hand and left in silence.

Steve served two tours of duty as a Vietnam marine He returned home a decorated and tired soldier, trying to move back into society. Unfortunately, Steve carried the anguish of those terrible years with him. Steve turned to alcohol and drugs to help ease the loneliness and disgust of the war. He lost his wife and children. He found comfort with his brethren in the Vietnam Veterans of America. However, Steve lived a pretty solitary life.

On his first day of chemotherapy, Steve was in control and silent. When the nurse tried to insert the needle for the intravenous delivery of the chemotherapy, Steve got very anxious. He began pacing and verbalizing his dislike of the procedure. I intervened. I sat with Steve, explained the procedure, and reviewed the information I had taught him. I held his hand. I was able to start his IV on the first try. With relief, Steve sighed and tolerated his first chemotherapy treatment.

Over the next nine months, I was present at all of Steve's chemotherapy treatments and clinic appointments. I visited him every time he was admitted in the hospital. I intervened on his behalf with the physicians regarding his symptom management. Steve learned to trust me and began to talk about his colorful life. No matter how angry or upset Steve was, when I walked into his room, his whole demeanor would relax. Steve's Vietnam brethren and the staff referred to me as "Steve's girl." To Steve, I was his angel.

I watched Steve's aggressive cancer get the best of him. Throughout his illness, he did not have a complaint but he did have one wish, to see the Vietnam War Memorial. Steve's brother, also a Vietnam veteran, worked with the Vietnam Veterans of America and the Purple Heart Association to get Steve his wish.

Steve would not go to Washington without me. His trip (which became our trip) was scheduled for Sweetest Day, 1991. Prior to the trip, I was given instruction on: what to do if Steve died in the air, how to handle his narcotics for pain, and how to deal with protestors and the press. I was overwhelmed!

Prior to the trip, Steve was in the hospital for pain management due to spinal metastasis. He looked thin, frail, and tired. When asked about his trip, Steve said, "I need to put to rest some nightmares before I die. Facing the wall of brethren is important to me." While squeezing his hand and looking into his tired blue eyes, I reassured him I would be with him on the trip. I was filled with emotions. I was also flattered, excited, scared, and disappointed that I would not be home for Sweetest Day. Saturday, Sweetest Day, the day of the trip, came quickly.

Steve's brother, a flight nurse, the pilot and I were the only people aboard the air ambulance. This was quite different than the crowd at the airport, which included his family, friends, numerous Vietnam vets, senators, and news media. In the air, Steve complained of pressure in his chest. I administered oxygen and he was able to breathe better. Steve was very awake and alert that day. He told me he wanted to keep a clear head for the trip, which meant he was going to tough it out with his pain and limit his narcotics.

When we arrived at the Vietnam War Memorial, we encountered our second set of media, press, and crowds. I could not believe my eyes. People were pushing and maneuvering to get a good picture of Steve. There were at least 25 camera crews. The ambulance attendants could not get Steve out of the ambulance because of the crowds. With my graceful "big mouth," I told everyone to give Steve space so he could get out of the ambulance and into a wheelchair.

I pushed the wheelchair over to a news podium where the conference was being held for Steve. He was getting nervous and restless. He just wanted to see the wall. The Secretary of the Department of Veteran Affairs and other dignitaries made speeches. I did not hear a word of the speeches as I stood behind Steve's wheelchair. After the speeches, the secretary wheeled Steve over to the corner of the wall. Steve's brother walked by his side with flowers. Steve took the flowers and said in a weak voice with numerous microphones near his chin, "This is in remembrance of all those Chicago soldiers who fell in Nam."

Steve did not have any quiet time at the memorial because the crowds were so thick. We decided to get back in the ambulance, take a tour of Washington, let the crowds clear out, and then return to the monument When we returned to the monument, Steve got back in his wheelchair and went to the wall. He looked for several names and began telling stories of how each man died an untimely death.

Steve told stories of carrying a man's leg back to a helicopter, closing a man's chest when he got shot, walking through a mine field with the rest of the platoon following him. For the first time, I saw this stoic, proud man cry. He sat staring at the wall with tears rolling down his face. When it was time to leave the memorial, Steve took one more moment, squeezed my hand and said, "Thank you."

The trip exhausted Steve. While in the air, Steve had tightness in his chest so oxygen was started. He also needed to be catheterized. As Steve slept on the plane, he began to have dreams and flashbacks to Vietnam. He began tossing, turning, tearing off his oxygen, and screaming, "Get down, incoming, Charlie, Charlie." Grabbing my arm, he pulled me down to the floor. He continued to scream, "Get down, incoming, get down." The flight nurse struggled to get a sedative into Steve, but he fought all the way. It took me several minutes to regain composure as the sedative took affect and Steve quieted down.

When we finally landed in Chicago, I could not wait to get Steve back to the hospital and go home. I had never been so scared in my life. This frail man had such strength. I wondered why Steve and I connected, and I wondered why he tried to protect me. When we arrived at the hospital, Steve was exhausted. As I left Steve's bedside,

he said, "I will love you forever." With tears of exhaustion in my eyes, I kissed his forehead and told him I would never forget our adventure. I wished him Happy Sweetest Day and a good night. On my drive home, I cried from exhaustion. I prayed to God for Steve's peace and freedom from pain. Steve died the day after Thanksgiving.

Prior to his death, Steve was in and out of flashbacks. He would tell me stories of life in Vietnam, stories about an 18-year-old boy becoming a man very quickly in order to survive in the war. He told stories about people not understanding what Vietnam soldiers had been through, yet judging them when they came home. He told stories about drugs being used to take away the realities of the war. When telling these stories, he became a very strong Marine, even though his body was dying and weak.

I was born in 1963. Prior to meeting Steve, I had no idea about the consequences of the Vietnam War on our soldiers or on our country. I thank Steve for our adventure together. I know I am a better human being for knowing of his courage. I also know if I died tomorrow, I would know I was a successful nurse because of Steve.

reflecting

PART V

NURSES REFLECTING ON THEIR STORIES

A GOOD WAY TO MAKE A LIVING

by Jo Anne Marcell

fter all is said and done, I believe nursing is a very good way to make a living and a fine way to spend my working life. My mother encouraged me to learn to type so I could earn a living as a secretary or receptionist, just as she had. Instead, knowing that was not what I had in mind for my life, I followed my own interests and took the standard college courses plus art history and painting.

During my fourth semester as a starving art student, I ran into my friend Ginny Long. She said she was graduating in a month and would be getting a job as a registered nurse. I was amazed. She and I were out of school for the same amount of time and she was assured a decent job, whereas I had no illusion of using my education in progress to further my socioeconomic status. "How?" I asked. "I went through the associate degree nursing program," she replied. I enrolled the very next day.

My first job as a graduate nurse was on the night shift in the intensive care unit (ICU). I cared for five patients, including a 13-year-old boy with a broken neck (on a Stryker frame that had to be flipped every two hours), a lady from the psych unit who was suffering from a lithium overdose, and a patient whose abdominal dressing change required four big bottles of Zero foam gauze. The other nurse in the unit was busy with an emergency trauma patient, giving many units of blood, and had no time to help me. Not too long after that night, I applied for a job with Delta Airlines as a flight attendant. I got the job because the interviewer liked the fact that I was a registered nurse.

Being a flight attendant was a little more glamorous than nursing. It was a little more fun and the uniforms were more stylish. However, the work of a flight attendant didn't seem as important or rewarding as the work of a nurse. The year was 1974, the year of a great recession. Everyone at my level of seniority was reassigned, so I left my glamorous, less meaningful job and went back to nursing. I got a job right away at the infirmary of a juvenile detention center close to my home. It served my purpose, although I was not overly enamored with the work.

Upon moving to Gainesville, Florida, I was offered a job in an operating room, an area in which I had never thought of working. It was valuable experience, but I distinctly remember saying more than once that "nurses should be at least as well respected as plumbers." Maybe then, we might even make comparable salaries.

I moved to Charleston and was immediately able to get a job. Nursing was fulfilling my expectations as a means of gainful employment, but it was more than just that. I loved patient contact and liked making a difference in a human being's process of healing. I felt that I could improve a patient's outcome, but there seemed to be so many obstacles. Nurses did not have the voice in 1978 that they have today. The work was stressful and exhausting, leaving every nurse I ever talked to feeling underpaid, under-appreciated, and frustrated. I often said, "I think I would like this job better if they paid us a little more."

I decided that I could make a difference by becoming more educated by getting a baccalaureate degree, so I started taking classes at the College of Charleston. During that time, I discovered the theater. I won great roles as an actress. I also designed and built costumes for five huge theatrical productions with casts of thousands. During all of this "theater exploration phase," I maintained a part-time job at the hospital, working when I was needed and when it fit into my course and play schedules. Few professions besides nursing could have allowed that level of flexibility.

I took a hiatus from nursing to pursue a career as a seamstress. It was not a good way to make a living. There are no benefits, no guaranteed hours, and the pay scale was nothing to write home about so I went back to nursing.

My last dalliance from nursing occurred when my children were very small. At the time, a nurse working 32 hours a week and a teacher working 10 months a year made the same pay. I reasoned that, if I were a teacher, I could spend summers off with my husband, a college professor, and my children. During the 18 months it took me to become certified for teaching elementary school in South Carolina, a great nursing change occurred-nurses' salaries increased by 50%. More importantly, nurses had a voice that had not been heard before. The higher pay was a manifestation of the higher regard for nurses. I went back to nursing again.

There were other reasons I went back to nursing, such as the prospects of having nursing experiences and having knowledge that could be used to make a difference in someone's life. I went back to nursing because I missed the camaraderie and bond that exists among nurses, the intellectual stimulation that comes with working in a teaching institution, all the new technology, and being elbow to elbow with medical miracles. I missed patients. I missed nursing.

A NURSE FOR ALL SEASONS

by Victoria C. Fron

t was early in the *spring* when Victoria Fron decided she wanted to become a nurse. Attending Catholic elementary and high schools had set the stage for Vicki to consider entering the convent. Her role model was Sister Leontine, a physiology teacher, a nun, and a nurse. It was Sister's enthusiasm for science and her "down to earth" nature that nudged Vicki into the nursing arena. Vicki decided to forgo the religious career and applied to nursing school.

She entered a diploma program where the Sisters used every extra hour of a student's life, without pay, for work on clinical units for the "experience of learning." Vicki was sure that 25% of the hospital's nursing staff were nursing students! It was while Vicki was learning how to give a bed bath to a blind patient that the news of John Kennedy's assassination was announced. Everyone went to the chapel to pray.

At the time Vicki was in school, a student nurse had to remain single and live in the hospital dorm. Vicki met John and took a detour from nursing to marry. Five years and three children later, Vicki returned to school to finish her nursing education. She studied into the night with the washer and dryer going full blast. But it sure paid off.

Vicki accepted an evening nursing position on a 25-bed patient ward. She and one nursing assistant worked on the ward. The variety of patients was as challenging as the moonlighting physicians. Vicki once called a code on a patient who was already deceased. The physicians were outraged but Vicki was not discouraged. As a result of this experience, she learned to check a patient's vital signs before calling the resuscitation team. Vicki was paid $4.64 an hour for this job!

Vicki was a natural for quickly absorbing pertinent facts. She transferred to the intensive care unit. The patients were more acutely ill. The nursing camaraderie was more intense, and the nurses worked in closer proximity to each other. The move to intensive care wasn't her only move. Despite being a "city girl" all her life, Vicki moved to the suburbs.

When Vicki went to register to vote in her new suburb, the parish priest mentioned that the fire department could use the help of a critical care nurse. Her family was surprised at her interest in the offer but supportive. Actually, Vicki thought the idea was wonderful. Soon she was putting on cervical collars and learning how to use extrication tools. Vicki found this volunteer work as a field nurse and paramedic exciting. She remembers crawling under a truck to start intravenous therapy on a motorcyclist, applying mayonnaise to the small feet of eight kids who ran across a newly tarred street, and teaching a pregnant diabetic about a balanced diet because she was having hypoglycemic seizures.

One sunny day, her pager opened with a "near drown." Vicki, who was in the ambulance, located and assembled the suction apparatus, intubation setup, etc. When she and the team entered the yard, they learned a small child had fallen into an unattended pool. Drowning protocol was initiated and the team began a rapid ambulance transport. On the way to the hospital, the ambulance was struck by a vehicle and the ambulance gas tank ruptured. Only a minute away from the hospital, Vicki made the decision to take the child the rest of the way in the paramedic's vehicle that had stopped at the ambulance accident scene. After several days in the intensive care unit, the child improved and is now a healthy adult.

Vicki became skeptical when informed that she would be doing fire suppression. She had no desire to become a firefighter. Nevertheless, she became a regular firefighter, advancing to the rank of engineer. Some firemen wondered how she could move with 40 pounds of gear on her small frame. "With brute strength," she would say. Some fire runs were extremely dangerous. Vicki remembers when an oil refinery blew up and she was sent to the center of the burning pipelines. Her job was to extinguish the fire and search for any survivors. Unfortunately, there were no survivors. A happier memory is sounding the fire engine siren for the neighborhood kids.

In the *summer* of her nursing career, Vicki was asked to be the evening supervisor of a 325-bed hospital. Next she became a manager in the sleep clinic, losing her own sleep while attaining a Master of Science in Nursing degree. She managed both school and her job while raising a teenager and a college student and working at the fire department.

In the *autumn* of her nursing career, Vicki worked at a university hospital as emergency department manager and emergency medical service (EMS) coordinator. One of her most satisfying jobs followed, that is, teaching student nurses. When teaching, Vicki felt the students got part of her, "Assertive Nursing 101." Vicki consistently told her students that "nursing opens up a world of opportunities for you." Vicki made a case study of herself. She shared the progression of her own career, consulting for the TV series "E.R."; working on a production set; being the only "first aid" personnel at a 400-employee picnic; volunteering for a medical mission in Cajamarca, Peru; setting up first aid classes for private businesses; becoming a cardiothoracic advanced practice nurse; and utilizing nursing skills in caring for family and friends.

The *winter* of Vicki's nursing career is still to come. She is certain that her love for family and nursing will continue to grow. She feels the knowledge she has gained and her love for nursing are gifts that enable her to care for her family and friends. She hopes that when the soft snows of winter days come to her life, she will leave large footprints in the path of nursing.

A NURSE'S MISSION

by Zenaida M. Sarmiento

s a five-year-old growing up in Pozorrubio, Pangasinan, a small barrio in the Philippines, my outlook on life was fairly simple. Because everyone seemed to know everyone in town, news traveled fast if a family member faced a near-death situation and was to be taken to the hospital. Perhaps it was this environment that influenced my perception of everyone's role in society. One of the roles assigned to the people in the barrio was that of a nurse. In my young eyes, a nurse was a pleasant lady dressed in white from head to toe with a little hat presiding over an ensemble of a starched white dress and white shoes. Usually, these lovely creatures walked arm in arm with doctors, using their "magic touch" to relieve pain from the ailing people that cried for help. This very image of a nurse was ingrained in my head; it was an image of someone whose mission was to grant health and wellness through service. Although, as a child, I was limited to catching only a glimpse of the identity of a nurse, my idea of her lot in life is truly not a far cry from what I consider her mission today.

Many lessons about life were learned at home and in church. Sunday school under a mango tree every week consisted of telling many parables. How fitting that my favorite was the parable of The Good Samaritan. At home, my mother stressed the importance of a selfless attitude through serving others. Being an ambitious woman, she often lived vicariously through me, as if she'd lost her chance at carrying out her mission to "serve the world" after having endured

many hardships brought about by World War II. My father, who also possessed the same ideals of service to others, pushed me as well. I was encouraged to rise from our less-than-affluent life to pursue a career that used prestige to help the less fortunate. In light of these expectations, I grew up with a mission to help others, to be the one who could bring hope to the lives of those in need. Call it divine intervention; it seemed the path that carried my mission was paved with many signs, whether it was my future husband writing "Rodolfo A. Sarmiento, M.D." in the dirt when we played as children or my grandfather who prophesied that I, out of all his countless grandchildren, would be the one who would someday go to America. When destiny calls your name, it cannot be ignored.

With the passing years, I became that trusted individual in Pozorrubio when it came to needing medical assistance. Title or not, my nursing days started as a student, aiding my neighbor having a baby or rescuing someone having a seizure. It was experiences like this that kept the image of the saintly "lady in white" fresh in my mind. When my husband and I left the Philippines for America as doctor and nurse, we set out to help others as we walked arm in arm.

When you are middle-aged and have finished creating a family and establishing stability, your goal returns to fulfilling your life's calling. At this point in my life, my husband and I looked for ways

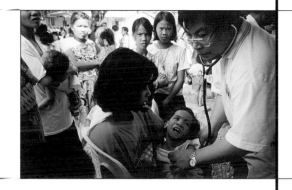

to carry out our mission statement as healthcare providers. Achieving the "American Dream" and living well had occurred as a result of staying true to the ethics my parents had instilled in me as well as my desire to help others. Therefore, in spite of the good and comfortable life I had been blessed with in America, I never forgot from where I came and the needs of the people of Pozorrubio.

Our opportunity finally came. As leaders of the Pozorrubians Midwest USA, an organization of people from my hometown whose goal is to unite fellow members of the Filipino-American community in the Chicago-Midwest area, we elected to use our combined talents and resources to attempt to make a difference in the world. This goal motivated us to launch Medical Mission, a project to offer free medical and dental services to those who could not afford adequate healthcare in Pozorrubio. After a year of preparing medical supply boxes and a team of willing workers, I was ready.

For three days, the team and I serviced whoever registered for the free care we provided, whether it was an acute or lingering illness. Our team offered medicine, medical advice, referrals to specialists, and encouragement to set higher goals for their lives. As living proof that success and prosperity are attainable to those with desire even in the face of humble beginnings, I inspired others. After all, being a nurse is not limited to treating physical wounds; it also involves treating the soul of a sick patient. This is how the lady in white from my memory puts smiles on the faces of patients.

With the limited means we were given, improvising was not an option but a necessity. Makeshift examination tables were created under trees. We crossed rivers to reach those who were not willing to travel to our first venue. I suppose that's why they call it "overseas." A multitude of children required de-worming or ointment for their skin disorders. Families lined up to receive a small package containing essentials including toothbrushes, toiletries, and food. Neither the team nor I expected to treat as many people as we did.

If we ran out of supplies, the money to acquire more had to come from our own pockets. The overwhelming need to be serviced was prevalent, and it was our goal to see that no family left empty-handed. The image that will forever be in my mind is that of an ailing mother whose blood pressure was being taken as she nursed her baby as still another of her children clung to her skirt. This powerful picture of need further augmented my belief that I was fulfilling my life's duty as a nurse.

To know that I was part of something that made a difference in the lives of over 3,500 people in Pozorrubio gave me much more than a sense of gratification. Words cannot express how fulfilling it was to experience this Medical Mission. Working day in and day out with a great deal of needy patients exhausted our bodies, minds, and wallets. Any extra items we brought with us were easily relinquished without a second thought to those who wore the smiles I had given them.

In the end, I left with empty hands and an overflowing heart. It is my belief that this spirit of generosity and selflessness is part of the true nature of nursing. I truly believe nursing is not just a profession; it is a way of life. Whether or not I wear the white clothing today, I am still a nurse, ready and willing to serve those in need.

My mission does not end here. Following the end of Medical Mission, the organization regularly sends care packages to the people of Pozorrubio to keep them smiling. In 2004, the Pozorrubians Midwest USA plans to embark on a second Medical Mission to our hometown. Having seen the impact on the lives of others as well as my own life, I anxiously await the next opportunity to fulfill my life's mission as a nurse.

aren chose to major in nursing because she wanted to care for people and pursue a love for science, the perfect career combination. She graduated from a baccalaureate nursing program in 1976, our nation's bicentennial year. There was much cause for celebration-four years of hard work successfully completed and a bright future ahead.

Following graduation, Karen accepted a position as a staff nurse on a gastroenterology unit at a large teaching hospital. She was struck by the *incredible* responsibility for human life that was placed in her hands. "Nursing school had not prepared me for this. Not only was I responsible and accountable to my patients' physical lives, I was also expected to know and help people in their most vulnerable moments, when they were most frightened, lonely, embarrassed, anxious, happy, or sad." These were moments to which sometimes even the closest family members were not privy.

"Will my girlfriend still love me, knowing I may not be able to have children?"
"What will my friends think when they find out I have an ostomy?"
"How will I ever go back to work with this nasogastric tube in my nose?"
"Will my wife still be able to be close to me when she finds out I have cancer?"

Patients trusted Karen with their physical, psychological, and spiritual selves, even though she may not have had the answers. She began to apply the professional skills learned in her undergraduate nursing program, such as therapeutic communication, listening, confidentiality, and a caring presence. These professional strategies helped facilitate the therapeutic relationship between the patient and nurse, as well as establish a human connection. This human-to-human connection was the true essence of nursing. It was the critical vehicle through which she could understand her patients' needs and intervene appropriately. Along with this connection came a deepened responsibility and vigilance in the nursing care provided. As she developed her abilities, she began to feel she was an instrument for a greater purpose.

Many times in caring for patients, Karen felt the connection between patient and nurse transcend the objective physical findings and measurements. Knowledge went beyond a blood pressure within a normal range or skin that was pale in color. Her connection with patients sometimes went beyond the patients' verbal statements. Her connections with patients provided a deeper level of perceptiveness. She recalled saving a woman's life, because after Karen left the patient's room, a voice inside said, "Go back and check on her" even though there was no objective reason.

I was working the day shift and got my usual assignment of four primary patients. I had cared for them all week. One of my patients, Mrs. Walker in Room 327-1, was a somewhat anxious lady who was having a liver biopsy at 8:00 a.m. Dr. Rub, a gastrointestinal fellow, was to do the biopsy. The procedure was done at the bedside and I was present to assist. There were two items of significance during the biopsy. First, I didn't have a lot of confidence in Dr. Rub's abilities (we called him the Black Cloud, because one seemed to follow him wherever he went). Secondly, during the liver biopsy, Mrs. Walker complained of pain with the needle puncture. Patients usually get numbing medicine prior to the procedure, and they usually don't complain of any pain.

Following the biopsy, Mrs. Walker was instructed to lie on her right side to apply pressure to the liver and prevent bleeding. I began taking her vital signs every 15 minutes. Her vital signs were stable; she was in no distress, just a little anxious. I tried to allay her anxiety with patient teaching and a consistent, caring presence. Mrs. Walker put her call light on frequently between the 15-minute vital sign measurements. Other nurses working that day commented on her "neediness" and suggested I should stop running to her so much. I'm glad I didn't listen to them. I couldn't help it, that's the way I was. My patients' needs came first, and patient anxiety is never relieved by ignoring the patient's feelings!

Everything was looking good for Mrs. Walker. It was now 10:00 a.m. Her vital signs were still stable and her color was good. There was no bleeding at the puncture site, and there were no physiological signs of a problem. I walked out of her room and to the nursing station, not 30 feet away. Within 20 seconds, her call light was on. The first urge might have been to continue what I was doing. After all, I had three other patients to care for, but a little inner voice said to me, "Go back and check her." The voice carried a sense of urgency. I listened to that voice and immediately returned to her room, only to find Mrs. Walker lying on her back with no blood pressure, no pulse, and unconscious. I called a code, and we successfully resuscitated her. One-to-one nursing care was provided for the next two hours as the surgery service was called and she was prepared for the operating room. In the OR, the surgeon found a large liver laceration that had apparently occurred during the biopsy and opened when she turned onto her back. She had been hemorrhaging internally, but the laceration was successfully repaired. Mrs. Walker came back to thank Karen several days later. What was the source of that inner voice that made Karen go back when there was no apparent reason to do so? What would have happened if she hadn't been receptive? It would only have been a matter of minutes before Mrs. Walker would have died. Karen wishes that she could listen and be receptive to the inner voice in all her ministering to patients. It is sometimes that "listening to the spirit" that leads nurses to do extraordinary things to help people.

Although this experience occurred in Karen's first year of nursing practice, she will never forget it. It has become a sentinel experience that has shaped her philosophy of nursing practice throughout a lifetime. However, Karen doesn't feel it is unique from other nurses' experiences. This story could be any nurse's story. She has asked that her name be changed and wishes to remain anonymous. She does not feel this story is about her but rather a tribute to nursing practice and the impact nurses have on the lives of those for whom they care.

The names of all the individuals in this story have been changed.

A SECOND CHANCE

by Shannon Bright Smith

ho would think that a day could so significantly change a life! I woke up early that humid Charleston morning and arrived at the hospital minutes before my 6:00 a.m. schedule. Assisted by a very pleasant nurse, I was soon ready for the operation. I was nervous, but excited. I would be rid of my problems and go back to normalcy as part of the hustle and bustle of my nine to five job at the police station. I'd be happy again. After all, I was a small-town country girl who had achieved the American dream. I had a wonderful husband, a son, a daughter, a cat, a dog, a great job, two cars, and a great home! Who could ask for more? My experiences over the next year would completely reorder my priorities.

After surgery, Dr. S. entered my hospital room with an ominous look on his face. He said, "We found cancer in your ovaries." I didn't hear anything else he said until, "If it was my wife or daughter, I'd want her to see Dr. L." At first I was furious—not at him, just at the fact that someone like me should have this disease. After all, I was hard-working, loving, and compassionate to others. I was a mother of small children. I had plans, and they didn't include hospitals, chemotherapy, and being sick. My fury turned to pity and then to fear. How would I get through this? Would I get through this?

During the following 10 months, I came to know nurses in a new light. They weren't just the people who passed out pills and started IVs. Nurses became my friends, my confidants, and my care providers. They laughed with me and yes, they cried with me too. They supported my belief and faith in God. The gentle rub on the shoulder when my body was wracked with nausea was so encouraging. The gentle "hang in there" gave me strength to continue the chemotherapy treatments.

The fear that had once conquered me soon turned to hope for a better tomorrow. A year went by—CANCER FREE! Then two and then three years passed. I reflected on my life and the second chance I had been given. Suddenly, material possessions weren't so important. I was grateful to God for my family and for being alive. I thought about those wonderful nurses who gave me such great care and decided I wanted to be like them.

Now 13 years cancer free, I thank my family for the sacrifices they made so that I might go to school to become a nurse. I enjoy being a nurse. I treat my patients like those superb nurses treated me. And when times get tough, I reflect on my experience and renew my innermost convictions because they give me encouragement to continue. After all, a second chance comes only once.

FAMILY CARE

by Linda M. Bond

here are times when our families become our patients. My father became my patient a few years ago. I had asked him several times to move in with me, but his desire for independence won out. He had had prostate cancer with surgical intervention 10 years before. The cancer was back within five years, but with hormonal treatment at the Mayo Clinic, Jacksonville, the cancer was kept at bay. He did have hot flashes from time to time and developed empathy for menopausal women.

When my father came to visit one Christmas, cancer had spread to his bones but no one knew it. Neurological changes landed him at the hospital. As I was moving him from the bed to the chair, he became unresponsive; I switched quickly into the nurse mode. I called for a nurse on the floor and yelled, "I need a blood pressure cuff, I need neuro STAT, I need an EKG, and I need IV fluids!" The floor nurses responded quickly and stayed at my side.

I didn't know what had happened, but I knew that it was bad. I drew blood on my own father. The lab results indicated that he was bleeding. Neurology called for a surgical consult. I watched the blood pressure monitor and saw 68/40. I said to the doctor, "Would some-body please do something!" He ordered a CT scan of the abdomen. The scan showed a pathological fracture of the iliac crest. My father was confused and was put in restraints. It was 3:00 a.m. before they finally inserted a femoral line and I was allowed to see him. The iliac vessel tear would be discovered later. I knew many of the residents who came to treat him. I was so glad my father was at the hospital where I was a practicing nurse. I was in an environment I knew. Two weeks and 10 units of blood later, he was ready for rehabilitation.

I drove to Florida to close his bank accounts and move his things. My sister and brother-in-law stayed with him to help quicken his rehabilitation. He ultimately moved to assisted living next to the nursing home where he had been. The drive was a distance, so I made the decision to move him to a James Island assisted living facility. He was excited about the move but after the arrangements had been made I went to see him and he asked, "Why won't you let me live with you?" I told him I had tried to do that for a year and now I didn't see how I could possibly do it because I had to work.

After a sleepless night, I asked my daughter whether she would be willing to help me bring her grandfather home. I would adjust my schedule around her school schedule. She never once hesitated. The answer was, "Yes." When we arrived to move him, he was sitting in his wheel chair and I said, "You are coming home with us." He just smiled.

I learned a lot about caring for the dying patient at home. I set up an assisted living room in my bedroom. The first night he became very ill and was vomiting. He said, "I am so sorry," and I said, "Dad, I'm a nurse, this is what I do-it's OK."

For a while, he was well, but then became weaker and more confused. Hospice provided everything we needed, a bedside commode, hospital bed, pastoral care, and weekly assessments. I initially slept in another room with a baby monitor, but eventually I was on the couch to be there when he climbed out of bed or when he needed to be comforted. I would play his favorite music, Sarah Brightman, Charlotte Church, John Denver, and James Taylor. He often mistook me for my mother and asked when his deceased brother was coming. My daughter Kathy helped him as much as she could, which was a big responsibility for a 21-year-old.

Staff nurses on my unit and the manager were very supportive. I did not start family leave until the last week of his life. A nurse from my unit came to my home to help bathe my father the last Sunday of his life. Hospice nurses came when I didn't understand his agitation, even with the Ativan. He needed more Ativan, and he was in "terminal restlessness," a term I had never heard but one that every hospice nurse knows. It occurs during the transition between consciousness and coma. Soon he was resting and, the last night he had with us, both my daughter and I talked to him. I woke up at 5:00 a.m. and started the CD player with his favorite music. Hearing is the last thing to go, they say, so hopefully I eased his passing. When I awoke at 6:00 a.m., I couldn't hear his breathing and knew he had passed on.

I am so happy I could do this for my father. I know that not everyone would be able to or would want to do what I did. But my years of experience as a nurse came into play for a very important patient, my father. I am a nurse!

HOPE

by Michelle Williams

very time I tell someone I am a nurse who works with cancer patients, the first response is, "Oh, that must be so sad." Being an oncology nurse can be sad but it is very rewarding and a privilege. The greatest gift given to me is how to really appreciate life. "If it's chocolate cake you want for breakfast, then chocolate cake is what you shall have."

While in nursing school, I had no idea that I would be working with cancer and bone marrow transplant patients. In the fall of 1996, I made the decision to move from South Carolina back home to Minnesota to pursue my education in nursing. In my second school quarter, two days before Christmas Eve, my grandfather and I were doing some last minute errands. The sunshine sparked liked diamonds off the snow. How could anything terrible happen that beautiful day?

By the time we arrived at home, my grandfather was ashen gray and could barely breathe. I called my mother and then took my grandfather to the local hospital. He was diagnosed with leukemia. Coupled with his age and previous medical health, it was a poor prognosis. He was airlifted to the University of Minnesota where they began treatment. The doctors didn't think he would make it through the night, and if he did, the survival rate would be only 5 percent. He spent the next four months going through grueling chemotherapy treatments. Every problem that could develop did. It was April when he finally came home. He had a close resemblance to *Kojak* and everyone was giving him gifts of lollipops.

The following spring, I was sitting on the living room floor, looking through an application I had received from Medical University of South Carolina. The 8 West "Hope" unit caught my eye. I said to my grandfather, "How wonderful it would be to help people like you who have cancer!" I thought that it was only a dream. Why would they hire someone like me with no experience?

I've been a nurse on the "Hope" unit for almost four years now. It was my only interview and the only job I've had as a registered nurse. I have a love/hate relationship with the Hope unit. Most days I want to quit. However, it's those special moments, like being the one to assist during a bone marrow transplant or caring for dying patients and knowing that you made them comfortable and their passing bearable for their family, that keep me coming back to work every day.

During the Christmas season of 2001, I went home to Minnesota with my first-born son and celebrated my grandfather's five years in remission. He is one in only five percent, which is a true miracle.

IS THERE A NURSE ON BOARD?

by Linda Heitman

In June 2001, I boarded a connecting flight in another country on my way to Copenhagen, Denmark. After recently completing my PhD in nursing at Saint Louis University, I was looking forward to presenting my research at the 22nd Quadrennial Congress of the International Council of Nursing. Approximately 45 minutes after takeoff, a flight attendant appeared at the aisle and asked, "Is there a physician on board? If so, please make yourself known." There was no response. Since a physician was summoned, I did not reply. A couple of minutes later, the same flight attendant reappeared and repeated his request, "Is there a physician on board?" Again, no response. Within moments, the attendant appeared for the third time, and now his plea was urgent, "Please, if there is a physician on board, make yourself known!" Noting the tone of his voice I answered, "I am a nurse, may I help you?" He immediately said, "Please, madam, would you follow me?" I removed my seat belt and followed him down the aisle to the rear of the plane. There, to my dismay, I observed a woman lying on the floor. I immediately dropped to my knees and did an assessment. There was no response, no spontaneous breathing. I palpated a faint heartbeat, so I began CPR.

The crew was trained in first aid but not in CPR. I instructed them to ask any of the passengers who knew CPR to assist me. There were no airways, no automatic defibrillator, only an Ambu bag. Within minutes, two men joined me to help with resuscitation. I asked the flight attendants, encircling us as we knelt on the floor, if anyone was traveling with the lady. They brought her husband to me. He was crying and immediately began speaking to me in Swedish. I explained to him that I was an American and asked if he could speak English. He replied in English and told me that he and his wife had been "on holiday." She had experienced chest pain two days earlier and had been seen at a hospital in the city they were visiting. After being told that her symptoms were "epigastric" in origin, they decided to fly home to Sweden. I explained to him what we were doing. I urged him to kneel beside me and talk to his wife, to tell her he was there, and that we were trying to help her. He thanked me and proceeded to follow my suggestions.

By this time, we had been taking turns providing CPR for approximately 20 minutes. The seven flight attendants were still encircling us. It occurred to me I had heard no mention of landing, so I looked up and asked, "Are we still flying toward Copenhagen?" "Yes," they replied. In a rather high pitched tone I replied, "Go tell the captain to turn this thing around! We need to land and get help for this lady!" One of the attendants replied, "Yes, ma'am!" and proceeded to run from the back of the plane to the cockpit. He returned to report that the captain was turning the plane around and that we were returning to the city from which we had departed slightly more than an hour earlier. The three of us continued taking turns with the CPR, with the lady's husband begging us to continue. We still had no response, no spontaneous respirations, but could feel a faint pulse. After almost 90 minutes of CPR, a flight attendant tapped me on the shoulder and said, "Madam, the captain is preparing to land, and he is concerned that the three of you do not have seat belts on and may roll around during landing." I informed him that there was no way we could leave the lady and return to our seats. I agreed that we might roll around a bit, but we could not stop. The flight attendants found seats and fastened their seat belts. As the plane landed, the three of us on the floor DID roll around a bit.

Within minutes, I heard footsteps thundering down the aisle of the plane. I looked up to see the emergency team carrying an array of equipment. One team member intubated the lady and continued ventilation, while the other continued chest compressions. An IV was started and medications administered. She was defibrillated once. A small heart beat was noted, and a monitor was put into place. I explained to her husband what was being done and why. We quickly said our good-byes and wished them our best as the emergency team took the lady from the plane and into an ambulance directly outside the aircraft.

Weary and a bit disheveled, I returned to my seat. The attendant who had made the original plea for a physician approached me. He smiled and said, "I didn't know a nurse could do that! We always ask if there is a physician on board. From now on, we'll ask for a nurse!" Interesting, I thought, working to save a life, organizing others in crisis, teaching and comforting a worried family member, these are skills that are the hallmarks of good nursing care. Yet, how often even we take them for granted. This time I was glad I carried them aboard.

We departed again for Denmark. Just before landing, the flight attendant returned to say, "Madam, the captain would like to speak with you." The captain, in a white uniform, smiled, bowed, and said, "Madam, the crew and I wish to thank you for helping one of our passengers. We are grateful that you responded." One month after returning home, I received a letter from the airline thanking me for offering help to a fellow passenger. I was given one free round trip ticket anywhere in the world as a token of their appreciation.

Although receiving the round trip ticket was a pleasant surprise, my true reward had been given much earlier. Approximately two hours after the patient has been evacuated from the plane, the flight attendant came to my seat. Smiling, he handed me a piece of paper and said, "Madam, the captain thought you would like to see this." The e-mail read, "Patient admitted to intensive care unit in stable condition." This is truly one of the true rewards of nursing . . . saving a life.

Although receiving the round trip ticket was a pleasant surprise, my true reward had been given much earlier.

JULIA'S STORY

by Julia T. O'Malley

ife and all of its challenges have shaped me into the woman I am today. A major part of who I am is that I am a nurse. I never dreamed that I would find a career so challenging, so frustrating, and yet so rewarding. While still in high school, I knew that I wanted to work with people. I just had to be led to a career that allowed me to do that. Being diagnosed with cancer at the age of 15 directed me toward the way I could help others.

At the end of my freshman year of high school, I suddenly fell ill with some sort of immune disorder that placed me in a local hospital. As the disease progressed, I was ultimately sent to Children's Memorial Hospital in Chicago. My doctors at Children's were brilliant clinicians and researchers that never gave up until they had a diagnosis and treatment plan. After exploratory surgery, a five-day trip to the ICU with ventilation support, numerous IVs, tests and procedures, I was given little hope. With a lot of prayers, I did recover. This first part of my journey lasted almost two months and caused my family to truly unite and look at life in a new way. I was discharged in July, thinking this awful experience was in the past.

In mid-October of my sophomore year of high school, I had just recovered from a horrible cold, made the sophomore basketball team, and was ready for all that life had to offer. Life as I knew it suddenly ended when again I became very ill. I had swollen glands in my neck, axilla, and groin that grew overnight. I finally told my mom about these bumps. I was referred back to Dr. Elaine Morgan, an oncologist at Children's Memorial Hospital. I had a neck lymph node biopsy and numerous lab tests. My life changed forever.

I distinctly remember being in school a day after that visit, sitting out of practice due to fatigue and soreness, going home and eating dinner with my family like any other normal Monday. The phone rang and it was Dr. Morgan. She told my parents that I had cancer. My mom and dad entered the room where I was watching TV with my siblings. They were crying. I knew it was bad when I saw my dad crying because he never cried. They told all of us together that I had non-Hodgkin's lymphoma. I said, "No big deal. At least it's not cancer!" My dad sat next to me, held me tight, and said, "No, Julia, you do have cancer."

In the following days, weeks, and months, my mom, dad, and I (and occasionally my grandfather), ventured to Children's Memorial for chemotherapy, and bone and CT scans. At that time, I never believed that there was an end. I met some very dedicated nurses at Children's who cared for me unconditionally. They treated a stranger's child as if I were their own. I met Cora, Karen, and Theresa, who were my in-patient nurses who would fight to keep my primary nursing team consistent. On several occasions, they kept my mom from crumbling when I was too sick to care for myself and when my dad was unable to come due to work. "V," my lab tech, was the best. She never missed a vein. She always said that I was beautiful, despite my horrible cushnoid appearance from taking prednisone three times a day. My clinic nurse, Jackie, always made me laugh as she started my weekly IVs. She encouraged me to never quit. And then there were the nurses in the hospital who made sure that the aroma of food was never brought into my room or gave me something to drown out the smell so I would not get nauseated. These exceptional nurses always kept my parents and me included in my daily plan. The nurses would always explain changes or why new side effects were happening. These extraordinary women made days better for me as well as my parents.

Life after cancer went on. I graduated on time from high school and went to nursing school. I was determined to work at Children's Memorial Hospital, the same place I had received my care. I knew that my path in life was planned. Being treated and then working at Children's is where I was supposed to be. Working with cancer children and their families is an amazing gift. Many people cannot understand why I love my job. I was given cancer for a reason; it directed my life. I have cared for amazing children who were so strong, so funny, and so loving. I believe each patient I care for is brought into my life for a reason. All of these special people have taught me something new about life and, hopefully, I made some impact on their lives.

Part of my journey as a nurse and cancer survivor is to promote living life to its utmost capacity. I have learned to never let life's roadblocks keep me from reaching my dreams. In 2000, I met a patient named Mark Staehely. We shared the same dreams and inspired each other to promote survivorship. This past year, Mark, his mom Sue, and I started a cancer survivor foundation called The SOCS Foundation, Inc. (The Staehely O'Malley Cancer Survivor Foundation, Inc.). Together, with the help of our friends and family, we will raise funds to support our mission to promote, empower, and educate cancer survivors so they can "reach for their dreams." The money we raise goes to the STAR program (Survivors Taking Action and Responsibility) at Children's Memorial Hospital. This is Children's long-term pediatric cancer survivor program that provides comprehensive follow-up care education and promotes healthy living. This program follows survivors into adulthood at Northwestern Memorial Hospital in Chicago. Hopefully, the money raised will help to empower other survivors not to let cancer get in the way of their dreams.

Every day is a new learning experience. I hope to remain a lifelong learner as long as I can.

I have learned to never let life's roadblocks keep me from reaching my dreams.

LESSONS FROM A HOSPICE NURSE

by Melanie Morrisey Dines

did not become a nurse to watch my family die. Yet, that is precisely what I did. I was working as a hospice nurse and still recall the day my father-in-law called. "They took off two quarts of beer-colored fluid," he said with glee, knowing that I would enjoy hearing the gory details. After thanking him for his call, I thought, "He has cancer." Why would I think anything else? After all, that's all I knew. I had been an oncology nurse since the day I graduated.

It was a death sentence. Glen, my father-in-law, was diagnosed with mesothelioma. I needed to be his daughter-in-law, but I also felt the urge to be his nurse. With much encouragement, we got Glen hospice care. I chose his doctor, his nurse, and his case manager. I also attended the office and home visits with his doctor. I was both his nurse and his daughter-in-law.

We couldn't have asked for a more peaceful and meaningful death. I stood at the kitchen sink, washing out morphine syringes and heard my husband reading one of Glen's stories to our five-year-old son, Nathan. Glen's wife, Rickie, listened too. I looked over at Glen and could no longer see the rise and fall of his chest. "He's gone," I announced. Rickie crawled into Glen's bed to give him one last hug. As I walked over to console Rickie and my husband, I felt like someone was looking at me. There, outside the window, stood a big, strong buck staring at me. He held his gaze just long enough for all of us to look his way. "Glen's spirit is now one with the deer," I said, trying to comfort my son as well as myself. "Now his suffering is over."

"How can you do that type of nursing?" "How can I not?" I reply. I didn't always have that snappy kind of comeback. Early in my career, I used to say, "It's not for everyone. Just like emergency department nursing isn't for me." However, as I grew in my career and moved from acute care to hospice nursing, I truly knew what my nurse life was about.

I am involved in people's lives when they are most vulnerable. It is an honor and a privilege to be involved in people's lives. Where else can one walk into a stranger's living room, sit down, and talk about dying? I like my patients to understand what's happening, so I give them and their families as much information as they are ready to process. One of the most poignant hospice moments comes when I sit down with the patient and the family and talk about their declining status.

Usually the family has observed changes in the patient, yet no one is willing to discuss them. And probably no one is talking with the patient about dying because they don't know what to say. I say to the patient, "What do you think is happening?" If they say, "I don't know," I'll ask them if they want to know. If they do, I gently tell them that they are dying and explain what it is that I'm seeing. Most times, there is relief because the topic of "death and dying" is out in the open.

This time it's my father. He had metastatic renal cancer. His symptoms were similar to my father-in-law's with fluid in the lung after what he thought was an upper respiratory illness. Having just moved to Oregon with my husband and son, I felt helpless and in shock as he told me his news. No amount of chemotherapy or radiation therapy was going to help. Dad didn't look too different, but my mom was a wreck. When talking with my parents, I slipped into my hospice mode. I spoke with them about how helpful hospice could be for both of them. Seeing my mom cry, I asked dad to consider hospice, if not for his sake, then for hers.

My dad agreed to sign up for hospice. Sitting together on the bed, I said, "As sad as this is, try to think of this as a 'gift.' The gift of knowing your life will be over soon and you can begin saying 'goodbye' and 'I love you' to friends and family."

The next time I saw my dad was at Thanksgiving. He had lost weight, was more short-of-breath, and tired easily. My dad was also a little "goofy" from the morphine. He had started the process of "life review" with his pastor and good friend, Bart. I suggested that Bart tape-record my father's life story. In telling his story, my father was able to spend time with Bart, reminisce about old times, and pass on his legacy.

I wanted to pay tribute to my father by making a photo videotape set to the music of two songs, one that I chose and one that he chose. I asked my father what song he wanted; he replied, "The party's over." Since my father was a poet, I asked him to read one of his poems for the video. When my father received the video, he called and said, "I am so touched I wanted to type you a thank-you note, but I couldn't figure out how to type." With tears sliding down my cheeks, I cried and told him that I loved him.

I got "the call" from my mom at the beginning of Christmas vacation. "It's time to come down," she said. I had promised my father that I would take care of him at the end. There sat my father, on the couch with the dog on his lap, oxygen tubing hanging from his nose and a crossword puzzle by his side. To my husband and son, he didn't seem too bad. But I knew different. That night, while sleeping on the living room couch, I awakened at 2:00 a.m. by the sound of my father and mother talking in the bathroom. "No, Bill, it's not time to get up and get dressed," said my mother. I could hear the edge of exasperation and exhaustion in her voice. This was not the first time he was confused.

The next day, a hospice nurse and a social worker came to visit. It was time for a hospital bed, medication for his agitation, and diapers. Normally, this is a huge adjustment for patients and families. That evening, not too long before bed, my father rose from the couch and stood still for a while. I asked him what he was doing and he said, "I'm waiting for the bus." "Where are you going, Dad?" "Home," he replied. Instead of trying to reassure him that he was already home, I simply said, "Oh." I understood him to mean that he was getting ready to die. The next morning, he was comatose. When he died, I cried and screamed, "It's not fair!"

While out in the garden the spring after my father died, I heard the call of a lone mourning dove sitting on top of our roof. I looked up, waved, and said, "Hi Dad! You finally made it. What do you think?" My father never got a chance to visit us in our new home. I felt sad about that and often wished he were close by. Now he is visiting our home appearing in the form of the dove. As crazy as this sounds, it is reassuring to me as I live my life without dad.

In the garden, I can set aside my nursing persona and return to being a child. Digging in the dirt and planting new life is therapeutic and life affirming. Sometimes, in our nursing lives, we don't always see the results of our good work. With gardening, I see results and also am able to refuel at the same time, so that I'm ready to give once again.

Life is short—appreciate it.
Tell your loved ones that you love them.
Don't wait until they are dying.
You may never get the chance. Have fun.
Laugh. Don't take yourself too seriously.
Say "good-bye" as if it were the last time.

MAKING A DIFFERENCE AROUND THE WORLD

by Debra Dunn

ashkent, Uzbekistan; Damascus, Syria; Yerevan, Armenia; Varna, Bulgaria, are countries and cities most of us have never heard of. They are countries and cities that have not heard of us. However, these countries have something in common, Debra Dunn. Debra receives many letters from diverse, underprivileged countries like the ones already mentioned. All the letters have similar sentiments as excerpted from the following two letters:

Debby, I whole-heartedly thank you for your kind assistance as we continue our mission of helping Armenia's underprivileged. A great amount of thanks also comes from our staff and patients. Without your help, our staff would not be able to provide the safe treatment to our patients whose lives truly depend on it.
Appreciatively,
S. D. AGBU
(Armenian General Benevolent Union),
Office of Armenia Aid, Medical Programs.

Dear Debra:
Healing the Children wishes to thank you for your assistance in recycling supplies for our International Medical Program. Some of these medical supplies have already been used on our most recent trip to the Dominican Republic. We are able to help the children because of volunteers like you.
Sincerely,
R.D. Director of International Medical Trips,
Healing the Children, Midlantic, Inc.

Debra often wondered if one person could make a difference in the world." The answer she found is a resounding *"YES!"* "You never know where a road will lead. It's amazing how life's twists and turns take you, unexpectedly, down so many different paths. Several years ago, I was reading an article in a professional journal, *AORN Journal* (Association of peri-Operative Registered Nursing). The article described a recycling program developed at Yale University School of Medicine in conjunction with Yale-New Haven Hospital. The program was called REMEDY.

"The purpose of the REMEDY program was to collect surgical supplies that were not used during surgery at Yale-New Haven Hospital and to send them to developing nations around the world. Countries that receive these supplies are in desperate need of proper medical and surgical supplies to treat patients. The article and the idea of helping individuals around the world not only helped answer my question about making a difference, it also really captured my interest."

Debra was aware that there were many people in this world who were disadvantaged or who lived at poverty levels. Debra knew a program like REMEDY could do wonders for helping individuals who did not have the resources to receive proper medical treatment. Debra, being an operating room nurse, pursued the REMEDY program in her own institution. She wrote a proposal for her hospital, St. Joseph's Wayne Hospital, to develop a program to ship unused medical supplies to eleven different charitable organizations. One of the most recent experiences at St. Joseph's Wayne was to ship medical supplies to Turkey after a major earthquake. Another project was to ship supplies to a city in Poland, where one of St. Joseph's Wayne Hospital's physicians was born.

The recycling program is multistep and technical in nature. Supplies opened for surgery, but not used, are collected in a closed decontaminated bin (i.e., no microorganisms present), sorted, counted, and packaged for pickup. The charitable organizations that receive the medical supplies have to be proficient in overseas transportation, customs clearance, and supply distribution.

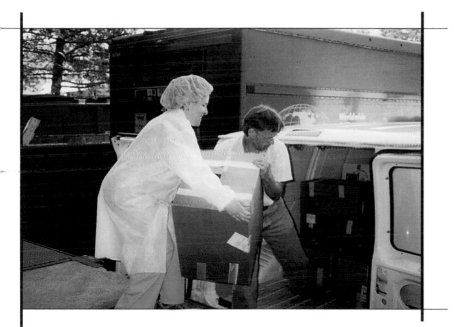

The development as well as the implementation of the program did not seem insurmountable to Debra. She believed a program like REMEDY was an excellent humanitarian option for countries that subsisted on the bare medical essentials. She wanted someone in need to have access to the supplies that were wasted in the operating room in the U.S. Waste that occurred when medical supplies were opened but not used for surgical procedures, when items fell to the floor or were contaminated, and when surgical cases were cancelled were excellent materials for shipping to those in need.

Gowns, surgical drapes, electrocautery pencils, scratch pads, skin staple guns, suction tubing, Yankauer tips, and needle boards are just a few of the medical items that are shipped. The items are not always used in the manner for which they were intended. For example, latex gloves with holes are not used as gloves but recycled as penrose drains. Half drape sheets may be cut into surgical drapes.

Debra tells about the letters of thanks she receives from some of the charitable organizations. "The letters make the project very rewarding." Debra reads the literature the organizations send her. She looks over the snapshots of children who have benefited from the supplies. When looking at the children and some of their deformities, Debra feels close to the children. "It really is heartrending. Although these people and children are so very far away, I know in some way I have touched their lives. I feel that in my own small, little world I have made a difference. Making a difference is what counts. Nursing has provided me the opportunity to touch so many lives. Nursing has given me the ability to make a difference around the world."

MY CHILD SHOWED ME THE WAY

by Trudie Kidwell Hart

lthough I worked as a mental health aide, I can't say I really considered nursing when I was growing up. I'd been married for six years when we discovered I was finally pregnant. Thrilled, our dreams turned to ashes quickly when I miscarried at three months. Though sad, my faith and philosophy of life is, "It goes on."

The following year, my husband, Everett, also known as "Coach" and I learned I was once again with child. We were happy, but I'd just lost 60 pounds and was not looking forward to gaining back any weight.

Brenden Blair Hart was born at 34 weeks gestation by emergency caesarian section on February 4, 1981, at 2:31 a.m., weighing 5 lbs, 15 ounces, 46.5 cm in length with a low apgar score, which meant trouble. I had developed increased amniotic fluid, had premature rupture of membranes for six days, and Brenden was showing poor respiratory effort. Our neonatal intensive care experience was about to begin.

Brenden was intubated, lines were placed, and a full sepsis work-up with antibiotics was started. It was soon discovered that even the smallest nasogastric tube could not be passed down either nostril. His nasal cultures were positive for "beta" strep. The primary diagnosis was bilateral choanal atresia; the final diagnosis was CHARGE syndrome, a multi-system problem. CHARGE means: C for coloboma; H for heart disease; A for atresia of the choanal; R for retarded growth and development; G for genitourinary anomalies; E for ear anomalies or deafness. After genetic counseling, we learned that this diagnosis carried its own devastating prognosis. In all likelihood, our son, Brenden, would die within the first few months of life.

I got to see Brenden on the fourth day of his life in all his glory. He was beautiful, but of course, every mom feels that way. He was surrounded by much high-tech equipment, living in an isolette on a cardiorespiratory monitor with an airway tube taped to his face. If he closed his mouth, he would not be able to breathe.

For three months, I admired, watched, spoke with, and learned from the many nurses who cared for Brenden and us. We sat through surgeries at Albert Einstein and North Shore hospitals. We witnessed many procedures and lessons on everyday care. We had our ups and downs, good days and bad. Most likely we wouldn't have remained sane without the nurses. They took the time to show us the way.

As unrealistic as it may seem, in my naivety, I thought that if we just "fixed" each problem, then Brenden would be alright. We would beat the odds and my "perfect child" would come home. You see, we believed in the miracle of prayer. The glass for us was always half full, not half empty.

On the bright side, Brenden was our joy. Our situation brought out the goodness, kindness, and support of family and friends. Every occasion was celebrated. I still have every card, letter, and note I received.

The day did arrive when Brenden came home along with oxygen, suctioning equipment, an apnea monitor for nighttime use, feeding tubes, medication, and a large collection of medical supplies and follow-up appointments. I will always treasure my memories of those 11 days he spent at home.

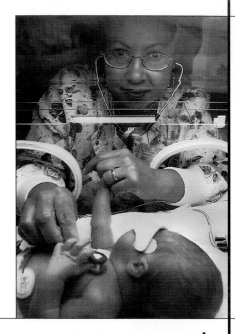

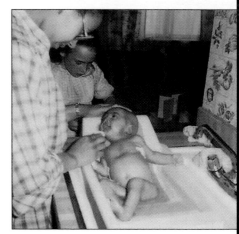

Brenden unexpectedly died on May 19, 1981, in his car seat on the way home from a meeting. I immediately knew something was terribly wrong. All I'd learned went out the window as I screamed.

My world had fallen apart. Yes, I knew Brenden would die, but denial is a strong emotion. In my heart, I felt that it was too soon! I remember afterwards being supportive and calm for family and friends, as a slow anger began to grow beneath the surface, eroding away my faith and belief in God. The "why me" syndrome had begun.

The grieving process is odd. Everyone does it in a different way and at a different rate. To keep myself occupied, I reapplied to school. I'd just spent the last three months around the medical and nursing professions, admiring the nurses I'd met. I admired their skills, patience, compassion, and teaching methods. I finally decided I would return to school. By June 1, I was back in the classroom. Still not dealing with my loss, or was I?

At some point that summer, I was contacted by the SIDS Foundation. Although Brenden wasn't technically a SIDS case, I'd been referred to them, and they were reaching out to us. The crying, guilt, and shame began to surface. By November, doubts about nursing began to creep in, but I took the time to speak with a guidance counselor and submitted my application to the school of nursing. I didn't think I stood a chance, but to my surprise, I was accepted for the September 1982 semester.

I found the program challenging and difficult. As a full-time student with a full-time job, I was still struggling to come to terms with the "Why me, God?" questions. Upon graduation, I thought I was ready for the neonatal intensive care unit (NICU). I wasn't even close. I hadn't prepared myself for the return to the unit, and as I recall, it wasn't a memorable interview. In actuality, it required several more years to work through my grief and guilt. My gradual return to church and my religious roots put me back on track. I was then ready to move forward.

By now, I was comfortable working with the mentally disabled. I'd been there for six years and wasn't looking to change my position. My NICU dream was fading fast. In mid-January of 1990, a *Newsday* ad noted, "Nursing Opportunities to Start February 1—

Will Train." It wasn't unusual for my colleagues and I to occasionally check out these ads.

After speaking to the nurse recruiter, I decided to pick up an application since the jobs were to start in approximately three weeks. To my surprise, they wanted to interview me right then and there. Thank goodness the NICU assistant director of nursing wasn't available. I was able to return the next day, a little more prepared.

The interview went well. When asked what I could offer, I said, "I know I'll understand what the parents feel when their baby is in NICU." I was willing to learn new skills and all it entailed to care for a neonate. I'd admired the nurses who'd cared for my family years before, and although I was currently a nurse, my scope of practice was very different. I've always compared it to apples and oranges. They are both fruit, but different fruit. A new saga was about to begin. This time it was to be on the other side of the door.

Here I was beginning over. My journey with Brenden had brought me full circle. I admit I felt terrified and nervous going back to class, doing a preceptorship, gaining new knowledge, and learning totally different skills. It was enough to give me palpitations as I walked through the hospital door. Never mind how I felt crossing the threshold of the NICU.

I had the best unit educator, preceptor, and NICU staff to guide me in those early days. These colleagues, now my close friends, are the most knowledgeable, caring men and women you will ever meet. This made my love of the NICU increase over the years. Now don't get me wrong, like any job, we have our ups, downs, changes, and moments of despair, but we take solace in knowing that there is always a light at the end of the tunnel, be it in the form of a kind word or a card.

It's been 21 years since Brenden was born. Because of him, I know that I've been given a purpose. I have a collection of pictures, cards, and letters from parents that tell me I've always been at the right place at the right time, as a nurse and also as a mother. In some way, I have had the privilege of touching the lives of other moms and dads and their newborns. I guess this is where I truly belong. Thank you, Brenden.

Because of him, I know that I've been given a purpose. I have a collection of pictures, cards, and letters from parents that tell me I've always been at the right place at the right time, as a nurse and also as a mother.

RECOLLECTIONS OF SEPTEMBER 11, 2001

Excerpts from NURSES REMEMBER 9/11
by Students, Faculty, and Alumni of the Division of Nursing, The Steinhardt School of Education, New York University
The project supported by the Division of Nursing and the Upsilon Chapter of the Honor Society of Nursing, Sigma Theta Tau International
The project was coordinated by Hila Richardson and Barbara Mellor with participation from Angela Apuzzo, Alphonse Falcone, Terry Fulmer, Judith Haber, Carla Mariano, Sandee McClowry, and Elizabeth Norman.

The nation and, in fact, the world watched in horror as New York City reacted to the events of September 11, 2001. Faculty and staff of the New York University Division of Nursing were among the first to respond. Students and professors alike were deployed to Ground Zero, emergency rooms in the World Trade District, triage centers at Chelsea Piers, and our own NYU Medical Center.

"Professional nurses are always among the first to respond during times of tragedy, but never was the need more profound than on September 11. The voices in the stories that follow tell a compelling story that gives some sense to the emotions experienced and care provided by students and faculty on that day and in the days and months that followed."

> —*Terry Fulmer, The Erline Perkins McGriff*
> *Professor of Nursing, Head, Division of Nursing,*
> *The Steinhardt School of Education, New York University*

For the students at New York University's Steinhardt School of Education, Division of Nursing, the memories of their first day of clinical in September of 2001 will remain with them forever. The students were scheduled to take a medication-administration math exam, review clinical policy and procedures, and spend the afternoon at hospital clinical sites. Normally, students would recall this day as one filled with the usual fears and anxieties, colored by the uncertainty of their own knowledge. But September 11, 2001, was different. The first day of clinical coincided with the terrorist attack on the World Trade Center in New York City.

"By 10:00 a.m., our world was completely transformed. We were stunned, shocked, angry, and grief-stricken. Our lives would never be the same. But we are nurses and we did what nurses do. We prioritized, improvised, and mobilized and went where we were needed. And so, within an hour of those horrific events of September 11, a group of NYU nursing faculty and students arrived at Tisch Hospital to lend support in any way we could.

"This was not the clinical orientation we had envisioned, but it was an orientation of sorts. It was trial by fire, literally and figuratively. It was an orientation to reality and to tragedy and to the incredibly important role nurses play in the face of such tragedy.

"Without knowing exactly where we were going or what we would be doing, we volunteered to work at Ground Zero. As thousands of people evacuated lower Manhattan, we headed toward it, armed with nothing but our stethoscopes and a handful of latex gloves. As we got closer to our destination, the air became thicker and more acrid, full of smoke and dust and the smell of hot steel and pulverized concrete. Our eyes stung and our throats burned. We were scared for our own safety and for what we would encounter."

> —*Melissa Offenhartz, Faculty, NYU Division of Nursing*

"We watched in horror as planes crashed into the World Trade Center. Our emotions were uncontrollable. All we wanted to do was turn around and go home to our families. No, that would not happen. Somber and shocked, we looked at each other and knew what we had to do."

> —*Sheila Amyth-Giambanco, Faculty, NYU Division of Nursing*

"We sent the critical care instructors in first and when they asked for more volunteers, I took medical and nursing students in a caravan to Chelsea Piers, where a makeshift emergency treatment center was being established. On the ride, I explained to them what we might see. I needed to assess what skills they had. And then I tried to prepare them for the kinds of injuries that they might see and how the triage system worked.

"As the minutes turned to hours, the waiting became our enemy. I knew this was not a good sign. First, the hospitals should be filled with patients, and then we should start getting victims, I thought. In a strange irony of healthcare, for the first time there were enough nurses and doctors, but no patients. All our skills and abilities were waiting to heal the victims of this terrible tragedy, but where were the patients? It was unthinkable . . . there would be no patients.

"Later that evening, the first wave of exhausted rescue workers arrived. I set about showing my students how to nurse. We asked questions of those who were injured to decide who needed treatment first. We gave priority to those with breathing problems or chest pains. We gave them oxygen and other treatments to help them breathe better. We immediately took EKGs to see how their hearts were doing. My students and I washed out their burning eyes with a

solution of salt water called normal saline—although no amount of normal saline could flush the sights they had seen from their eyes. 'Here's how you improvise and can use an intravenous IV bag to rinse out the eyes,' I told my students."

—*Elizabeth Ayello, Faculty, NYU Division of Nursing*

"Humvees were passing exhausted MDs, EMTs, and nurses. The New York City firemen had soiled masks. I helped them change to clean ones as they were leaning up against their trucks or sitting on pieces of twisted steel. I had to touch them in order for them to realize that someone was talking to them.

"I stayed with the surgeons who were used to an operating room. They would yell out, 'Angela, get me O_2, get me Proventil, get me gauze.' One asked for a suture set up. I looked at him through the falling debris and reminded him that wounds couldn't be sutured because everything was contaminated. 'Treat it, tape it shut, and transport him out of here' he replied. As the ambulance crew prepared to take him away, I called out to remind him to ask for a tetanus shot.

"I realize what I have defined was triage on September 11. 'Tag patients with level of injury, treat what you can, tape what you can't, and transport out of the area. Tag, treat, tape, transport, tetanus.'"

—*Angela Apuzzo, Faculty, NYU Division of Nursing*

"The doctor brought us to Firehouse 10, located at Greenwich and Liberty. I stood in amazement, taking in the environment that would be my home for the next few days. There was not a front door or wall to the station house because it had been blown out. It was dark, dim, and filthy, with thick layers of dust, ash, and debris from the fallout. There were two small tables, one gurney, and a coat rack that was fashioned into a makeshift IV pole, hung with a few bags of solution and tubing. There were also a few tanks of oxygen, a defibrillator, and an emergency crash box. Two other people, a retired lawyer turned EMT from Pennsylvania and a medical resident, walked into the station and joined us. We all sat down and looked out. For the first time that day, I really saw what no photograph, news report, or television footage could ever capture. Ground Zero was a mountain of concrete, mangled steel, dirt, debris, and rubble. It was absolute devastation and destruction. Silently we sat, exchanging a sober moment. There was nothing for us to do. Or was there?

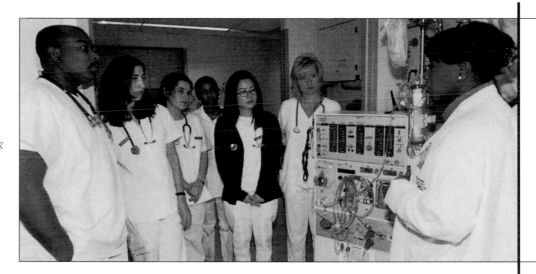

"Hundreds of people were working in a synchronized bucket brigade. A community banded together on their hands and knees, trying to clear and unearth anything to bring home to thousands who were waiting to celebrate or mourn. Our duty was right there in front of us. We joined the digging effort. On our hands and knees we dug with a purposeful rhythm. The ground underneath me was very hot and the air was dense with choking fumes. I filled buckets with dirt and debris. Then signs of what once was a workforce of thousands began to appear.

"First it was the occasional business card, part of a day planner with smeared notes, then pieces of a briefcase. This brought me closer to what I feared the most, a shoe and then the foot. I called out to the rescue worker, a towering man, rough and filthy from the day's events. He placed the remains carefully into a container and walked it down the mountain, cradling them like a baby. I said a silent prayer for this kind man who had just taught me one of the greatest lessons a nurse could learn: in life we celebrate, in death we respect."

—*Maria Gatto, Student, NYU Division of Nursing*

(Excerpts printed with permission from New York University, Steinhardt School of Education, Division of Nursing)

THE BIRTH OF A PEDIATRIC NURSE

by Stephanie L. Morris

here to begin? I guess I should start by saying that I knew I wanted to be a nurse in high school. However, due to the lack of funds and family support, it was not an option. So I chose to marry my high school sweetheart and start a family. I don't regret this, and I am still happily married. We have a wonderful family.

I have helped many friends through crises. They would say, "You should be a nurse." I would think, someday! Finally, in 1994, my husband's Naval career made it possible for me to start school. I could finally pursue my dream of becoming a nurse. My husband was assigned to shore duty for four years, we had three children, and I entered nursing school.

I did well in my college core courses and was on my way to start the clinical experience. Then I learned I was unexpectedly pregnant. After much consideration, we decided to take a chance and continue with my schooling. All was going well, even through the semester that Zackary was born. Then, during my five-week pediatric rotation, when Zack was nine months old, things started to go wrong.

We were studying children with cancer. Zackary got sick, and I noticed similarities between the cancer children and my son Zackary. He was bruising easily and was pale. During Thanksgiving week, our doctor confirmed our worst fears, Zackary had leukemia. He was admitted to the unit where I was having my clinical experience. I learned so much more as a parent than I did as a student. With the love and support of my husband, my in-laws, and a wonderful clinical instructor, I made it through those trying weeks until Christmas break.

Zackary was the best baby, considering how sick he was. As the next semester was ready to begin, so were the plans for Zackary. He was to have a bone marrow transplant. I finished my last semester of school with my husband's support and encouragement. I would stay at night with my baby in the hospital and go to clinicals the next morning. My husband or my in-laws would stay with Zack while I was in school.

It was all very difficult, but things were falling into place until my very last clinical day. I was at Trident Hospital doing my management clinicals when I got the call that Zackary had gone into septic shock and respiratory failure. He was put on a ventilator in the pediatric intensive care unit (PICU). I thought I had been through the worst, but now it was even worse than before. We were told that Zack and the doctors were fighting for his life hour by hour. No one, as I learned later, had ever survived being put on a ventilator so soon after a bone marrow transplant, especially a baby. But, somehow, with great care and the power of prayer, he did. At the same time, I passed my last exam and became a registered nurse.

Before going through my ordeal with Zackary, my goal had been to become a labor and delivery nurse, but I believe things happen for a reason. I initially became a newborn nursery nurse and a year later joined a pediatric team.

My strong desire to help others and my experience as a parent of four boys with one very ill has prepared me to get and give the most I can for pediatric patients and their families. I will never forget how it feels to have your child's life, the one over whom you have been the main caretaker, handed over to medical professionals who are strangers. Even my husband, who was a successful military professional, felt helpless because he lacked any medical knowledge. I learned, through the experience with Zack, how important it is for patients and families to have information.

I will never forget how a compassionate ear or shoulder to cry on, when nothing else could be done, made everything a little better. I have learned the importance of incorporating and empowering family members to be a part of the team for healing their child.

I am happy to say that Zackary is now seven years old and very happy and healthy. We have struggles ahead of us, but we will pull through. I can truly say I absolutely love being a nurse. When I care for my patients and their families, my goal is to make sure that they know how much I like my job, love the profession of nursing, and enjoy caring for their loved ones.

THE GIFT OF INTUITION

by Katherine L. Smith-McEwen

he best gifts are often those that cannot be purchased from a store. I have been given one of those gifts, intuition, from both my grandmother, "Grammy," Eva Ferguson, and from my mother, Jane Smith. I believe just as heirlooms can be passed on from generation to generation, so too can personal attributes such as intuition be passed on.

My Grammy Eva was a nurse. She decided to become a nurse as a second career. In her 40s, she began nursing school at Cook County Hospital in Chicago. She graduated in 1961, the same year I was born.

Grammy was a nurse in the recovery room at Lutheran Deaconess Hospital. As a child, I remember Grammy dressed in her perfectly white dress with her perfectly white shoes and hose. I also observed her polishing her nursing shoes nightly. But the best thing I remember about Grammy was her professionalism as a nurse. She took her job very seriously and was not just "putting in time" to get paid. Nursing was her vocation, a way of life.

When I was a child, Grammy taught me lessons in nursing such as how to "miter" the corners while making my bed. I was aware Grammy could take in large amounts of patient information, get to the roots of issues, and determine the correct nursing course. She also had this skill in her everyday life, outside of nursing. Although the term was not and still may not be broadly used, it could be said that Grammy had a tremendous sense of *intuition.* Grammy was well respected by the most influential physicians, including those who are now internationally known. For these and other reasons, she was selected to fulfill a variety of leadership positions.

Grammy intervened daily on behalf of her patients and her staff, using knowledge and *intuition.* She passed on her gift of *intuition* to her daughter, my mother, Jane. Mom told me daily when she did or did not "feel" right about something. To my amazement, she was always right, just like Grammy.

I knew that I needed to work in a medical field, because I had a strong desire to help others and to learn anatomy, physiology, pharmacology, and chemistry. I became a radiologic technologist but because I wanted to spend more time with the patients, I decided to become a nurse, just like Grammy.

In 1984, I was a new graduate nurse. I graduated from Loyola University in Chicago and had the good fortune of being one of the first new grads hired into a critical care unit. I knew I would enjoy this fast-paced nursing environment. I remembered how my Grammy had worked in the recovery room. She and I both enjoyed high acuity patients.

I have many fond memories of nursing at Loyola University Medical Center, the most significant of which is caring for Mr. H. Mr. H., a 41-year-old, had been driving on the Eisenhower expressway when his automobile was struck by another vehicle. Mr. H. incurred multiple fractures of his ribs, humerus, bilateral femurs, parietal skull, and neck (C-1 and C-2). He also had a myocardial infarct and subsequent cardiac arrest during the accident. Mr. H. received nursing care on our unit for approximately six months. Despite the predictability of his unpredictable condition, his course continued to be enigmatic. For example, despite his spinal and neck fractures, a cardiopulmonary resuscitation, and an intubation, he was not paralyzed! He was ventilated on a RotoRest bed and was on some Class III anti-arrhythmias to treat his arrhythmias. He would frequently flip into supra ventricular tachycardia, followed by ventricular tachycardia. This was especially true when the RotoRest bed was turning. I was always nervous when caring for Mr. H. I knew caring for him would always be very "active" and "unpredictable."

One night, during the Christmas season, I was asked to be the night charge nurse. I was scared and questioned my abilities but was encouraged by my supervisor's faith in me. Most of our senior nurses had moved to the day shift, and I recognized it was time for me to become a leader. Although I accepted the position, I still thought, "Why now? I have been out of nursing school for only six months. There are more than 20 patients and I am concerned for their safety." On that fateful night of being the charge nurse, I also took a nursing assignment of patients, Mr. H. being one of them. He was a bit tachycardic, with a heart rate of 112-120, a systolic blood pressure of 140 and a diastolic pressure of 90. To my horror, as I was making rounds on the unit, I heard Mr. H.'s monitor begin to ring out. *Intuition* told me this was not a good situation. As I ran for the room, I asked one of the nurses to call his doctor. Mr. H.'s heart rate had reached 220, and his systolic blood pressure had dropped to 90.

The rhythm appeared to be ventricular tachycardia, yet I somehow "thought differently." I remember evaluating this rhythm for what seemed to be hours. I also remember thinking the stakes were very high for Mr. H. because he was the head of his household with several children.

The doctor suggested I administer Lidocaine intravenously. My "gut instinct" told me to do otherwise. I developed tachycardia myself searching for the "right intervention." I hesitated then told the intern I did not believe Mr. H.'s present heart rhythm was ventricular tachycardia (VT). By this time, the chief surgical resident had arrived in the room. I told him I was very familiar with Mr. H.'s heart rhythm and that this one was significantly different than the way his rhythms had been previously. During this discussion, Mr. H.'s systolic blood pressure dropped into the 60s. I knew that Mr. H.'s cardiac output had dropped significantly. I told the chief surgical resident that we should "shock" the patient. I grabbed the defibrillator that was in the room and with a lump in my throat and fear that I was wrong, I administered the shock. Mr. H. immediately flipped into a sinus rhythm with a rate of 90. With tears in my eyes and a sick stomach, I asked about Mr. H.'s rhythm. The cardiology fellow said that Mr. H. had been in Torsades de Pointe. (Although well known today, it was not well understood by the nursing community in the 1980s.) The fellow continued to tell us that, for Mr. H.'s condition, Lidocaine would have been contraindicated and most likely would have resulted in sustained cardiac arrest and death. That night, while acting as the charge nurse and while caring for Mr. H., I learned to trust my "gut instinct" and *intuition* when caring for patients. I recognized that my Grammy and my mother had passed on the *gift of intuition* to me.

Several months after Mr. H. was discharged, he was readmitted for a coronary artery bypass surgery. I remember thinking the nurses would have many issues to address while caring for Mr. H. However, my "gut" told me he would be fine and indeed he did quite well. He had an uneventful bypass surgery and was discharged soon afterward.

Since this episode, I have had hundreds, if not thousands, of circumstances where my head has told me to do one thing and my "gut" has told me to do another. I have learned to use both attributes synergistically to provide my patients and the staff with the the best outcomes possible.

Even though my mother is not a nurse, she nursed my family through a multitude of illnesses. She stayed with my Grammy and grandfather when they were dying and instinctively and *intuitively* knew what to do.

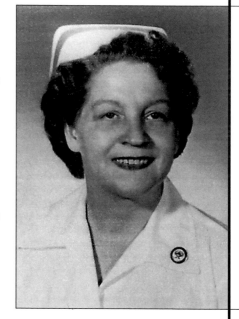

It has been a long time since Grammy passed away. She lived boldly and honestly and, even in death, her *intuition* was evident. After suffering from end-stage emphysema and cardiac arrhythmias, the doctors tried to be encouraging to Grammy. She pulled out her mirror, looked at her tongue, and told my mother that she was dying. She knew because of the tongue cyanosis and the "rattling" in her lungs. Grammy boldly told me not to dwell on her death with my mom because she did not want her to worry. This was good advice and good *intuition*. The advice was too late. My mom told me she "knew" Grammy was dying.

I visited Grammy during her last hospitalization with my infant daughter, Brooke. As Brooke was pulling on Grammy's oxygen tubing, I whispered in Grammy's ear that I had been a nurse because of her. I told her she had taught me so much and that her *gift* to my mother and me would live on. I held Brooke close to Grammy and said, "Maybe you have given Brooke the gift as well, *the gift of intuition.*"

THE TAPESTRY OF NURSING

by Nancy Carol Parks

nce you're a nurse, you're always a nurse. To me, the nursing profession is a strong, bright thread in the *tapestry of my life*. It runs continuously throughout the piece, popping up in all kinds of beautiful patterns. This thread shapes my identity. It integrates the work I do in the hospital with my faith in God and my commitment to my community. I have known nurses who, in a moment of frustration, have said, "It's just a job . . . it doesn't matter." I have never been able to say that. It's been impossible for me to separate myself from my profession.

A few years ago, I was helping spring-clean my church. One of the men asked me whether I had considered going on the family mission work trip. I had not. I had no experience at doing those kinds of things. I had never even stood on a ladder, not to mention a roof. My toolbox had everything I needed for hanging artwork, but roofing was definitely out of my league. That was five years and five work trips ago. I've been roofing ever since.

The objective of my church's family mission work trip is to make vital repairs to the homes of people who, because of age, poverty, or illness, are unable to manage the work themselves. We take one week each summer and travel north to a little town near Lake Ontario. Once there, we collaborate with a local church-based group to make these repairs. Most of our work involves roofing, but we have also converted homes for wheelchair access by putting in lifts and ramps, as well as building first-floor additions.

Imagine what it must be like if you are elderly and living alone in a rural setting. Your home is in a region that receives more then eight feet of snow each winter. Your roof is leaking. You can't fix it yourself and you have no money to hire someone to do it. You pray to God for help. One day, a group of men, women, and children show up with tools, ladders, and roofing material. They tear off your old roof and put on a new one. You start to feel your life is important when you learn that these rowdy Presbyterians have traveled 300 miles just to fix your roof.

This is community nursing in the broadest sense. We all have a basic human need for a safe, dry, accessible place to live. Making vital home repairs might involve repairing roofs, but we are also mending lives. A grandfather who now needs a wheelchair can remain at home with his family with the addition of a lift or a ramp. An elderly woman with emphysema breathes more easily when her new roof keeps out the damp and chill. The question, "Just who is my neighbor?" is answered on a daily basis.

Community care also involves caring for our children and ourselves. We allow children as young as 10 to join these trips. It may take longer to teach a kid to hammer than to do it yourself, but the benefits make it worth the effort. The child's self-esteem is strengthened when a skill is mastered. The child beams with pride when adults treat him/her as a valuable member of the team. On a personal level, these experiences have helped me discover new skills and hidden talents.

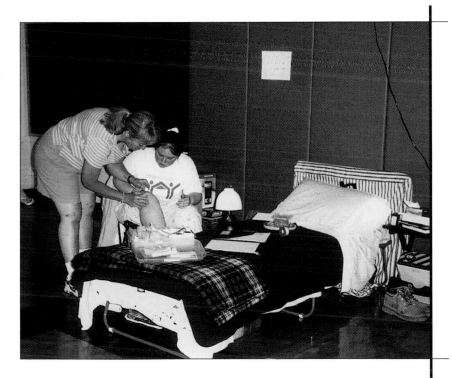

There have been situations on these work trips where it was the caregivers who needed the care. Every morning and evening, I would open my "Boo-Boo Clinic." This is where the minor bumps and bruises, cuts and scrapes were cared for with bandages, icepacks, and a kiss on the forehead. Two years ago, I found myself dealing with much more than "boo-boos." One of our workers, a retired school-teacher named Shirley, fell head first off an eight-foot roof. I was at the site and the only nurse. She was unconscious but breathing. Another worker had been a volunteer on an ambulance squad. She knew exactly what to do when I asked her to stabilize Shirley's head. We maintained her airway and immobilized a fractured clavicle and wrist. Even though we were in a rural setting, the Emergency Medical Transport (EMT) arrived quickly. Shirley had two hairline fractures in her cervical vertebrae but no spinal cord damage. She has since made a full recovery.

One might think the nursing profession, an active spiritual life, and roofing have nothing in common. I believe they are different expressions of the same devotion and discipline. In nursing, we speak of the five "rights" when administering medication (the right person, the right drug, the right time, the right dosage, and the right method). In the Judeo-Christian tradition, we follow the Ten Commandments. In roofing, there are specific rules for safety that must be followed.

Compassion for humans in need is a guiding principle for entering the nursing profession. One of the fundamental commandments of the Judeo-Christianity ethic is to love our neighbor as we love ourselves. Spending one's summer vacation replacing a neighbor's roof is compassion mixed with action, just as nursing is compassion mixed with action.

I have prayed for my patients, visited ailing members of my congregation, and provided first aid on the work sites. I believe that a nurse is always a nurse. That which brings you into the profession is exhibited in all areas of your life. Nursing is the thread. Unexpected patterns may emerge, but the vibrant radiance of the thread of nursing is always visible in *the tapestry of one's life.*

TOUCHY-FEELY STUFF

by Sally Bellerose

n 1977, while I was in nursing school, I had to write an essay entitled, "Inspiration, Aspiration, Vocation: Why I Want to Become a Nurse." This title suggested motivations more lofty than mine were in favor at the school.

Job security and a living wage, not a burning desire to care for the sick, drew me to nursing. I was as compassionate as the next child of Woodstock, but to be honest, I would have chosen raising sheepdogs, becoming a folk singer, or being the girlfriend of a rock star first. If Jerry Garcia had shown any interest in me, I never would have gone to a community college to become a registered nurse.

At the time, I hadn't written an essay since I was in high school. I was working in the lingerie department at Sears and didn't see how my ability to make a guy feel comfortable selecting a nightgown for his wife was a skill I could use in nursing. So, as I sat cross-legged on my beanbag chair (every self-respecting former hippie owned one), I wrote about Anne, a hospital roommate from a few years earlier who I met when I had a total colectomy. While recuperating, my main pastime (besides watching television and pitying myself) was talking to Anne, who was afflicted by a wicked neurological disease that made her twitch and jerk.

The only medical professional I saw respond appropriately to Anne's complaint of shoulder pain was a gray-haired nurse. She would perform her tasks, i.e., neurological checks, blood pressure measurements, administration of medications, and the fine-tuning of the therapeutic equipment, and then she would fold her hands and ask Anne, "What do we need to do today?" She used the term "we" literally, meaning how could they both make Anne more comfortable?

I watched her massage Anne's back and I listened to their conversations, noting how she became Anne's trusted confidant and informed advocate. It looked so easy and natural. I wondered, "How hard can it be to focus for five minutes on the needs of a patient?" I was a witness to the "art of nursing." With the grace of a skilled professional, Anne's nurse made it look simple.

In nursing school, however, I was overwhelmed by how much I didn't know. By that time, I had decided the *touchy-feely stuff* was all well and good, but it seemed a luxury compared to learning the signs of diabetic shock.

But I sweated through that essay, piling on the sensitivity like the former flower child I was. I wrote what I thought would establish my potential as a nurse whose strength was exhibiting compassion. Consequently, the essay I submitted was not so much untrue as incomplete.

During my tenure in nursing school, I decided to leave the ability "to stand still while holding chaos in the palm of the hand" to the Dalai Lama. But I could not entirely abandon the notion that someday I would become a nurse who calmed the tumult of the working day by folding her hands and listening to her patients. In the meantime, I strove to fill the frontal lobes of my brain with practical information that would get me through the next clinical trial. I had my eyes on the prize. I was going to graduate, pass the national nurse licensing examine, obtain a job, and buy a car that didn't require a screwdriver to shift gears.

One month after graduation and the day after test-driving a cherry-red Mustang, I located a job. On the first day, I faced a ward of 32 severely handicapped and developmentally disabled patients. I felt like an outsider, a frightened witness with medications to give, treatments to administer, and conditions to assess. Then, I met the gaze of a 42-pound woman named Daisy, whose small body was enfolded in a beanbag chair.

I knelt in front of her and made my first attempt to get a patient to take a medication. She glared at me and clenched her teeth. I looked to the aide, "What do we do to get her to take this pill?" "We say 'hello' before doing anything with Daisy," she replied. The aide grinned at Daisy and made a loud guttural sound. Daisy responded with a corresponding "grrr."

Daisy took her medication, but the nebulizer treatment was another matter. I felt as though I were teetering on the edge of incompetence much of that day, but the memory of the gray-haired nurse kept luring me back to solid ground. Sometimes I snarled at her saint-like image, but I always restored my composure when I interacted with patients. That weekend, I drove home in a new Ford Escort, thinking about Daisy and my life as a nurse. The car wasn't as sexy as a Mustang, but it was cherry red and had a dynamite sound system that handled my tapes of the Dalai Lama and the Grateful Dead with equal ease.

[Reprinted with permission from *American Journal of Nursing* (2002), 102(7), 25.]

WHEN DISASTER STRIKES

by Loretta Jean Aiken

anuary 13, 1982, I stood by my huge picture window watching the heavy snow come down. I thought, "It will take more than ten minutes to get to work today." Traffic was already a mess, schools had closed early. I hoped this storm wouldn't be as bad as the infamous George Washington Birthday Blizzard of 1977 (three days in the intensive care unit (ICU) with no extra food or clean underwear). I mentally checked off a list of essentials I needed to pack for this pilgrimage to work. Today, I would just have to toughen up and be like a postman, even if it meant going through sleet, rain, snow, and the dark of night to get to the ICU patients

One friend, a co-worker, offered to give me a ride to work. I lived on a hill and feared her car would not make the steep incline. Another co-worker called and begged me to pick up a pack of Salem Lights. I did not like the thought of buying cigarettes, but she was a friend. The grocery stores were full of customers and I was irritated by the delays. As I waited in line, I thought, "My neighbors were lucky, they could stay in their homes and be warm, safe, and comfortable, while I had to go out in the storm to get to work."

When I was leaving the parking garage, I saw an elderly woman walking with a cane. From the corner of my eye, I noticed she slipped, fell, and couldn't get up. Another delay I thought, but the nurse in me made me stop to make sure she was alright. I helped her up, brushed her off, and offered her a ride downtown.

The snow came down in blizzard waves and we could barely see 20 feet in front of our car. "Almost 4:00 p.m. and we've only gone a mile," I wondered aloud if I would arrive on time. Two hours in snarled traffic brought us to a dead stop on the Fourteenth Street Bridge.

My rear defroster was useless. I got out of my car to wipe off the back window. My passenger got out of the car to stretch her legs. I heard a God-awful thud. I watched the car shake. The bridge felt like it was moving under my feet. I thought, "An earthquake and the bridge is going to collapse into the river!" I heard screaming and saw people running. The bridge was cracking and the noise was getting louder.

I was too scared to move, someone was yelling, "A plane hit the bridge and there might be an explosion!" The profound stench of gasoline hit me like a sledgehammer. My adrenalin kicked in when I thought of a fireball and I felt nauseated from the smell.

I screamed to my passenger, "We need to run and get off the bridge!" Thoughts of an explosion whirled through my mind. I ran but I couldn't seem to get off the bridge. People were jerking open car doors to see what happened. I was wildly looking around for my passenger, but I could not see her in the confusion.

People were running away from the bridge, yet some people were in a rush to get on the bridge. Someone ran into me. I slid and fell on the snow-covered concrete road. My feet couldn't find enough traction to stand. Hundreds of people were running and jumping over my feet. I knew I was about to be trampled.

My fingers were "stepped on." A baby was crying beside me, and I realized loud sobs were coming from a woman, perhaps the baby's mother. A person was lying across my feet. For this brief second, time stopped. I had trouble catching my breath.

Maybe I had been knocked out cold. Maybe I had fainted from fright. Suddenly, my mind focused on my fingers and I knew I was alive. As I came back to awareness, I could feel the pain in my fingers and the coldness of the snow. People were lying in a heap and I was at the bottom of the pile.

My fear mounted as we tried to get untangled. I was sure we were going to die. But out of nowhere came a big warm hand. The hand was reaching out and pulling me up. The heat of the human contact was like a jolt of electricity. As I got up, I grabbed the baby and held on to the woman who was clinging to me.

My eyes caught the missing piece of the bridge. I got a glimpse of the huge plane floating in the river. The scene was surreal. I stared at the grotesque site of the plane. My knees were sinking again because of the weight of the woman and baby, but the big man held on to us. The baby screamed, the woman sobbed, and I bordered on hysteria.

A helicopter was overhead. I could hear sirens in the distance. I looked up and as if by a miracle, the visibility cleared and we all knew the people of Washington were on their way to help. "Please, please God, let them get here fast" was the repeated thought in my mind. I was already frozen stiff and could only imagine the icy water below. "Maybe some of the passengers were still alive," we kept saying over and over again to each other. I was crying and begging God to "Let the people get out of the water."

Policemen, firemen, and other rescue workers were on the bridge. I questioned myself, "Had I been out for a while or had my mind just gone numb?" I looked up and held my breath as I watched the big inner tube from the helicopter swing to and fro. I kept saying, "Thank you God, someone is here to help." The sirens were so loud I couldn't hear anything else. I lost contact with the mother and baby. I lost contact with my passenger. An older black woman looked over the edge of the bridge and started singing the old hymn *We Shall Gather at the River.* The effect of the singing was mesmerizing.

I cried, prayed, and felt profound grief as I realized the magnitude of the tragedy. I was caught up in the very pinnacle of horror. I remember just standing on the edge of the bridge, in the blowing snow, and feeling powerless. I could not help the people in the water. I was an ICU nurse, I was alive, and I wanted to help those in need but could not.

It was dark. I was chilled to the bone. My clothes were wet and my feet felt frostbitten. I had a huge lump on my head and I was sure that my fingers were broken. A policeman put a paper in my hand. I stared at him as he kept asking me over and over again, "Are you okay?" I was so overwhelmed by the death and destruction I could not speak.

I realized my friend Wendy, who offered me a ride to work, was on the bridge along with other co-workers. I did not know where or how they were. I had lost the mother and baby and never laid eyes again on the elderly woman who was my passenger. As I left the scene and walked back to my home, I kept asking, "Why me, why me?" For some reason, I was still living and able to walk away from the river. "Why me?" I asked. "Why was I still alive?" Air Florida Flight 90 had 79 people on board and only five survived the crash. I was fine, my friends, co-workers, and neighbors were fine. I did not move on with my life until all the bodies were recovered from the river.

While I struggled with survivor guilt, my ICU staff nurse job was a godsend. I was able to throw myself into my work. I focused on others instead of myself. I was the textbook picture of post-traumatic stress syndrome. I had to keep busy. I volunteered to teach classes at work, took on arts and crafts fund-raising projects at my church, and adopted a grandparent through Arlington County Social Services. In my heart, I knew if I had not bought the cigarettes or helped the older lady in the snow, I might have been a victim instead of a survivor. To this day, I still smile when I see Salem Lights and always look for little old ladies in snowstorms.

Nearly 20 years later, I witnessed another plane crash. Once again right in my own neighborhood. I stood on my own front steps and watched the flames from the Pentagon. I smelled the horrible gasoline stench and remembered the crash of that snowy day so many years before. I once again felt feelings of despair, yet I knew the country would get through the tragedy. The people of Washington rallied again to help the victims. The grief and death were penetrating because I dearly missed my dear friend Wendy, a nurse, who had died of cancer only three months earlier. Wendy was my friend who survived the bridge crash nearly 20 years before.

Just like 20 years ago, I reached out to my nursing friends, my profession, and my patients for strength and solace. Just like the "warm hand" in the snow storm, my colleagues, patients, and friends, and the profession of nursing have been my rock. I salute you all!

Just like 20 years ago, I reached out to my nursing friends, my profession, and my patients for strength and solace.

WHY I BECAME A NURSE

by Christine D. Rowland

ll right, I'll admit it. I was a spoiled rotten little brat. The youngest of seven, I was the type of child who made adults suck their teeth and shake their heads in disgust. I became involved with the school and church choirs as early as kindergarten. As puberty started to push me forward, a wise counselor suggested that I pursue the theater as a venue for my ever-surging energy, a direction I continued to travel through junior high and high school. Roles became larger, solos more common, and my independence and confidence grew. I was going to be a Broadway star!

With my senior year quickly approaching, I discussed my desire to attend college to study theater with my father. I can still remember the look on his face that sunny afternoon as we stood on the deck overlooking his mini-kiwi farm. He put his hand on my shoulder, indicated that I was not one of the most scholarly students, and said, "You should focus your energies on marrying well." All my pleading, whining, foot stomping, and tears could not persuade him otherwise.

As my senior year progressed, my interest in the theater dwindled. I got a job as a waitress in a very popular beachfront restaurant and I fell in love. That summer, my parents took an extended European vacation, no doubt to celebrate the graduation of their last child. During their absence, I took the placement test, paid all the fees, and was actively enrolled at Trident Technical College. I was going to be a legal secretary!

A few years later, after working for several different law firms, I earned a position on the Charleston County Planning Board. It was an exciting and challenging position that I adored. It wasn't long before I married my love and I could not have been happier, except for one thing. I attended many late night meetings with the county council, and my newlywed husband found this very disruptive. A few short months later, with some reluctance, I resigned my position. I was going to start a family!

Nobody in my circle of friends ever discussed difficulty getting pregnant. At last, a little over a year later, I became pregnant. Unfortunately, I was very ill and on absolute bed rest. At 35 weeks, my daughter was delivered by emergency cesarean section. When she was three, after trying for two years, I became pregnant again, only to lose the child early in the second trimester. I was devastated. What did I do to deserve the life growing inside me to be extinguished? After crying for days, I realized I had to pay some emotional penance.

I decided to become a volunteer at one of the local hospitals. Something clicked deep inside me when I walked into the hospital. I was doing things I never, in my wildest dreams, ever pictured myself doing. The staff was thanking me for my help and giving me greater responsibility. One physician asked me if I were a medical student. I told him I was just a mommy. He said that I was wasting a "beautiful talent" and that I should return to school and study medicine. I was shocked. I couldn't believe my ears. Within three months, I became pregnant with my son.

Due to the high-risk nature of my pregnancy, I was placed on immediate and absolute bed rest. During the next eight months, I wrote to all the local colleges, requesting information on their nursing programs. My son was born in early June and by the middle of August, I had begun night and weekend classes at Trident Tech. In two years, I had completed all the prerequisite courses for the Bachelor of Science in Nursing degree program. I applied and was accepted to begin the following year. I was going to be a nurse!

Everything fell into place perfectly, as if the missing pieces of a life-long puzzle were finally within my grasp. The student loans came through without a hitch, and I was awarded a full fellowship to Medical Universiy of South Carolina. I knew it was going to be difficult but had no idea just how difficult. Ironically, in my second year, I learned I was pregnant again. Yet again due to the high-risk nature of my pregnancies, I was monitored closely. Everything was going fine, no problems at all. We decided that it was time to tell my parents. Two days later, my father suddenly and unexpectedly died.

It never occurred to me just how dependent my mother was on my father. She barely knew how to write a check, much less handle the household business. Needless to say, I took over. Her health was rapidly declining with mutiple angina attacks and frequent transient ischemia attacks (TIAs). So in my third trimester, taking care of her, my family, and my academics, I cut back to part-time student status. In early June, I gave birth to my daughter, who, oddly enough, looks exactly like my father.

I returned to school in the fall. I still had the responsibility of running two households and maintaining my studies. It was a struggle. I had good days, bad days, and days when I just wanted to quit everything. I am not sure what kept me going, what power was pushing me onward. Yet, the following May, two days after my son graduated from kindergarten, I (in cap and gown) took the short walk up the horseshoe to the portico and received my degree.

I can't tell you what power put me on this road or what power prevented me from jumping off and running away with my tail between my legs. I can't tell you where this power will lead me in the future. However, there is one thing I can definitely say without hesitation. I am, have always been, and will always be a nurse!

tribute

PART VI

TRIBUTE TO A SPECIAL NURSE

ooks about nurses are scarce, but stories about nurses who have accomplished extraordinary feats in their everyday lives are rarely told. *Ordinary People, Extraordinary Lives: the Stories of Nurses* is a book that breaks that trend. This book is about nurses who, in their daily lives, make outstanding contributions in extraordinary ways as nurse caregivers in their community. In March of 2002, we posted a request for stories honoring nurses in clinical practice. In three short months we received over 80 stories affirming our intention to raise the public's awareness about nursing and that a book containing nurses' stories would have a powerful impact. Many of the nurses featured in the book have had traditional nursing roles; some have had very non-traditional roles. All, however, have touched others lives in a special way and give us cause to celebrate the profession's continuing contributions. These are stories about nurses who dedicate themselves each day to the concern and care of others in often invisible yet elegant ways. From around the globe, we have assembled stories that provide images of nurses guaranteed to make you laugh, cry, and applaud as you learn of their accomplishments. Through the use of narratives and photography, each story shows how the individual nurse applied his or her talents to improve the quality of life for others. Stories in this book capture the diversity, intensity, and heroism of nursing. The stories taken together form a fascinating mosaic describing the fullness of the nursing profession and give us cause for celebration!

This book only captures 107 stories. We are certain that there are many more. In fact we know that you too have a story to tell—a story that honors the caring work that has touched your life. We believe that stories serve to preserve important values and deeds, the culture of a people. They also serve to build community; just ask anyone who has been a part of this project. We believe that as a community we can use our stories to build a collective vision that can be used to guide policy makers and visionaries in designing a culture of care.

We invite you to join with us by chronicling your own story or the story of a special nurse on the following page. Help us to keep this message visible. This book would not be complete without the story that has yet to be told. . . .

TRIBUTE TO A SPECIAL NURSE, THE STORY OF . . .

by _____

This story is a tribute to a special nurse, a nurse that in many ways is an ordinary person, but living an extraordinary life. This story is about . . . .

Debbie Downey Afasano, RN, BSN, RNC/CDONA. Debbie is the assistant director of quality assurance at the Florida Health Care Association. Debbie's career and home life emphasize the importance of quality time centered on people, faith, values, life purpose, and making each day count for something special. Her greatest joys come from her husband, Ray, twin sons, Benjamin and Scott, and her calling to healthcare ministry for the elderly.

Loretta Jean Aiken, RN, MSN. Loretta is a clinical nurse specialist in the Cardiac Intensive Care Unit at the National Naval Medical Center in Bethesda, Maryland. Loretta has traveled extensively throughout the world and is now pursuing a post-graduate certificate in International Health at George Mason University in Fairfax, Virginia.

Sheila Kelly Ames, BA. Sheila is a wife, daughter, sister, and mother of three grown children who are the greatest joy in her life. Sheila feels particularly blessed with dear and amazing friends.

Ida M. Androwich, RN, PhD, BC, FAAN. When Ida is not engaged in teaching as a professor at Loyola University Chicago, she is enjoying her sixteen grandchildren at the family lake cottage.

Heather R. Beebe, MBA. After leaving the harried life of a health-care consultant, Heather now leads the harried life as mom to Laura and Anna.

Sally Bellerose, RN. For 20 years Sally worked in the Monson Development Center caring for individuals who were retarded or handicapped. Today Sally is a creative writer. She also is mastering skills and pleasures in her garden. Sally has a fellowship from the National Endowment of Art so she can pursue her interest in writing.

Pam Berreth, BS, MMgt. Pam works in the marketing department of St. Alexius Medical Center, Bismarck, North Dakota. Pam enjoys spending time with her family and friends.

Patricia Birck. Patty is co-founder of Turnkey Facilities, a healthcare services company, and is a consultant for Reed Illinois Corporation, a sixth generation family business. Patty's weekends are spent at the family's Wisconsin farm, where she and her husband trap shoot, fly-fish, and derive much pleasure from being with their children, their children's spouses, and their one-year-old grandson.

Susan A. Bisol, RN, MSN, CNOR. Susan is the operations vice president for Cardinal Health Consulting and Services. When Susan is not visiting client sites in her project management role, with the consultant teams, or vacationing, she enjoys being at home with her husband, Tom, in their garden. Susan enjoys making jams and jellies, reading, and writing.

Janet Boivin, RN. Janet is the editorial director of the Greater Chicago/Tri-State edition of Nursing Spectrum. Janet is a nurse/journalist who has written extensively about military medicine.

Linda M. Bond, RN, MSN, CPAN. Linda is a clinical nurse III at the Medical University of South Carolina in Charleston. Linda is active in state and national professional organizations. Linda enjoys reading, horseback riding, and traveling.

Sister Mary Stephen Brueggeman, PHJC, MEd. Sister Mary Stephen Brueggeman presently volunteers in a childcare facility for abused and neglected children, where her nursing skills are still relevant. She functioned as a nurse and administrator in healthcare for 61 years.

Elly Burns-Prestage, RN, BA. Elly is a healthcare consultant at PricewaterhouseCoopers. Elly enjoys spending time with her grandchildren, Alexandra, Hank, and Hannah. Elly and her husband, Tony, enjoy fishing and watching a multitude of wild birds at their country home in Eudora, Mississippi.

Rebecca Caldwell, RN, BSN. When Becky is not working as the director of a medical-surgical unit at Bon Secours St. Francis Health System in Greenville, South Carolina, she is raising two sons, ages six and three. Together they enjoy sports and outdoor activities.

Judy Lau Carino, RN, BSN, MSN. Judy is a nurse at Cardiovascular Associates in Elk Grove Village, Illinois. Judy enjoys running, reading, and spending time with family.

Carol Ann Cavouras, RN, MS. Throughout her career in education, administration, and most recently as the co-owner/senior consultant of Labor Management Institute, Carol has embraced the value of oral and written stories to assist staff in finding meaning in and energy for their work.

Linda L. Chlan, RN, PhD. When Linda is not conducting research, teaching, or providing community service as an assistant professor at the University of Minnesota School of Nursing, she is enjoying music, nature, and all things feline.

Peggy Daly, RN, MA. Peggy is a home care nurse at Bayada Nurses in Prussia, Pennsylvania. When she is not working, she is cooking, babysitting her two grandchildren, or planning her next trip.

Nancy Lynn Dextrom, RN, MPA, CAN. Nancy is the executive director of Rogers City Rehabilitation Hospital in Rogers City, Michigan. In addition to enjoying her work, she "plays hard" as a participant in many outdoor activities year around.

Melanie Morrisey Dines, RN, MSN, FNP. Melanie enjoys gardening and spending time with her family when not working in palliative care at Rogue Valley Medical Center in Medford, Oregon.

Marie Duffy, RN, MSN, BC, CS, CNA, CNAA. Aside from being a nurse administrator at St. Mary's Hospital in New Jersey, Marie is a devoted mother of two boys, Kenneth and Sean.

Debra Dunn, RN, MBA, CNOR. After spending the day managing the operating room at St. Joseph's Wayne Hospital in New Jersey, chauffeuring her two children to various activities, trying to have a conversation with her husband, walking the dog, and taking care of the house, Debra writes articles for nursing journals.

Elizabeth (Betty) J. Corso Falter, RN, MS, CNAA, BC. When Betty in not consulting or teaching, she is traveling to see family or photographing the desert. She is president of Falter & Associates, Inc. and is adjunct clinical associate professor at the University of Arizona and Georgetown University Center for Professional Development.

Lori Fewster, RN, MSN. Lori was most recently corporate manager for patient safety at Children's Memorial Hospital, Chicago. Lori is now a new mom and part-time research consultant.

Lori L. Fischer. When Lori is not working as a senior placement consultant at Cross Country Travcorp or traveling for pleasure, she is enjoying entertaining or cooking for family and friends.

Elizabeth Fredeboelling, RN, MSN. Elizabeth is the director of nursing of the Pediatric Emergency Department at the Bristol-Myers Squibb Children's Hospital at Robert Wood Johnson University Hospital. Elizabeth is a wife, mother, and nurse who enjoys the challenge of finding the right balance in all three.

Victoria C. Fron, RN, MSN APN, CEN, NEMT-P. Keeping up with her fast-paced life style, Vicki enjoys motorcycling, camping, and restful times for reading and gardening. Vicki is a cardiovascular thoracic advance practice nurse at Loyola University Medical Center.

Deb Gauldin, RN, PMS. Deb is a professional speaker and entertainer specializing in healthcare morale and women's well-being. The inspiration for her original music, humor, and cartoons comes from over 20 years as an obstetric nurse and having served many years on the board of the PTA. Deb also practices therapeutic humor on her husband and two children.

Janie Lea Gawrys, RN, MS. Janie is passionate about nursing, children, and people with chronic illnesses. Janie is the director of Pediatrics/Pediatric Intensive Care at the University of Chicago Children's Hospital. She also enjoys ocean cruises.

Carole L. Hamm, RN, MBA, CCHP. Carole is excited about starting her new job as corrections account specialist for Agouron Pharmaceuticals, a division of Pfizer. Carole also enjoyed her previous career and challenges in the Correctional Health Care Industry and loves to play golf, ski, travel, and ride her Harley.

Trudie Kidwell Hart, RN. Trudie is a nurse in the Neonatal Intensive Care Unit at Stony Brook University Hospital in New York. When she is not working as a nurse, she can be found on the golf course, traveling with her family or just relaxing with a good book.

Sharon Brody Heath, RN, BSN, CCRN. Sharon is an intensive care nurse at Underwood Memorial Hospital, Woodbury, New Jersey. When Sharon is not being a nurse, wife, mother, daughter, sister, or aunt, she is enjoying caring for and spending loving time with her many friends young and old. Sharon also enjoys reading.

Linda Heitman, RN, PhS, CSm. Linda is an assistant professor of nursing at Southeast Missouri State University in Cape Girardeau, Missouri. Linda enjoys traveling, photography, and participating in church choral activities.

Donna Horrocks, RN, CCRN. Donna is a nurse in the Intensive Care Unit at Kent Hospital. When she is not working, she loves to just spend time with her family.

Carol Hutelmyer, RN, MSN. Carol is a nurse practitioner in an HIV Program at Albert Einstein Medical Center in Philadelphia. Carol enjoys spending time with her family and friends, hiking the Poconos and vacationing in foreign lands.

Sister Judith Jackson, BA, MA, Certified Chaplain, SCL. Sister Judith is the vice president of sponsorship at the Sisters of Charity of the Leavenworth Health System in Kansas. Sister Judith's passion in life is to influence the level of trust and compassionate care in healthcare delivery. She balances her life with reading novels and biographies; watching movies; attending cultural events; and having fun with her family, the religious community, and her circle of friends.

Judith (Judi) A. Jennrich, RN, PhD, ACNP, CCRN. Judi is an associate professor in the Marcella Niehoff School of Nursing at Loyola University Chicago. Judi enjoys being with her friends, family, and current and former students. She also enjoys biking, camping, smelling the roses, or preparing for the next trip to Belize.

Sarah Ann Johnson, RN, MSN. When Sarah is not at work in the post-anesthesia care unit at the Medical University of South Carolina, Charleston, she is spending her time studying in a PhD program.

Elizabeth Burn Joosten, RN, MSN. Beth is committed to working as a management consultant in the business she founded, Health Care Management. She is also devoted to her family and to nursing.

Sue Kamrad-Marrone, RN, MSN, MBA. When Sue is not working as a director of nursing at Medix Staffing Solutions, she is spending time with her wonderful husband, Paul, and their golden retriever, Sam. Sue believes balancing work with other life events is the key to a quality career within a healthy lifestyle.

Geraldine Kelly-Mancuso, RN, BSN. When Geraldine is not working as a clinical nurse manager at St. John's Riverside Hospital, H.O.P.E. Center in Yonkers, New York, she is spending time with her young children.

Vicki Keough, RN, PhD, ACNP, CCRN. Vicki, along with Judi Jennrich, is associate professor and coordinator of the Marcella Niehoff School of Nursing's Acute Care Nurse Practitioner Program at Loyola University Chicago. In her leisure time, Vicki enjoys being with family and friends, boating, and reading.

Katherine (Katie) Koehn, RN, OCN. Katie is a clinical manager at the Patty Berg Cancer Center at Southwest Regional Medical Center in Fort Myers, Florida. Katie enjoys spending time with her beautiful daughter, Emily, and her husband, Jason.

Linda Knodel, RN, BS, MHA, FACHE, CNA, BC, CPQA. Linda is the assistant administrator at St. Alexius Medical Center Bismarck, South Dakota. When not at the medical center, Linda enjoys being with her husband and three college-age daughters.

Ann Kobs, RN, MS. Ann is president and CEO of Ann Kobs & Associates, Inc. She spends most of her time traveling throughout the United States consulting and speaking. Because of her business travel, she is often able to take a detour and visit her grandchildren.

Alma Joel Labunski, RN, MS, EdD. Alma is professor emeritus and former director of North Park University School of Nursing. Currently, Alma is an educational consultant for Educational Challenges with Global Culture Consulting Services. Alma has dedicated 48 years of her life to nursing as an educator, administrator, scholar, and clinician. She continues to volunteer her services to hospitals, long-term care facilities, and programs for the homebound. She serves on numerous boards of organizations and universities as a committee member or chair. Alma is a choral member and an expert classical and sacred music pianist.

Carole Leomporra, RN, BA. Carole is a care manager at The Long Term Care Group in Eden Prairie, Minnesota. Carole has devoted the past 21 years to rearing two wonderful daughters, Sarah and Annie, who are now 21 and 18 years old.

Terry R. Light, MD. Terry is chair of the Department of Orthopaedic Surgery and Rehabilitation of the Stritch School of Medicine, Loyola University, the Dr. William M. Scholl Professor of Orthopaedic Surgery, and a surgeon at the Shriners Hospital for Children, Chicago Unit. Terry enjoys relaxing with his family, cheering for the Chicago White Sox and Blackhawks, collecting early 20th century pottery, and solving jigsaw puzzles.

Deborah Mandel, RNC, MSN, PNNT. Deborah is the regional perinatal nurse coordinator for St. Vincent's Catholic Medical Center in Stratton, New York. When not working in the medical center, she is busy creating gourmet meals and candy confections.

Jo Anne Marcell, RN, ADN, BFA, MAT, CAPAN. Jo Ann is a nurse at the Medical University of South Carolina, Charleston. She enjoys her family, gardening, reading, and singing.

Pamela A. Martyn-Nemeth, RN, MS. Pamela is an assistant professor in the College of Nursing and Health Professions at Lewis University in Romeoville, Illinois. Pam is also a doctoral student in the PhD program at Loyola University Chicago.

Mary Ann McDermott, RN, EdD, FAAN. Mary Ann is a professor at Loyola University Chicago, Marcella Neihoff School of Nursing and a trustee and past chairperson of Advocate Health System, Oak Brook, Ill. Mary Ann enjoys singing, volunteering, teaching, and nursing. Mary Ann has found she can do all of these activities while working with nurses in churches.

Fran McGibbon, RN, MSN, FNP. Fran is a faculty member at Hunter Bellevue School of Nursing in New York. She enjoys teaching nursing students, her private surgery practice, and spending time with family and friends.

Kimberly A. McNally, RN, MN. When Kimberly isn't coaching healthcare executives as president of her firm, McNally & Associates, she is enjoying traveling with her husband, attending theater, playing tennis, and/or hanging out with her friends.

Sheila McNally, RN. Sheila is a nurse at Rush University Medical Center. She also works as the manager of her father's plastic surgery practice. Sheila enjoys spending time with her children, with her parents in Lake Geneva, and with church reflective activities.

Pat Mezzina, RN. Pat is the head nurse on an Orthopaedic/Medical-Surgical Unit at St. Mary's Hospital in Hoboken. Pat enjoys scuba diving, traveling, and motorcycling.

Peggy Miller, RN, BSN. Peggy is the director of Risk & Insurance Management at Ancilla Systems Incorporated, a healthcare corporation, in Hobart, Indiana. Peggy obtained her BSN at the University of Iowa and lives in LaGrange, Illinois, with her adored animals, Punk, Muzzy, and Sugar, all rescued and living the good life!

Judith S. Mitiguy, RN, MS. When not working as an associate corporate editorial director for the Western Region for Nursing Spectrum, Judith is reading and writing.

Jorie Moberley, RN, MSN, CPNP. Jorie is a pediatric clinical instructor at Loyola University Chicago, Marcella Neihoff School of Nursing. Jorie's greatest inspirations, both personally and professionally, are her family and friends.

Stephanie L. Morris, RN, ADN. Stephanie splits her work schedule between a pediatric unit of Children's Hospital at the Medical University of South Carolina and the newborn nursery of St. Francis Hospital. Stephanie is a busy mom with four boys ages 18, 16, 12, and 8.

Betty J. Noyes, RN, MS. Betty was a volunteer/candy striper at 13, chief nurse executive of a 500-bed hospital at 27, and a CEO at 43. Betty is still finding challenges at 59 as president of her own health-care firm, Noyes & Associates, in Brainbridge Island, Washington.

Kerry L. O'Brien, RN, MPH. Kerry is the cerebral vascular coordinator at Winthrop-University Hospital. Kerry enjoys walking the boardwalk and building sand castles with her husband and two daughters.

Julia T. O'Malley, BSN, CPON. Julia is a nurse at Children's Memorial Hospital in Chicago and is president and co-founder of The Staehely O'Malley Cancer Survivor Foundation (SOCS).

Susan O'Neill, RN, CCRN. Susan works as a patient care coordinator in the Trauma Neuro Intensive Care Unit at Lehigh Valley Hospital, Allentown, Pennsylvania. After raising two sons, Seth and Conner, Susan is now reflecting and sharing her lifetime stories of nursing.

Nancy Carol Parks, RN, BSN student. When Nancy is not busy helping to bring babies into the world as a clinical nurse III in Labor and Delivery at Thomas Jefferson University Hospital in Philadelphia, she is active in her church and sings in the Jefferson University Choir.

Phyllis Powell Pelt, RN, MS. When Phyllis is not learning how to improve her online school nurse courses as the director of School Nurse Certification for the Department of Public Health at the University of Illinois at Chicago College of Nursing, she is working with grandparents who are the primary care givers of children. Phyllis loves reading stories to children and singing in the choir at her church.

Diane Henley Peters, RN, MSN. Diane is the vice president for cardiothoracic and the Ford Road Campus at Thomas Jefferson University Hospital in Pennsylvania. She also serves as nurse executive at Wills Eye Hospital. Diane is an avid gardener who enjoys needlecrafts.

Alicia Pufundt, RN, MSN, EMT-P. Alicia is the program manager of Patient Safety at the Metropolitan Chicago Healthcare Council. She is currently working to form a volunteer nurse's group to respond to disasters.

Susan Randall, RN, MSN, CFNP. Susan is the director of Nursing External Affairs at INOVA Health System. She enjoys reading mysteries, cooking, completing crossword puzzles, and working to improve the image of nursing at INOVA Health System.

Bernie Rimgale. When Bernie isn't busy being the administrative assistant for the Admissions Office of Vanderbilt University School of Nursing, she is keeping up with family and friends via e-mail. She also enjoys quilting, boating, and exercising. Bernie has a wonderful sense of humor and enjoys making others laugh.

Susan Rimgale, RN, MSN, ACNP. Susan currently resides in Nashville where she is a critical care nurse practitioner for Cardiothoracic Surgical Services at St. Thomas Hospital.

Jacqueline Rohaly-Davis, RN, MS, AOCN. Jacqueline is a clinical nurse specialist for Joliet Oncology Hematology Associates, Ltd. Jacqueline is a dedicated mother and wife. She is also a doctoral student at Loyola University Chicago.

Christine D. Rowland, RN, BSN. When Christine has free time from working in the peri-anesthesia unit at the Medical University of South Carolina or from raising her three children, she enjoys cooking, the beach, and writing both short stories and poetry.

Jackie L. Sallade, RN, CRRN. When Jackie isn't working as a supervisor of nursing at Bayada Nurses in Wayne, Pennsylvania, she is enjoying her seven grandchildren, gardening, writing, or traveling with her husband.

Sally A. Sample, RN, MN, FAAN, Honorary DSc in Nursing. After 40 years in nursing administration and many years on non-profit healthcare boards, Sally is enjoying a new lifestyle of travel, playing golf, and hiking. She is on the local library board and University of Vermont's College of Nursing advisory board.

Zenaida M. Sarmiento, RN. Zenaida is the general office manager and nurse for Midwest Pediatrics, Ltd. in Lombard, Illinois. Fulfilling her lifelong dream of becoming a nurse and marrying her childhood sweetheart, Dr. Rodolfo Sarmiento, Zenaida and her husband continue to serve the community as a dynamic nurse-doctor team both in the United States and abroad in the Philippines.

Diane Scheb, RNC, MSN. Diane is the acute pain program coordinator and a clinical specialist at Sarasota Memorial Hospital. She is the proud mother of two wonderful children, Ryan and Amy.

Kathleen Archibald Simon, RN, HNC. Kathleen is founder and president of Health Care Futures, Inc. She also is a clinical associate at the University of Illinois at Chicago College of Nursing and Great Lakes Centers in the School of Public Health. As a futurist and writer, Kathleen has an unwavering belief in the art of healing and dedicates her work/life to this activity.

Carolyn Hope Smeltzer, RN, EdD, FACHE, FAAN. When not consulting, participating as a trustee for the Advocate Health System or Sisters of Charity of Leavenworth Health System, coaching executives, or performing project management in healthcare as a partner at PricewaterhouseCoopers, Carolyn can be found golfing, swimming, tutoring, or writing.

Shannon Bright Smith, RN, MSN. Shannon is a gastroenterology inpatient staff nurse at the Medical University Hospital Authority, Charleston, South Carolina. Shannon enjoys playing the piano and organ at her church, as well as mentoring youth.

Katherine L. Smith-McEwen, RN, BSN, MBA. When Kathy is not working as a manager at Clarian Health Partners at Methodist Hospital in Indianapolis, she is going to the theater, swimming, or reading books with her daughters, Brooke and Kelly.

Anne E. Solak, RN, MSN. Anne has spent the majority of her nursing career as an educator at Ravenswood Hospital School of Nursing and as a director of nursing at the University of Chicago Hospitals. Anne spends much of her free time with her beloved pets, tending her rose garden, and volunteering at the Brookfield Zoo.

P. Ann Solari-Twadell, RN, PhD, MPA. Ann is new to academia. Prior to teaching at Loyola University, Ann was employed at Advocate Health Care for 25 years as the director of the International Parish Nurse Resource Center. When not teaching, Ann has fun playing with her four grandchildren, Nathan and Clara Kuhlman, and Kaitlyn and Lauren Twadell.

Angela Renee Starkweather, RN, MSN, ACNP. Angela is an acute care nurse practitioner in the Department of Neurological Surgery at Loyola University Medical Center. Angela is striving to walk in the footsteps of her mother—her greatest inspiration—by pursuing a doctoral degree in nursing.

Irene Stemler, RN, BSN, CRRN. Irene is a principal with Creating Spirit. She creatively focuses on exploring diversity within nursing. She has a traveling national exhibit titled, "Heroic Acts in Humble Shoes." The exhibit displays well-worn nursing shoes and tells the stories of nurses who wore the shoes.

Students, Faculty, and Alumni of The Steinhardt School of Education, Division of Nursing, New York University, Upsilon Chapter of Sigma Theta Tau International. Project coordinated by Hila Richardson, Barbara Mellor, Angela Apuzzo, Alphonse Falcone, Terry Fulmer, Judith Haber, Carla Mariano, Sandee McClowry, and Elizabeth Norman.

Carol J. Swenson, RN, MS, OCN. Carol has always loved the Northwoods and whenever she can get away from her work as the director of the Outreach and Development Program at Swedish-American Health System in Rockford, Illinois, she can be found kayaking on the lake, hiking, or tending her perennial gardens.

Helen Jean Talbot-Bond, MS. Helen is the coordinator for the Talented and Gifted Program of Madison Metropolitan School District. When Helen is not working or spending time with educators, students, parents, and her grandchildren, she is sailing with her husband or traveling somewhere in the world.

Rhiannon E. Tennant, BS. Rhiannon is currently enrolled in the MSN program at DePaul University, Chicago. She is the daughter of a nurse, Anne Solak, the great-granddaughter of Nana (see Nana story), the niece of several nurses, and the godchild of a nurse. Rhiannon's destiny is clear. Rhiannon lives in Lincoln Park in Chicago with her four cats.

Mary Grace Tighe, RN, MSN. Mary is a nurse at Thomas Jefferson University Hospitals, Inc. Mary Grace enjoys gardening and volunteering at her children's school and parish.

Cheryl Vajdik, RN, MS. When Cheryl is not working at Northwestern Memorial Hospital in Chicago, she enjoys spending time with family and friends. She is a devoted mother and daughter.

Carol Vandrey, RN, BSN, MS, CCRN. Carol is the deputy director of the Critical Care Nursing Course at Walter Reed Army Medical Center. When Carol is not teaching critical care nursing, she is kayaking, biking, or hiking on Maryland's eastern shore.

Chris Harris Vlasses, BS. Chris is a research assistant and medical student. He hopes to return to Rwanda soon to continue working with its many wonderful healthcare professionals, nurses, and physicians.

Frances R. Vlasses, RN, PhD. Fran enjoys teaching as an assistant professor at Loyola University Chicago in the Marcella Niehoff School of Nursing. She also enjoys friends and family, volunteering at her church, and traveling. Fran is always listening for *the story* with her current "Assistance Dog in Training" at her side.

Barb Ward. After ten years in healthcare marketing and communication, Barb started a home-based marketing and communication firm, Marketing Innovative Ink, Marketing and Communication, LLC. Having her own home-based firm allows her to spend time with her two-year-old son Joshua.

JoEllen Wilbur, RN, PhD, APN, FAAN. When JoEllen is not working as a professor and associate dean for research services and administration at the University of Illinois at Chicago College of Nursing, she is enjoying family time with her husband, 9-year-old son, and adult daughter. JoEllen also enjoys biking and running.

Mary Beth Williams, RN, MN. Mary Beth is the deputy chief nursing officer at the University of Chicago Children's Hospital. Mary Beth never ceases to be inspired by the nurses she meets and remains deeply grateful to be in their presence.

Michelle Williams, RN, BAA. When Michelle is not working at the Medical University of South Carolina, she is busy with her 18-month-old son, Carlton.